Praise for *The Visual Basic .NET Prog[...]*

"There is no substitute to getting the inside scoop direc[...] father of a programming language such as Bjarne Strou[...] [...] Gosling for Java and Alan Cooper for the original version of Visual Basic. Paul Vick, the father of Visual Basic .NET, explains the whys and hows of this exciting new language better than any other human being on the planet." —*Ted Pattison, Barracuda.NET*

"*The Visual Basic .NET Programming Language* includes nuances that in all my use and study of VB .NET, I haven't seen discussed anywhere else. For example, I learned that you can use the Imports statement to import an Enum name, so that you needn't refer to the enum in all its uses. In addition, I learned that the dictionary lookup operator, '!', works in VB .NET—I thought this one had been retired. In any case, if you're searching for a book that covers all the language syntax issues, and more, Paul Vick's book is a great place to look." —*Ken Getz, Senior Consultant, MCW Technologies, LLC*

"This book is an excellent stepping stone for Visual Basic developers wanting to get their toes wet in the .NET waters. Paul's presentation of the core topics all VB developers should tackle first is clear, concise, and unlike other books in the genre, does not overwhelm the reader. The VB6 vs. VB.NET task-oriented approach guides you through the new language and OO features, and then moves to basic threading and other CLR topics—as well as to the key points in the COM to .NET transition—in a well thought-out sequence. If you've been holding out on VB .NET, this is a great book to get you started."
　　　　　　—*Klaus H. Probst, Sr. Consultant/Architect, Spherion Technology Services, Microsoft MVP*

"There is no shortage of VB .NET books in the market, but this is the only book straight from the creators. While that is an excellent reason in itself for reading this book, it is the brevity and clarity of the content, along with the examples, that makes this book a must-have." —*Amit Kalani, Developer*

"Overall, I liked this book and it definitely benefited me. I learned new things I didn't see anywhere else and I'll certainly put these to good use in the future. Paul's book makes a great reference manual for intermediate and advanced VB .NET developers."
　　　　　　—*Philip Williams, System Engineer, LDC Direct*

"This book contains a lot of great information I have seen nowhere else and addresses issues that other books do not."
　　　　　　—*Ethan Roberts, .NET Architect, General Casualty*

"This book is full of useful information and provides a good historical background for the Visual Basic .NET Language."
　　　　　　—*Dave Vitter, Technical Lead Developer and author of* Designing Visual Basic .NET Applications *(Coriolis, 2001)*

Microsoft .NET Development Series

John Montgomery, *Series Advisor*
Don Box, *Series Advisor*
Martin Heller, *Series Editor*

The **Microsoft .NET Development Series** is supported and developed by the leaders and experts of Microsoft development technologies including Microsoft architects and DevelopMentor instructors. The books in this series provide a core resource of information and understanding every developer needs in order to write effective applications and managed code. Learn from the leaders how to maximize your use of the .NET Framework and its programming languages.

Titles in the Series

Brad Abrams, *.NET Framework Standard Library Annotated Reference Volume 1*, 0-321-15489-4

Keith Ballinger, *.NET Web Services: Architecture and Implementation*, 0-321-11359-4

Don Box with Chris Sells, *Essential .NET, Volume 1: The Common Language Runtime*, 0-201-73411-7

Mahesh Chand, *Graphics Programming with GDI+*, 0-321-16077-0

Anders Hejlsberg, Scott Wiltamuth, Peter Golde, *The C# Programming Language*, 0-321-15491-6

Alex Homer, Dave Sussman, Mark Fussell, *A First Look at ADO.NET and System.Xml v. 2.0*, 0-321-22839-1

Alex Homer, Dave Sussman, Rob Howard, *A First Look at ASP.NET v. 2.0*, 0-321-22896-0

James S. Miller and Susann Ragsdale, *The Common Language Infrastructure Annotated Standard*, 0-321-15493-2

Fritz Onion, *Essential ASP.NET with Examples in C#*, 0-201-76040-1

Fritz Onion, *Essential ASP.NET with Examples in Visual Basic .NET*, 0-201-76039-8

Ted Pattison and Dr. Joe Hummel, *Building Applications and Components with Visual Basic .NET*, 0-201-73495-8

Chris Sells, *Windows Forms Programming in C#*, 0-321-11620-8

Chris Sells and Justin Gehtland, *Windows Forms Programming in Visual Basic .NET*, 0-321-12519-3

Paul Vick, *The Visual Basic .NET Programming Language*, 0-321-16951-4

Damien Watkins, Mark Hammond, Brad Abrams, *Programming in the .NET Environment*, 0-201-77018-0

Shawn Wildermuth, *Pragmatic ADO.NET: Data Access for the Internet World*, 0-201-74568-2

The Visual Basic .NET Programming Language

■ Paul Vick

✦✦ Addison-Wesley

Boston • San Francisco • New York • Toronto • Montreal
London • Munich • Paris • Madrid
Capetown • Sydney • Tokyo • Singapore • Mexico City

Many of the designations used by manufacturers and sellers to distinguish their products are claimed as trademarks. Where those designations appear in this book, and Addison-Wesley was aware of a trademark claim, the designations have been printed with initial capital letters or in all capitals.

The .NET logo is either a registered trademark or trademark of Microsoft Corporation in the United States and/or other countries and is used under license from Microsoft.

The author and publisher have taken care in the preparation of this book, but make no expressed or implied warranty of any kind and assume no responsibility for errors or omissions. No liability is assumed for incidental or consequential damages in connection with or arising out of the use of the information or programs contained herein.

The publisher offers discounts on this book when ordered in quantity for bulk purchases and special sales. For more information, please contact:

U.S. Corporate and Government Sales
(800) 382-3419
corpsales@pearsontechgroup.com

For sales outside of the U.S., please contact:

International Sales
(317) 581-3793
international@pearsontechgroup.com

Visit Addison-Wesley on the Web:
www.awprofessional.com

Library of Congress Cataloging-in-Publication Data

Vick, Paul.
   The Visual Basic .NET programming language
   / Paul Vick
   p. cm.
   ISBN 0-321-16951-4 (alk. paper)
   1. Microsoft Visual Basic for Windows.   2.
BASIC (Computer program language)   3.
Microsoft .NET.   I. Title.

QA76.73.B3V484 2004
005.13'3--dc22

                                    2003069632

ISBN 0-321-16951-4
Text printed on recycled paper
1 2 3 4 5 6 7 8 9 10—CRS—0807060504
First printing, February 2004

To my wife Andrea,
Without whose love and support
This book never would have been finished

Contents

Figures

Tables

Chapter 1: Language Overview

Chapter 3: Fundamental Types

Chapter 5: Operators

Chapter 7: Exceptions

Chapter 15: Attributes

Appendix A: Runtime Functions

Preface

PERHAPS NO COMPANY'S fortunes have been more closely tied to those of a single programming language than Microsoft's has been with BASIC. Since Bill Gates and Paul Allen formed Microsoft over 25 years ago to sell their Altair MIPS BASIC interpreter, the corporation's successes have been linked with the BASIC programming language. From MS-DOS to Windows to the .NET Framework, BASIC has played a key role in attracting millions of developers to every major Microsoft platform.

And of all the incarnations of BASIC produced by Microsoft, none has been more successful than Visual Basic. The introduction of Visual Basic played a large part in the phenomenal success of the Windows platform and the Office productivity suite. The language also boasts the most developers—over 3 million at last counting—of any computer language, making it the most successful computer programming language ever. Much of the success of Visual Basic has come from the fundamental design tenets of the language: simplicity, straightforwardness, and ease of use. Visual Basic is a language designed for first-time programmers and experienced programmers alike. It makes learning computer programming easy by being approachable and understandable while providing maximum productivity and power suitable for the most advanced kind of applications. It is a versatile language that is an important part of any programmer's toolbox.

About This Book

This book contains a detailed description of the Visual Basic .NET programming language. It is intended to help new programmers to learn to program in Visual Basic .NET and to serve as a reference for experienced Visual Basic .NET programmers. In general, this book does not cover topics that are unrelated to the language itself, such as how to use the Windows Forms libraries to do GUI programming or the underlying design of the Common Language Runtime. It focuses first and foremost on the language itself, and discusses topics outside the language only to the degree that they are necessary to understand some part of the language design.

The book is laid out as follows: After a general overview of the language is given, concepts are arranged in order from the simplest to the most advanced. The book is intended to be read sequentially, although programmers with some prior experience in Visual Basic might find that skipping back and forth through the book will work just as well. The progression of concepts through the book starts with the basics of the language such as statements and expressions, moves on to the object-oriented programming (OOP) features of the language such as classes, and then finishes with advanced topics such as inheritance and versioning. Readers who are familiar with prior versions of Visual Basic are still encouraged to read through each chapter; changes occurred throughout the language when moving to the .NET Framework, and so even familiar topics may contain new features.

In general, when a concept is discussed, it is discussed in detail. For the reader new to programming, the .NET Framework, or Visual Basic, some of the details may seem difficult to grasp. Advanced concepts are usually highlighted and are not required for a working understanding of the language—in practice, they can be skipped. Readers are encouraged not to get hung up on things that may not make sense, but instead to plow ahead and circle back later. Many times, advanced concepts earlier in the book may be simpler to understand once later concepts have been digested.

> **■ NOTE**
>
> The Visual Basic .NET language as discussed in this book corresponds to Visual Studio .NET 2003 and the .NET Framework 1.1.

A Short, Unofficial History of Visual Basic

The original BASIC programming language was defined by John G. Kemeny and Thomas E. Kurtz at Dartmouth College in 1964. BASIC is an acronym for **B**eginner's **A**ll-purpose **S**ymbolic **I**nstruction **C**ode, and the language was intended to be easy for beginners to learn, yet powerful enough to write general-purpose programs. In 1975, a couple of programmers named Bill Gates and Paul Allen developed a version of BASIC for the Altair MIPS and started selling it through a small corporation they set up. That version of BASIC helped launch the Microsoft Corporation to some extraordinary heights, and since then Microsoft has had a BASIC product available in one form or another.

In 1991, BASIC at Microsoft took a major step forward with the introduction of Visual Basic. Based on an idea originally developed by Alan Cooper, Visual Basic wedded a version of the BASIC language to the new Windows user interface, resulting in a powerful tool for developing Windows applications. The concept took off, and today Visual Basic is the most widely used programming tool in existence. The fourth version of the Visual Basic product marked the introduction of the Common Object Model (COM), a framework for developing components that could plug into one another. COM was also extremely successful, forming a foundation technology for Windows and being used to build millions of components.

As successful as COM was, it had limitations. One of the biggest was that it was not always designed to work well with languages other than Visual Basic. This meant that, for example, programmers who used C++ often found it difficult and time consuming to program against COM components, especially those written in VB. Another problem was that COM only defined how components were *supposed* to interact with each other, leaving the actual details of this interaction, especially in terms of such things as component lifetime and memory management, up to the component author. Although Visual Basic provided these services to its programmers, other popular languages, such as C++, did not. Because each C++ programmer was required to implement these services themselves, implementations were not always compatible or complete, resulting in not only more work but also more bugs (and, by extension, more user anguish).

To try to address some of the shortcomings of COM, Microsoft began developing a replacement technology, the Common Language Runtime (CLR). In addition to defining component interactions, the CLR also took on the job of managing such things as memory and component lifetime, taking over those responsibilities from the programmer. Microsoft also began developing the .NET Framework, a set of class libraries that provided capabilities equivalent to the Win32 API, on top of the CLR. Together, the .NET Framework and the CLR form the foundation of the next generation of Windows programming.

Although the CLR is intended as a replacement for COM, there are many differences between the two, some major, some extremely subtle. Because Visual Basic had become so integrated with COM, it was necessary to make corresponding changes to the language, some of which significantly altered the way programs were written in VB. As a result, Visual Basic .NET, a new and distinct version of the Visual Basic language, was developed. Although most of the language came through unchanged by the transition, some details of the language were modified, and many new concepts were added.

Where practical, things that have changed from previous versions of Visual Basic are pointed out in a box labeled Compatibility, but a full accounting of the changes in the language between Visual Basic 6.0 and Visual Basic .NET is beyond the scope of this book.

Style and Preferences

The style and practice of writing BASIC code has changed significantly since the language was introduced almost 40 years ago, and continues to evolve. More than any other programming language, BASIC has been adapted to almost every conceivable purpose and used in almost every possible computing environment. It is, perhaps, the most nonstandard computer language ever developed. Thus, the idea of suggesting a particular style or usage of the language may seem quaint, but is nonetheless part of the purpose of this book. As the previous section should have made clear,

Visual Basic .NET represents a huge leap forward for the Visual Basic language. Parts of the language have been dropped, other parts have been significantly altered, and still other parts are completely new. Where possible, the book offers suggestions on how best to use the language and provides rationale for those suggestions. Some suggestions are based on practical considerations; others are purely stylistic, bordering on pure personal preference. Readers are, of course, always free to ignore such suggestions—one of the joys of programming is the freedom to write code as one sees fit.

Acknowledgments

Without all the people who contributed to the creation of Visual Basic .NET, this book would not have been possible. In particular, my thanks go to the core group of people who worked together with me to come up with the language design for Visual Basic .NET, and especially Alan Carter, Sam Spencer, John Hamby, and Cameron McColl. They all managed to stick it out through what was often a long and extremely difficult transition from Visual Basic to Visual Basic .NET. Without their tireless work and passion for the product, we never would have made it.

Thanks also go to the larger Visual Basic .NET team, who translated the language designs into reality, and to the C# team, our partners in crime (as it were). Thank go especially to Anders Hejlsberg, Peter Golde, and Scott Wiltamuth, who all provided valuable insight into language design from a decidedly different vantage point. The CLR and .NET Framework teams also played an invaluable role in bringing Visual Basic .NET to fruition, and many thanks are due to the efforts of Brad Abrams and Jim Miller, who patiently spent many an hour explaining some aspect or another of the new platform!

This book itself would not have been possible without the enthusiastic support and enduring patience of Stephane Thomas and Michael Mullen at Addison-Wesley, and the editing skills of Martin Heller. Thanks go to Ken Getz, Amit Kalani, Rex Jaeschke, Rocky Lhotka, David Vitter, Phillip Williams, Ethan Roberts, Joe Hummel, and Klaus Probst for their willingness to review the book and offer helpful and enlightening comments and suggestions. And there would have been no way that I would have been able to complete the book without the willingness of Julia Liuson and Paul Kuklinski to give me time to work on it (and to understand when other things didn't necessarily get done on time!).

And finally, none of this would have been possible without the love and support of my family, especially my wife, Andrea. I can never thank them enough.

■ 1 ■
Language Overview

This chapter provides a high-level overview of the entire Visual Basic .NET language. It is intended to quickly give readers a general familiarity with the features of the language and to help new programmers get up to speed in writing programs as soon as possible. Everything covered in this chapter is discussed in more detail in the following chapters; if you don't need or want an overview of the language before starting to learn about Visual Basic .NET, you can safely skip this chapter and start reading with Chapter 2.

Hello, World!

By long-standing custom, the first example in any programming language book is the following program.

```
Module HelloWorld
  Public Sub Main()
    Console.WriteLine("Hello, world!")
    Console.ReadLine()
  End Sub
End Module
```

This Visual Basic .NET program simply writes the text Hello, world! to the output window and waits for the user to hit the Return key. It declares a module, HelloWorld, that contains a single method, Main, that is run when the program executes. The `Main` method calls a system-defined method, `WriteLine`, on the `System.Console` class. The `WriteLine` method takes a string of characters and writes that string to the output window. Then the system-defined method `ReadLine` on the `System.Console` class is called. This method waits for the user to enter a string of characters and hit the Return key. The `ReadLine` call ensures that the output window does not immediately disappear.

Although compiling, executing, and debugging a Visual Basic .NET program is not discussed in detail in this book, a few helpful pointers can be discussed. If a machine has Visual Basic .NET installed as part of Visual Studio .NET, the following steps will compile and run the program.

1. Start Visual Studio .NET.
2. Create a new Visual Basic .NET Console Application project.
3. Replace the code in the file `Module1.vb` with the previous code.
4. Run the program by hitting the F5 key.

Alternatively, if a machine has only the .NET Framework installed, the following steps will compile and run the program.

1. Use a text editor such as Notepad to create a new file named `HelloWorld.vb`, and type in the previous code.
2. Find the Visual Basic .NET compiler, `vbc.exe`, provided by the .NET Framework.
3. Run the Visual Basic .NET compiler on the source file you created, by typing `vbc.exe HelloWorld.vb` at a command prompt.
4. Run the resulting program, `HelloWorld.exe`, by typing `HelloWorld` at a command prompt.

Running the Visual Basic .NET compiler causes the source code to be compiled from text into an assembly. An *assembly* is a file with an EXE or DLL extension that the .NET Framework can load and run. An assembly has a name (in this case, `HelloWorld`) that distinguishes it from other assemblies and allows the .NET Framework to identify which assemblies need to be loaded to run a particular program. Inside an assembly are two things created by the compiler—*intermediate language* instructions (*IL*) and *metadata*. IL is a machine language that the .NET Framework understands and can execute. Metadata is extra information about the program above and beyond what is stored in the IL. Metadata is used by the .NET Framework to ensure that the IL can be executed correctly and securely, and is also used by the .NET Framework Reflection APIs. You can learn more about the internals of the .NET Framework in the book *Programming in the .NET Environment,* by Damien Watkins, Mark Hammond, and Brad Abrams (Addison-Wesley, 2003).

Fundamental Types

The Visual Basic .NET language predefines fundamental types that can be used to perform numeric, Boolean, and text operations (see Table 1-1). The fundamental numeric types split into three categories: integers of varying ranges (Byte, Short, Integer, and Long), floating-point numbers of vary-

TABLE 1-1: Fundamental Types

Type	Description
Boolean	A Boolean (true/false) value
Byte	A 1-byte unsigned integer
Short	A 2-byte signed integer
Integer	A 4-byte signed integer
Long	An 8-byte signed integer
Decimal	A 16-byte scaled decimal number
Single	A 2-byte single precision floating-point number
Double	A 4-byte double precision floating-point number
Date	A time/date value
Char	A single Unicode character
String	A string of Unicode characters

ing ranges and precision (`Single`, `Double`), and a decimal number with a fixed range and precision (`Decimal`).

The language defines operators that can be used to perform standard arithmetic operations on the numeric types (see Table 1-2).

The `Boolean` type, which represents a true/false value, can be used to express the result of conditional expressions. The logical operators are listed in Table 1-3.

The comparison operators listed in Table 1-4 can also be used to form comparison expressions.

The `String` and `Char` types represent Unicode strings and characters, respectively. The string operators are listed in Table 1-5.

String comparisons are special in that they can be evaluated in one of two ways. If the `Option Compare Binary` statement is specified at the beginning of a file, strings are compared using a code-point comparison.

TABLE 1-2: Numeric Operators

Operator	Description
+	Addition
–	Subtraction and negation
*	Multiplication
/	Floating-point division
\	Integer division
Mod	Integer remainder
^	Exponentiation
Not	Bitwise NOT
And	Bitwise AND
Or	Bitwise OR
Xor	Bitwise Exclusive OR

TABLE 1-3: Logical Operators

Operator	Description
Not	Logical NOT
And	Logical AND
Or	Logical OR
Xor	Logical Exclusive OR
AndAlso	Short-circuiting logical AND
OrElse	Short-circuiting logical OR

TABLE 1-4: Comparison Operators

Operator	Description
=	Equality
<>	Inequality
<	Less than
>	Greater than
<=	Less than or equal to
>=	Greater than or equal to

TABLE 1-5: String Operators

Operator	Description
&	Concatenation
Like	Pattern matching

That is, two strings match if the value of each corresponding Unicode character in the two strings matches exactly. If the Option Compare Text statement is specified at the beginning of a file, strings are compared using a locale-sensitive comparison. That is, two strings match if each character is considered equivalent in the current Framework culture at runtime. In some cultures, two different Unicode values may represent the same character, so a text comparison may produce a different result than a binary comparison. If no Option Compare statement is specified at the top of a file, the default is Option Compare Binary.

The Date type represents date and time values. Date and time values are specified by surrounding the date or time with hash marks.

```
Dim x As Date
x = #8/23/1970 4:34:12 AM#
x = #4/22/1972#
x = #3:41:00 PM#
```

The fundamental numeric types can be augmented with *enumerated* numeric types. Enumerated numeric types are Byte, Short, Integer, or Long types that have assigned names to specific numeric values. By default, enumerations that do not explicitly declare an underlying type are Integer. For example, the following defines an enumerated Integer type called Color that gives the name Red to the value 1, the name Blue to the value 2, and the name Green to the value 3. It also defines an enumerated Byte type called SwitchValue that gives the name Off to the value 0 and On to the value 1.

```
Enum Color
  Red = 1
  Blue = 2
  Green = 3
End Enum

Enum SwitchValue As Byte
  Off
  [On]
End Enum
```

Once an enumeration has been defined, the enumerated values can be used in place of numbers.

```
Dim Background As Color

Background = Color.Red

If Background = Color.Green Then
  Console.WriteLine("Background is green.")
End If
```

The conversion operators allow converting values between compatible types. Conversion operators are defined for each fundamental type (see Table 1-6), and the general conversion operator CType can be used to convert between any two types.

By default, conversions between compatible types do not require use of a conversion operator; the compiler will implicitly attempt the conversion

TABLE 1-6: Conversion Operators

Operator	Description
CBool(x)	Boolean conversion
CByte(x)	Byte conversion
CShort(x)	Short conversion
CInt(x)	Integer conversion
CLng(x)	Long conversion
CSng(x)	Single conversion
CDbl(x)	Double conversion
CDec(x)	Decimal conversion
CChar(x)	Char conversion
CStr(x)	String conversion
CDate(x)	Date conversion
CObj(x)	Object conversion
CType(x, Type)	General conversion

at runtime. However, some conversions may fail at runtime—for example, converting a `Long` value to `Integer` may fail if the `Long` value is out of the range of `Integer`. Specifying the `Option Strict` statement at the top of a file will require all conversions that can fail to be stated explicitly.

Arrays

An *array* is a type that contains a set of variables of the same type. Each element of the array is accessed by its position in the array, called its *index* (see Figure 1-1). The starting index of an array is always zero.

The following example creates an array that has ten `Integer` variables and fills the array with the numbers 1 through 10.

```
Dim x(9) As Integer

For i As Integer = 0 To 9
  x(i) = i + 1
Next i
```

Arrays can be multidimensional; that is, they can be indexed by more than one dimension (see Figure 1-2).

The following example creates a two-dimensional array of 100 `Integer` variables and fills the array with the values 1 through 100.

```
Dim x(9, 9) As Integer

For i As Integer = 0 To 9
  For j As Integer = 0 To 9
    x(i, j) = (i * 10) + (j + 1)
  Next j
Next i
```

Array variables can be declared with a preinitialized size by specifying the size as part of the variable declaration. Sizes are always specified in

1	2	3	4	5	6	7	8	9	10	Values
0	1	2	3	4	5	6	7	8	9	Index

FIGURE 1-1: A One-Dimensional Array

Index	0	1	2	3	4	5	6	7	8	9
0	1	2	3	4	5	6	7	8	9	10
1	11	12	13	14	15	16	17	18	19	20
2	21	22	23	24	25	26	27	28	29	30
3	31	32	33	34	35	36	37	38	39	40
4	41	42	43	44	45	46	47	48	49	50
5	51	52	53	54	55	56	57	58	59	60
6	61	62	63	64	65	66	67	68	69	70
7	71	72	73	74	75	76	77	78	79	80
8	81	82	83	84	85	86	87	88	89	90
9	91	92	93	94	95	96	97	98	99	100

FIGURE 1-2: A Multidimensional Array

terms of the upper bound of each dimension; in the preceding example, the declaration x(9, 9) As Integer declared an array of 100 elements whose indices ranged from 0 to 9.

Array variables that omit bounds are not initialized to any size and must be created before they can be used. Arrays can be initialized using the ReDim statement.

```
Dim x(,) As Integer

ReDim x(9,9)

For i As Integer = 0 To 9
  For j As Integer = 0 To 9
    x(i, j) = (i * 10) + (j + 1)
  Next j
Next i
```

Unless the ReDim statement includes the Preserve modifier, an array with values already in it is cleared when it is redimensioned.

Arrays can also be created through an array creation expression. The list that follows the array creation expression either can be empty, indicating the array is not initialized with a set of values, or can contain the values to assign to the array. The following example creates an array of ten Integer values of 0 (the default value of Integer) and assigns it to the variable x. Then it creates an array of ten Integer values with the values 1 through 10 and assigns it to the variable y.

```
Dim x(), y() As Integer
x = New Integer(9) {}
y = New Integer() { 1, 2, 3, 4, 5, 6, 7, 8, 9, 10 }
```

The element type of an array can be an array type itself, in which case the element of the outer array is an inner array (see Figure 1-3), which must be created before it can be used. This is in contrast to a multidimensional array (see Figure 1-2), where all elements always exist.

In the following example, the variable x contains an array of ten one-dimensional arrays of Integer. Each element of the array must first be initialized with another array before it can be used. In contrast, the variable y contains a two-dimensional array of 100 Integer values. No extra initialization is required.

```
Dim x()() As Integer
Dim y(,) As Integer

x = New Integer(9)() {}
```

Index		0	1	2	3	4	5	6	7	8	9
0	→	1	2	3	4	5	6	7	8	9	10
1	→	11	12	13	14	15	16	17	18	19	20
2	→	21	22	23	24	25	26	27	28	29	30
3	→	31	32	33	34	35	36	37	38	39	40
4	→	41	42	43	44	45	46	47	48	49	50
5	→	51	52	53	54	55	56	57	58	59	60
6	→	61	62	63	64	65	66	67	68	69	70
7	→	71	72	73	74	75	76	77	78	79	80
8	→	81	82	83	84	85	86	87	88	89	90
9	→	91	92	93	94	95	96	97	98	99	100

FIGURE 1-3: An Array of Arrays

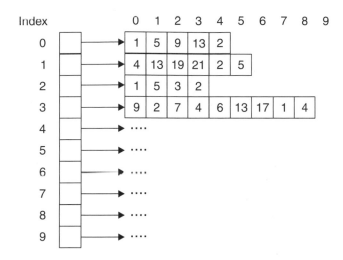

FIGURE 1-4: A Jagged Array

```
y = New Integer(9,9) {}

For i As Integer = 0 To 9
  x(i) = New Integer(9) {}

  For j As Integer = 0 To 9
    x(i)(j) = (i * 10) + (j + 1)
    y(i, j) = (i * 10) + (j + 1)
  Next j
Next i
```

Arrays of arrays can be *jagged*—that is, their dimensions can be uneven (see Figure 1-4)—while multidimensional arrays are always rectangular.

Statements

There are several kinds of statements.

- Assignment statements—In addition to the standard assignment statement (=), compound assignment operators use the left-hand side of the assignment as the left operand of the operator. The following example adds 10 to the value 5 and then divides the result by 3.

```
Dim x As Integer = 5

x += 10
x \= 3
```

- Looping statements—There are four kinds of loop statements: `While` statements, `Do` statements, `For` statements, and `For Each` statements. `While` and `Do` statements repeat a set of statements based on a condition.

```
Dim x As Integer

While x < 5
  x += 1
End While

Do
  x -= 1
Loop While x > 0
```

`For` statements increment a variable from one bound to another bound. A step value can be specified that indicates how much the variable should be incremented on each loop, and the step value can be negative. The following example loops from zero to ten, stepping by two each time.

```
For x As Integer = 0 To 10 Step 2
  Console.WriteLine(x)
Next x
```

`For Each` statements loop over all the items in an array or a list of values.

```
Dim c() As Integer = New Integer() { 1, 2, 3 }

For Each x As Integer In c
  Console.WriteLine(x)
Next x
```

- `With` statement—The `With` statement simplifies accessing multiple members of a value by allowing the repeated expression to be omitted. So the following code:

```
Dim c As ArrayList = New ArrayList()

c.Add(1)
c.Add(2)
c.Add(3)
```

can instead be written as follows:

```
Dim c As ArrayList = New ArrayList()

With c
  .Add(1)
  .Add(2)
  .Add(3)
End With
```

- Conditional statements—The If conditional statement executes code based on the value of a Boolean expression.

```
Dim x As Integer

If x < 0 Then
  Console.WriteLine("Less than zero.")
Else
  Console.WriteLine("Not less than zero.")
End If
```

The Select statement executes code based on a series of conditions.

```
Dim x As String

Select Case x
  Case "Red"
    Console.WriteLine("Red")
  Case "Green"
    Console.WriteLine("Green")
  Case "Blue"
    Console.WriteLine("Blue")
End Select
```

- Branching statements—Most block statements have a corresponding Exit statement that immediately exits the block.

```
Dim x As Integer

While True
```

```
   x = CInt(Console.ReadLine())

   If x = 0 Then
      Exit While
   End If
End While
```

Visual Basic .NET also supports the GoTo statement, which branches to a label.

```
Dim x As Integer

While True
   x = CInt(Console.ReadLine())

   If x = 0 Then
      GoTo ExitLoop
   End If
End While

ExitLoop:
Console.WriteLine("Finished.")
```

The Return statement exits a subroutine or function. Return can also specify the return value of a function.

```
Function Add(ByVal x As Integer, ByVal y As Integer) As Integer
   Return x + y
End Function
```

The Stop statement causes the application to stop executing and break into the debugger, if one is available. The End statement causes the application to stop executing entirely.

- SyncLock statement—The SyncLock statement can be used to prevent more than one thread of execution from executing the same block of code. The argument to the statement is a value that can be used by the Framework as a lock. The following example uses two threads of execution to fill up an array with 10,000 values. A lock is used to prevent the threads from writing to the same location in the array.

```
Imports System.Threading

Module Test
  Dim Values(10000) As Integer
  Dim CurrentIndex As Integer = 0

  Sub FillValues()
    For Number As Integer = 1 to 5000
      SyncLock Values.SyncRoot
        Values(CurrentIndex) = Number
        CurrentIndex += 1
      End SyncLock
    Next Number
  End Sub

  Sub Main()
    Dim t1 As Thread = New Thread(AddressOf FillValues)
    Dim t2 As Thread = New Thread(AddressOf FillValues)

    t1.Start()
    t2.Start()
  End Sub
End Module
```

Exception Handling

Errors that occur while a program is running can be handled through the use of *exceptions*. An exception is an object derived from the class System.Exception that represents information about an exceptional situation (usually an error) that has occurred in a program. When an exceptional situation occurs, the program can *throw* an exception using the Throw statement. The Error statement can also be used to throw an exception based on an exception number instead of the exception type. The following code throws the same kind of exception (an invalid index was specified) using the two different statements.

```
If x < 0 Then
  Throw New IndexOutOfRangeException()
End If

If y < 0 Then
  Error 9
End If
```

Thrown exceptions can be *caught* by code that is designed to handle the error. Exceptions can be handled in one of two ways: unstructured exception handling or structured exception handling.

Structured Exception Handling

Structured exception handling allows exceptions to be handled for only a specific block of code. A `Try` statement handles any exceptions that occur when the statements contained within the `Try` statement are executed. A `Try` statement can specify `Catch` statements that can catch particular types of exceptions. A `Catch` statement can catch exceptions on the basis of either the type of the exception or a filter expression. In the following example, the function `Divide` handles a division-by-zero exception by printing an error message, while the `Add` function ignores exceptions based on the value of a parameter.

```
Function Divide(ByVal x As Integer, ByVal y As Integer) As Integer
  Try
    Return x \ y
  Catch e As DivideByZeroException
    Console.WriteLine("Divide by zero.")
  End Try
End Function

Function Add(ByVal x As Integer, ByVal y As Integer, _
  ByVal IgnoreErrors As Boolean) As Integer
  Try
    Return x + y
  Catch When IgnoreErrors
    Console.WriteLine("Ignoring overflow.")
  End Try
End Function
```

A `Finally` statement can be used to execute statements regardless of whether an exception was thrown inside a `Try` block or not. This ensures that the code is run even if an exception occurs.

```
Sub DoWork(ByVal x As File)
  Try
    x.Open()
    ...
  Finally
    ' Ensure file is closed even if an exception occurs
```

```
        x.Close()
    End Try
End Sub
```

Unstructured Exception Handling

Unstructured exception handling works by using `On Error` statements to establish the "current" exception handler. When an exception occurs, `On Error GoTo` can be used to direct execution to a label. `On Error Resume Next` can be used to direct execution to the next line after the one that caused the exception. In the following example, the `Divide` function handles a division-by-zero exception by printing an error message, while the `Add` function handles all exceptions by continuing to execute.

```
Function Divide(ByVal x As Integer, ByVal y As Integer) As Integer
   On Error GoTo HandleError

   Return x \ y

HandleError:
   If Err.Number - 11 Then
      Console.WriteLine("Divide by zero.")
   End If
End Function

Function Add(ByVal x As Integer, ByVal y As Integer) As Integer
   On Error Resume Next

   Return x + y
End Function
```

Memory Management

Memory allocated by Visual Basic .NET programs is managed by the .NET Framework runtime environment. There are two kinds of types in the Visual Basic .NET type system—*reference types* and *value types*—that are distinguished by the way in which the Framework manages the memory used by the type. Reference types are stored by the Framework on the system *heap*. The heap is a pool of memory that the Framework keeps available for programs to use when allocating memory. When a value is allocated on the heap, the Framework finds a chunk of free memory large enough to hold

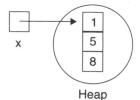

Heap

```
Class Test
    Public a As Integer
    Public b As Integer
    Public c As Integer
End Class

...
Dim x As Test = New Test()
x.a = 1
x.b = 5
x.c = 8
```

FIGURE 1-5: A Reference Type Variable and the Heap

the value, stores the value on the heap, and then returns a reference to where the value is stored on the heap. Variables that hold a reference type contain only a reference to the value on the heap, not the value itself (see Figure 1-5).

The Framework keeps track of all references to values on the heap and periodically reclaims memory on the heap by looking for values that are no longer being referenced and freeing them. This process is called *garbage collection*, and it ensures that the heap has memory available to fulfill allocation requests from the application.

In contrast to reference types, value types have values that are stored directly within another value, so they do not require allocating space on the heap (see Figure 1-6). Value types that are fields of a reference type are stored on the heap as part of the reference type; value types that are local variables or arguments are stored on the *stack*, which is a second pool of memory dedicated to local variables and method arguments.

Because a value type value is always contained within another value, a value type never requires memory to be allocated for it. Variables that hold value types can always have values stored into them, whereas variables that hold reference types have to first allocate space to hold their value.

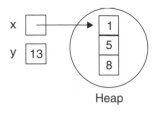

Dim y As Integer
y = 13

FIGURE 1-6: A Value Type Variable

Before storage is allocated to hold its value, a reference type variable contains the special value Nothing, which indicates that the variable does not refer to any value on the heap. Attempting to use a variable that contains Nothing generally will result in a System.NullReferenceException being thrown by the Framework.

Classes, Structures, and Modules

The fundamental types are not always sufficient for a program's needs, so new types can be defined. The simplest type that can be defined is a *module*. Modules can contain members, but only one instance of the module ever exists in an application. Modules are equivalent to a class or structure with only shared members, and are ideal for purely procedural code.

```
Module Test
  Dim i, j As Integer

  Function Add(ByVal x As Integer, ByVal y As Integer) As Integer
    Return x + y
  End Function

  Sub Main()
    i = 5
    j = 10

    Console.WriteLine(Add(i,j))
  End Sub
End Module
```

Classes and *structures*, on the other hand, behave more like the fundamental types and may have multiple instances. Classes and structures are distinguished from each other primarily by the fact that they have different memory management behaviors: Classes are reference types, while structures are value types.

```
Class C
  Public i, j As Integer
End Class

Structure S
  Public x, y As Integer
End Structure

Module Test
  Sub Main()
    Dim s1 As S  ' Declares an instance of structure S
    Dim c1 As C  ' Declares a reference to class C

    s1.x = 10    ' No need to create the structure because it is
    s1.y = 20    ' a value type

    c1 = New C() ' Because C is a class, it must be created before
    c1.i = 10    ' it can be assigned to.
    c1.j = 20
  End Sub
End Module
```

Classes and structures can contain both instance and shared members. Each instance of a class or structure has its own copy of an instance member, while all classes and structures of a particular type share the same copy of a shared member. Because instance members are unique to each instance, they must be qualified with an instance of the type. Shared members are qualified with the type name.

```
Class C
  Public Shared x As Integer
  Public y As Integer
End Class

Module Test
  Sub Main()
    Dim c1, c2 As C

    c1 = New C()
```

```
        c1.y = 10        ' Value is assigned to this instance only
        C.x = 20         ' Value is assigned to all instances

        c2 = New C()
        Console.WriteLine(c2.y) ' Prints out 0
        Console.WriteLine(C.x)  ' Prints out 20
    End Sub
End Module
```

Accessibility

Members of user-defined types always have an accessibility level that determines what code can access the member. `Public` members are accessible by any code, while `Private` members are not accessible outside of the type that declares it. `Friend` members are accessible only within the containing assembly. There are two other accessibility levels, `Protected` and `Protected Friend`, which will be covered in the Inheritance section later in this chapter.

By default, all type members have `Public` access except for fields in classes and modules, which default to `Private`.

Constructors

Constructors are methods that are executed when an instance of a class or structure is created, allowing for user-defined initialization of the type. Constructors look exactly like regular methods, except that they have the special name `New`. For example:

```
Class Customer
    Dim Name As String
    Dim Address As String
    Dim PhoneNumber As String

    Public Sub New(ByVal Name As String, ByVal Address As String)
        MyBase.New()
        Me.Name = Name
        Me.Address = Address
    End Sub
End Class

Module Test
    Sub Main()
        Dim Bob As Customer
```

```
      Bob = New Customer("Bob", "134 Main Street")
    End Sub
End Module
```

In this example, the `Customer` class defines a constructor that takes two parameters: a customer name and a customer address. It initializes the `Name` and `Address` fields with the values supplied. As shown in the example, arguments supplied to a `New` expression are passed to the constructor parameters. Like methods, constructors can be overloaded.

Every class or structure is required to have a constructor. If a class or structure doesn't define a constructor explicitly, the language assumes a default constructor, with no parameters, that does nothing. Each constructor must begin with a call to another constructor in the same class (`Me.New(...)`) or to another constructor in the base class (`MyBase-.New(...)`).

Constructors are primarily used to initialize instances of types, but they can also be used to initialize shared information in a type. A shared constructor is declared the same as a regular constructor except that it uses the `Shared` modifier, can have no parameters, and cannot be declared with an access level.

Nested Types

A type may be declared within another type and is called a *nested type*. For a nested type to be referred to from outside the type it is declared in, the type name must be qualified with the outer type's name.

```
Class Customer
  Class Address
    ...
  End Class

  ...
End Class

Module Test
  Sub Main()
    Dim a As New Customer.Address()
  End Sub
End Class
```

In this example, the address of a customer is stored in an `Address` type that is declared within the `Customer` type.

Fields

Fields are variables that are contained within user-defined types. Fields can be given an initial value by assigning an expression to the field in its declaration. Constructors can also be used to initialize fields in structures and classes. The following example shows different methods of declaring and initializing fields.

```
Class Test
  Public x, y As Integer
  Public z As Integer = 10
  Public a As New Test(10)

  Public Sub New(ByVal a As Integer)
    x = a
    y = a
  End Sub
End Class
```

Fields can be declared `ReadOnly`, which prevents their values from being changed after they are initialized. Read-only fields can only be assigned a value in a constructor or by an initializer—outside a constructor, the value of the field is read-only.

```
Class Customer
  ReadOnly Name As String
  ReadOnly ZIP As Integer = 98112

  Sub New(ByVal Name As String)
    Me.Name = Name
  End Sub

  Sub ChangeName(ByVal Name As String)
    ' Error: Name is ReadOnly
    Me.Name = Name
  End Sub
End Class
```

Constants are fields whose values are known at compile time and cannot be changed at runtime. Constants are more efficient than read-only fields because the compiler can substitute the constant value at compile time instead of having to read it at runtime.

```
Enum Color
   Red
   Blue
   Green
End Enum

Class Control
   Public BackColor As Color = DefaultColor
   Const DefaultColor As Color = Color.Red
End Class
```

Methods

A *method* is a set of executable statements. Methods come in two forms: functions, which return a value, and subroutines, which don't. The following example shows a function that adds two numbers and returns the result, and a subroutine that calls it and prints the result of the function.

```
Module Test
   Function Add(ByVal x As Integer, ByVal y As Integer) As Integer
      Return x + y
   End Function

   Sub Main()
      Console.WriteLine(Add(10, 20))
   End Sub
End Module
```

Parameters

Methods can have *parameters*, which allow passing values to and from the method. Values passed to parameters are called *arguments* to the method. By default, arguments are passed to parameters by value, which means the argument is copied into the parameter when the method is entered. Arguments can also be passed to parameters by reference, which means that the parameter gets a pointer to the argument itself, rather than a copy. Any changes to a reference parameter are reflected in the original argument. In the following example, the Add subroutine does not return a value—instead, it assigns the result value to the reference parameter Result. This changes the Result local variable in the Main subroutine.

```
Module Test
   Sub Add(ByVal x As Integer, ByVal y As Integer, _
           ByRef Result As Integer)
      Result = x + y
   End Sub

   Sub Main()
      Dim Result As Integer

      Add(10, 20, Result)
      Console.WriteLine(Result)
   End Sub
End Module
```

Parameters can be optional, with a default value that is supplied if no argument is given. Optional parameters must always be declared after required parameters. The following example declares the second parameter as optional, with a default value of 10. The Main subroutine prints the value 20.

```
Module Test
   Function Add(ByVal x As Integer, Optional ByVal y As Integer = 10) _
        As Integer
      Return x + y
   End Function

   Sub Main()
      Console.WriteLine(Add(10))
   End Sub
End Module
```

Parameters can also be *parameter arrays*. A parameter array is a parameter whose type is a special kind of array. A caller can pass zero or more arguments of the element type of the array, and they will be packaged into an array when the call is made. In the following example, the Add function now can add an arbitrarily large number of integers together.

```
Module Test
   Function Add(ByVal ParamArray Values() As Integer) As Integer
      Dim Result As Integer = 0
```

```
        For Index As Integer = 0 To Values.Length - 1
          Result += Values(Index)
        Next Index

        Return Result
    End Function

    Sub Main()
        Console.WriteLine(Add(10,20,30,40,50,60))
    End Sub
End Module
```

Methods can be *overloaded* with different parameter lists. At compile time, the best overload for the given arguments will be chosen. If a "best" overload cannot be chosen, an ambiguity error will be given. Methods cannot be overloaded solely by return type. In the following example, the `Add` method is now overloaded with both an `Integer` and a `Double` version. The compiler will choose to call one or the other based on which one the arguments best match.

```
Module Test
    Function Add(ByVal x As Integer, ByVal y As Integer) As Integer
        Return x + y
    End Function

    Function Add(ByVal x As Double, ByVal y As Double) As Double
        Return x + y
    End Function

    Sub Main()
        ' Calls Add(Integer, Integer)
        Console.WriteLine(Add(10,20))

        ' Calls Add(Double, Double)
        Console.WriteLine(Add(12.3, 31.4))
    End Sub
End Module
```

Declare Statements

It is sometimes necessary to call methods that exist outside the .NET Framework, such as Win32 APIs. These external methods are represented within the Framework by `Declare` statements. A `Declare` statement specifies the dynamic link library in which the external method resides and the method's parameters and return type. The following example shows a sample `Declare` statement that represents the Win32 API `GetWindows-DirectoryA`.

```
Module Test
  Declare Function GetWindowsDirectoryA Lib "kernel32" _
    (ByVal Buffer As String, ByVal Size As Integer) As Integer

  Sub Main()
    Dim s As String
    Dim Count As Integer

    s = Space(256)    ' Fill the string with spaces
    Count = GetWindowsDirectoryA(s, s.Length)

    If Count < 256 Then
      Console.WriteLine(s)
    End If
  End Sub
End Module
```

`Declare` statements can also provide an alias for the external method if the method name would conflict with an existing name or a different name is desired. The following example shows a sample `Declare` method for the `GetWindowsDirectoryA` external method that renames the method to `GetWindowsDirectory`.

```
Module Test
  Declare Function GetWindowsDirectory Lib "kernel32" _
    Alias "GetWindowsDirectoryA" _
    (ByVal Buffer As String, ByVal Size As Integer) As Integer

  Sub Main()
    Dim s As String
    Dim Count As Integer

    s = Space(256)    ' Fill the string with spaces
    Count = GetWindowsDirectory(s, s.Length)

    If Count < 256 Then
      Console.WriteLine(s)
    End If
  End Sub
End Module
```

Properties

A *property* is a cross between a field and a method. From the outside, a property looks and behaves like a field. But on the inside, there is not necessarily a variable storing the property's value. Instead, the property provides methods to get and set the value, called *accessors*. The accessors can deal with the value of the property in any way they see fit. The following example defines a Total property that calculates the Order total by multiplying Cost by Quantity. When the property is used, however, it appears just to be a field of the Order class.

```
Class Order
  Public Cost As Double
  Public Quantity As Integer

  Public ReadOnly Property Total() As Double
    Get
      Return Cost * Quantity
    End Get
  End Property
End Class

Module Test
  Sub Main()
    Dim Order As Order = New Order()

    Order.Cost = 34.32
    Order.Quantity = 5

    Console.WriteLine(Order.Total)
  End Sub
End Module
```

Properties can also have parameters; such properties are called *indexed properties* because the arguments are specified like array indexes. The following example defines a simple collection class that stores orders. When the Main subroutine fetches orders from the collection, it provides an index just as if the collection were an array.

```
Class Order
  Public Cost As Double
  Public Quantity As Integer
End Class
```

```
Class OrderCollection
  Private _Orders(9) As Order

  Public Property Orders(ByVal Index As Integer) As Order
    Get
      If _Orders(Index) Is Nothing Then
        _Orders(Index) = New Order()
      End If

      Return _Orders(Index)
    End Get

    Set (Value As Order)
      _Orders(Index) = Value
    End Set
  End Property
End Class

Module Test
  Sub Main()
    Dim OrderCollection As New OrderCollection()

    OrderCollection.Orders(5).Cost = 10.34
    Console.WriteLine(OrderCollection.Orders(5).Cost)
  End Sub
End Module
```

An indexed property can be declared as the *default property* for the type. This allows the type itself to be indexed directly as if it were the default property. In the following example, when the index is applied to the Customers variable, it is equivalent to applying the index to the default property of the CustomerCollection class.

```
Class Customer
  Public Name As String
End Class

Class CustomerCollection
  Private _Customers(9) As Customer

  Public Default Property Customer(ByVal Index As Integer) As Customer
    Get
      If _Customers(Index) Is Nothing Then
        _Customers(Index) = New Customer()
      End If
```

```
      Return _Customers(Index)
    End Get

    Set (Value As Customer)
      _Customers(Index) = Value
    End Set
  End Property
End Class

Module Test
  Sub Main()
    Dim Customers As New CustomerCollection()

    ' Customers(5).Name is equivalent to Customers.Customer(5).Name
    Customers(5).Name = "John Doe"
    Console.WriteLine(Customers(5).Name)
  End Sub
End Module
```

Default properties are most useful for defining collection types that
work like arrays.

Events

An *event* is a notification that is given when something specific happens in
a program, such as a button being clicked or a text box's value changing.
When an event occurs, the type that is giving the notification *raises* the
event, which allows other interested types to *handle* the event.

A type declares an event much in the same way that it declares a subroutine. The following example declares a `Click` and a `Moved` event.

```
Class Button
  Private X, Y As Integer

  Public Event Click()
  Public Event Moved(ByVal X As Integer, ByVal Y As Integer)
End Class
```

Events are raised by the `RaiseEvent` statement. The `RaiseEvent` statement has the same syntax as a method invocation.

```
Sub Move(ByVal X As Integer, ByVal Y As Integer)
  Me.X = X
  Me.Y = Y
```

```
      RaiseEvent Moved(X, Y)
   End Sub
```

Events can be handled in two ways: declaratively and dynamically.

Declarative Event Handling

Declarative event handling is the simplest way to handle events because it allows a type to declare what events it handles, and the compiler takes care of the rest. The first step in declarative event handling is declaring that a field contains something that may raise events. This is done by adding the WithEvents modifier to the beginning of a field declaration.

```
Class Form1
   Public WithEvents Button1 As Button
End Class
```

Methods can then declare that they handle specific events that are raised by the field. In this example, the Button1_Click method handles the Click event of the Button1 field.

```
Class Form1
   Public WithEvents Button1 As Button

   Public Sub Button1_Click() Handles Button1.Click
     MsgBox("Button1 was clicked!")
   End Sub
End Class
```

The Handles clause must specify a WithEvents variable followed by an event. The parameters of the method must exactly match the parameters of the event that it wishes to handle.

Dynamic Event Handling

Sometimes it is not possible or desirable to handle events declaratively. The AddHandler and RemoveHandler statements allow dynamically hooking up to and unhooking from events. Both statements take a delegate (covered later in the chapter) that specifies the method that handles the event. Once a handler has been added to the event, it will continue to be handled until the handler is removed. In the following example, when an instance of Button is created, the code adds a handler for the Click event. When all the `Button` instances are released, the code removes the handlers from the `Click` event.

```
Class Form1
  Public Buttons As New ArrayList()

  Public Sub CreateButton()
    Dim NewButton As New Button()

    AddHandler NewButton.Click, AddressOf Me.Button_Click
    Buttons.Add(NewButton)
  End Sub

  Public Sub DeleteAllButtons()
    For Each Button As Button in Buttons
      RemoveHandler Button.Click, AddressOf Me.Button_Click
    Next Button
  End Sub

  Public Sub Button_Click()
    MsgBox("Button1 was clicked!")
  End Sub
End Class
```

Namespaces

A *namespace* is a name that is used to organize related types within an assembly or across assemblies. For example, all the .NET Framework types are collected in the `System` namespace. All the .NET Framework types that relate to Windows Forms are collected into the `System.Windows.Forms` namespace, and so on. Namespaces are *open* in that multiple declarations can contribute to the same namespace—even across multiple assemblies. In the following example, both namespace declarations contribute to the same namespace, so the `MegaCorp.Controls` namespace contains both `Button` and `Label`.

```
Namespace MegaCorp.Controls
  Class Button
    ...
  End Class
End Namespace
```

```
Namespace MegaCorp.Controls
   Class Label
   . . .
   End Class
End Namespace
```

It is sometimes necessary to use the full name of the type when referring to it in code. The full name of a type includes the type's namespace—for example, `MegaCorp.Controls.Button`. This can become onerous, however, if the namespace is long and the type is frequently used. The `Imports` statement allows referring to a type without the need to include its namespace.

```
Imports MegaCorp.Controls

Module Test
  Sub Main()
    Dim x As Button = New Button()

    . . .
    End Sub
End Module
```

If the same type name exists in two different imported namespaces, it is not possible for the compiler to know which type the name refers to. The `Imports` statement can also be used to define an alias for a type or a namespace to allow disambiguation in this situation. In this example, the `Button` type is defined in both the `MegaCorp.Controls` namespace and the `Tiny-Corp.Controls` namespace. When the namespaces are imported, aliases are assigned to each namespace so that the code can make it clear which `Button` it is referring to.

```
Imports Mega = MegaCorp.Controls
Imports Tiny = TinyCorp.Controls

Namespace MegaCorp.Controls
   Class Button
   . . .
   End Class
End Namespace
```

```
Namespace TinyCorp.Controls
   Class Button
      . . .
   End Class
End Namespace

Module Test
   Sub Main()
      Dim x As Mega.Button
      Dim y As Tiny.Button

      . . .
   End Sub
End Module
```

The members of a type can also be imported using `Imports`. For instance, this can be used to refer to the names of enumerations without qualification.

```
Imports Color

Enum Color
   Red
   Green
   Blue
End Enum

Module Test
   Sub Main()
      Dim c As Color = Red
   End Sub
End Module
```

Delegates

A *delegate* is a type that represents a pointer to a method. A delegate type defines the parameters and return type of the kind of method that it can point to. Then, a delegate instance can be constructed around the address of any compatible method. A delegate instance can be invoked just as if it were a subroutine, and it will call the method that the delegate points to. For example, the following code creates a delegate instance that points to the method `Class1.S1` and then invokes it.

```
Delegate Sub SubroutineDelegate(ByVal x As Integer)
```

```
Class Class1
  Public Sub S1(ByVal x As Integer)
    MsgBox(x)
  End Sub
End Class

Module Test
  Sub Main()
    Dim s1 As SubroutineDelegate
    Dim t As New Class1()

    s1 = New SubroutineDelegate(AddressOf t.S1)
    s1(10)
  End Sub
End Module
```

A delegate instance stores both the address of the method and the instance given when the delegate was created (if the method is not shared). Delegates can be *multicast*, which means that multiple delegates can be combined into a single delegate that will invoke all the methods, one at a time. The following example creates a delegate that points to both Class1.S1 and Class1.S2. When the delegate is invoked, each method will be invoked in turn.

```
Delegate Sub SubroutineDelegate(ByVal x As Integer)

Class Class1
  Public Sub S1(ByVal x As Integer)
    MsgBox("S1: " & x)
  End Sub

  Public Sub S2(ByVal x As Integer)
    MsgBox("S2: " & x)
  End Sub
End Class

Module Test
  Sub Main()
    Dim s1, s2 As SubroutineDelegate
    Dim t As New Class1()

    s1 = New SubroutineDelegate(AddressOf t.S1)
    s2 = New SubroutineDelegate(AddressOf t.S2)
    s1 = [Delegate].Combine(s1, s2)
    s1(10)
  End Sub
End Module
```

Inheritance

A class can *inherit* members from another class. For example, a `Square` class can inherit members from a `Shape` class.

```
Class Shape
   Public x, y As Integer
End Class

Class Square
   Inherits Shape

   Public Width, Height As Integer

   Public Sub New(ByVal x As Integer, ByVal y As Integer, _
      ByVal Width As Integer, ByVal Height As Integer)
     Me.x = x
     Me.y = y
     Me.Width = Width
     Me.Height = Height
   End Sub
End Class
```

In this example, the `Square` class inherits members named x and y from the `Shape` class. The `Shape` class is called the *base class* of the `Square` class, and the `Square` class *derives from* the `Shape` class. A class can prevent other classes from inheriting from it by using the `NotInheritable` modifier on the class declaration.

Inheritance is most useful when multiple classes are defined that all share common traits. This allows code to be written that operates just on the common traits, which means the same routine can be used on many different classes.

```
Class Shape
   Public x, y As Integer

   Sub Move(ByVal x As Integer, ByVal y As Integer)
     Me.x = x
     Me.y = y
   End Sub
End Class

Class Square
   Inherits Shape

   Public Width, Height As Integer
```

```
      ...
   End Class

   Class RightTriangle
      Inherits Shape

      Public SideLengths() As Integer
      ...
   End Class

   Module Test
      Sub Main()
         Dim s As Square = New Square()
         Dim t As RightTriangle = New RightTriangle()

         s.Move(10, 20)
         t.Move(30, 40)
      End Sub
   End Module
```

Because a derived class contains all the members of its base classes, an instance of a derived class can always be treated as an instance of a base class. For example, the following code declares a method that works on instances of Shape. Instances of Square can be passed to the method because Square contains all the members that Shape does.

```
   Module Test
      Sub PrintLocation(ByVal Shape As Shape)
         Console.WriteLine(Shape.x & "," & Shape.y)
      End Sub

      Sub Main()
         Dim s As Square = New Square()

         PrintLocation(s)
      End Sub
   End Module
```

Protected Access

The Protected access level allows class members to be accessed only by more derived types. This is useful for members that contain internal state that can be used by more derived classes. In the following example, the Person class declares a field, SSN, that is Private just to the Person class, and a field, Password, that is accessible to any derived class.

```
Class Person
  Private SSN As String
  Protected Password As String
End Class

Class Employee
  Inherits Person

  Sub New()
    ' Error: SSN is private to Person
    SSN = "123-45-7890"

    ' OK: Password is protected and can be accessed
    Password = "password"
  End Sub
End Class
```

Access to a `Protected` member in a derived class must take place through an instance of that derived class. Without this rule, it would be possible to gain access to a `Protected` member of another type simply by deriving from a common base class.

```
Class Person
  Protected Password As String
End Class

Class Employee
  Inherits Person
End Class

Class Guest
  Inherits Person

  Public Sub PrintEmployeePassword(ByVal e As Employee)
    Console.WriteLine(e.Password)
  End Sub
End Class
```

In this example, `Guest` cannot access `Employee`'s protected field `Password`—it can only access the `Password` field of instances of `Guest`. `Protected` access can be combined with `Friend` access, in which case derived classes and types within the same assembly can access the member.

Overriding

A base class may wish to allow a derived class to provide a different implementation for a method defined in the base class. A base class can do this by declaring a method as *overridable*. This allows the derived class to *override* the implementation of that method. For example, the following code allows the method `PrintCoordinates` to be overridden. The derived type `Square` overrides the base class implementation so that it can print all four coordinates.

```
Class Shape
  Public x, y As Integer

  Overridable Sub PrintCoordinates()
    Console.Write(x & "," & y)
  End Sub
End Class

Class Square
  Inherits Shape

  Public Width, Height As Integer

  Overrides Sub PrintCoordinates()
    Console.Write(x & "," & y)
    Console.Write("-")
    Console.Write((x + Width) & "," & (y + Height))
  End Sub
End Class
```

When a class overrides a method that it inherits from a base class, the overriding method will be called regardless of the stated type of an instance. For example, the following code prints `1,1 - 4,4`, not `1,1`, because `Square`'s implementation of `PrintCoordinates` is still called even though it is typed as a `Shape`.

```
Module Test
  Sub Main()
    Dim Shape As Shape
    Dim Square As Square = New Square()

    Square.x = 1
    Square.y = 1
```

```
      Square.Width = 3
      Square.Height = 3

      Shape = Square
      Shape.PrintCoordinates()
   End Sub
End Module
```

If an overriding method wishes to use the base class's implementation, it can call the base implementation using the qualifier `MyBase`.

```
Overrides Sub PrintCoordinates()
  MyBase.PrintCoordinates()
  Console.Write("-")
  Console.Write((x + Width) & "," & (y + Height))
End Sub
```

A base class can also *require* that derived classes override a method by using the keyword `MustOverride` and providing no implementation for the method. A class that contains `MustOverride` methods cannot be created directly, because it contains methods that have no implementation—only derived classes that provide an implementation for the `MustOverride` methods can be created. A class with `MustOverride` methods must use the keyword `MustInherit`, which means that the class cannot be created directly. In the following example, the `MustInherit` class `Shape` defines a `MustOverride` method, `Paint`, that derived classes must provide an implementation for.

```
MustInherit Class Shape
   Public x, y As Integer

   MustOverride Sub Paint()
End Class

Class Square
  Inherits Shape

  Public Width, Height As Integer

  Overrides Sub Paint()
    ...
  End Sub
End Class
```

Finally, when a derived class overrides a method, it can prevent any further derived class from overriding the method by adding the `NotOverridable` modifier to the declaration.

Interfaces

An *interface* is a set of methods, events, and properties that a type can declare that it supports. When a type supports an interface, it is said to *implement* the interface. Interfaces are useful to allow types to declare general capabilities that they support. For example, the .NET Framework defines an interface, `IComparable`, that defines a `CompareTo` method.

```
Interface IComparable
    Function CompareTo(ByVal obj As Object) As Integer
End Interface
```

A type that implements `IComparable` can then be compared in a general way; for example, the Framework also defines an `Array.Sort` method that sorts arrays. This method requires that the type of the array implement `IComparable`, so that the sorting algorithm can determine whether one element of the array is "less than" another element of the array. If a type does not implement the interface, it cannot be sorted in an array. The following example shows a type implementing the `IComparable` interface.

```
Class Building
    Implements IComparable

    Public Height As Integer

    Public Function CompareTo(ByVal obj As Object) As Integer _
        Implements IComparable.CompareTo
      Dim OtherHeight As Integer

      If Not TypeOf obj Is Building Then
        Throw New ArgumentException()
      End If

      OtherHeight = CType(obj, Building).Height

      If Height < OtherHeight Then
        Return -1
```

```
      ElseIf Height > OtherHeight Then
        Return 1
      Else
        Return 0
      End If
  End Class
```

Interface implementation is different from inheritance in that implementing an interface provides no default implementation—instead, it simply names a set of members that the type must provide. Additionally, a type may implement as many interfaces as it wishes, while a class can only inherit from one base type. Interfaces, then, are primarily used to describe capabilities that many different kinds of types may support, while inheritance is primarily used to describe types that are closely related in some way.

Attributes

The language defines keywords such as `Public`, `ByRef`, and `Overridable` that can be applied to declarations to modify their meaning. These predefined modifiers can be augmented by user-defined *attributes* that can store extra declarative information about types and type members. For example, attributes can be used to declare that a type or type member is obsolete and should no longer be used.

```
<Obsolete("Use NewSquare class instead.")> _
Public Class Square
  ...
End Class

Public Class NewSquare
  ...

  <Obsolete("Use NewMove method instead.")> _
  Public Sub Move(ByVal x As Integer, ByVal y As Integer)
    ...
  End Sub

  Public Sub NewMove(ByVal x As Integer, ByVal y As Integer, _
      ByVal Refresh As Boolean)
    ...
  End Sub
End Class
```

Attributes are defined by declaring a class that inherits from the type `System.Attribute`. A `System.AttributeUsageAttribute` attribute must also be applied to the class. For example, the following type defines an `Author` attribute that can be used to name the author of a type.

```
<AttributeUsage(AttributeTargets.All)> _
Class AuthorAttribute
  Inherits Attribute

  Public Name As String
  Public Company As String

  Public Sub New(ByVal Name As String)
    Me.Name = Name
  End Sub
End Class
```

The parameters to the constructor of a user-defined attribute define the arguments that must be supplied when the attribute is specified on a type or type member. Fields and properties in the user-defined attribute can also be assigned to. For example:

```
<Author("John Doe", Company := "MegaCorp")> _
Module Test
  <Author("Jane Doe", Company := "Acme")> _
  Sub Main()
  End Sub
End Module
```

To retrieve attributes, the Framework reflection classes can be used.

```
<Author("John Doe", Company := "MegaCorp")> _
Class TestClass
End Class

Module Test
  Sub Main()
    Dim T As Type = GetType(TestClass)
    Dim AuthAttribute As AuthorAttribute

    AuthAttribute = CType(T.GetCustomAttributes(False)(0), _
      AuthorAttribute)
    Console.WriteLine(AuthAttribute.Name)
    Console.WriteLine(AuthAttribute.Company)
  End Sub
End Module
```

Versioning

Many applications and class libraries go through multiple release cycles during their lifetimes. When you are upgrading an application or library, it is not uncommon to add functionality in the form of new types and type members. When you are adding new types and type members, though, inheritance can cause a problem. For example, if version 1.0 of a class library contains the following:

```
Class Base
  Sub S1()
    ...
  End Sub
End Class
```

and version 2.0 adds a new method, as follows:

```
Class Base
  Sub S1()
    ...
  End Sub

  Sub S2()
    ...
  End Sub
End Class
```

then any class that derives from `Base` and defines its own member, `S2`, will break when compiled against version 2.0. To solve this problem, the `Shadows` and `Overloads` keywords can be used to allow a derived member to hide base members. The `Shadows` keyword causes a derived member to hide all base members with the same name; the `Overloads` keyword causes a derived member to hide only the base members with the same set of parameters. `Shadows` is the default because it protects implicitly against all changes, but `Overloads` is useful when a derived type does not wish to hide all the base members. For example:

```
Class Base
  Sub WriteLine(ByVal i As Integer)
    ...
  End Sub
```

```
    Sub Input()
      ...
    End Sub
End Class

Class Derived
    Inherits Base

    Overloads Sub WriteLine(ByVal d As Double)
      ...
    End Sub

    Shadows Sub Input()
      ...
    End Sub
End Class
```

In the case of `WriteLine`, the derived class is augmenting the list of methods; in the case of `Input`, it is hiding all other implementations.

Conclusion

This chapter has given a quick, high-level overview of the Visual Basic .NET language in its entirety. Keep in mind that many of the details of the language were not covered here in the interests of brevity—the later chapters in the book cover each topic in more thorough detail. However, the hope is that this overview will give the reader enough familiarity with the language to be able to sit down and start writing Visual Basic .NET programs. Having some practical experience with the language before continuing to the more detailed discussions that follow is recommended, but not required.

2

Basic Concepts

$\mathbf{B}$efore we dive fully into the language, it is first necessary to cover some basic concepts about the Visual Basic .NET language and the .NET Framework. This chapter covers some of the fundamental ideas that apply across the entire language. It also talks a little bit about the underlying design of the .NET Framework.

Language Fundamentals

If you take a look at the source code for the `HelloWorld` program from the previous chapter, several things should already be obvious. The first thing that should stand out is the way that the Visual Basic .NET language takes advantage of English words and syntax to make code as readable as possible. Compare the following Visual Basic .NET version of the "Hello, world!" program:

```
Module HelloWorld
  Public Sub Main()
    Console.WriteLine("Hello, world!")
    Console.ReadLine()
  End Sub
End Module
```

with the equivalent program in Visual C# .NET.

```
using System;
```

```
class HelloWorld
{
  public static void Main()
  {
    Console.WriteLine("Hello, world!");
    Console.ReadLine();
  }
}
```

In many ways the syntax of the two programs looks similar. But a closer look at how the `Main` subroutine is defined reveals some differences—in Visual Basic .NET, the subroutine `Main` starts with the statement `Sub Main` and ends with the statement `End Sub`. In Visual C# .NET, the subroutine `Main` starts with the statement `void Main` and an opening curly brace ({) and ends with a closing curly brace (}). While Visual C# .NET emphasizes conciseness at the cost of some readability, Visual Basic .NET emphasizes readability at the cost of some conciseness. This emphasis on using English (or English-like) words and syntax extends throughout the language and is intended to make reading Visual Basic .NET code as easy as possible. In most cases, keywords in the language describe what they do, and statements can be read as if they were sentences.

Case Insensitivity

Another aspect of Visual Basic .NET that is different from many other programming languages is that it is *case insensitive*. That is, the language does not care whether characters are uppercase or lowercase in a program. The following code compiles just the same as the original `HelloWorld` program shown earlier.

```
module HelloWorld
  SUB Main()
    console.writeline("Hello, world!")
    ConsolE.ReadlinE()
  EnD SuB
END MODULE
```

The fact that `module` is not capitalized has no effect on the program, nor does the fact that `END` is all uppercase.

Style

Although the language is very relaxed in regard to casing, it is always a good idea to use consistent casing because this increases the readability and understandability of code. The Visual Studio IDE will usually automatically correct casing to be consistent.

In the same way that the language is not strict about casing, the language is also relaxed in regard to parts of the language that can be understood implicitly. For example, the following version of the `HelloWorld` program is also equivalent to the first example.

```
Module HelloWorld
  Sub Main
    Console.WriteLine("Hello, World!")
    Console.ReadLine
  End Sub
End Module
```

This version of the `HelloWorld` program leaves off the parentheses after the `Sub Main` and `Console.ReadLine` statements. This is allowed because it can be reasonably inferred that leaving off the parentheses means that the subroutine has no parameters or arguments—the same thing that specifying empty parentheses indicates. There are many places in the language where pieces of syntax are optional when the intent is obvious.

Style

In general, it is best to specify syntax even if it is optional. The Visual Studio IDE will usually insert optional syntax if it is omitted.

Line Orientation

Another fundamental aspect of Visual Basic .NET may have become obvious if you tried typing in the `HelloWorld` program and didn't type it in exactly as it appeared on the page. Unlike some programming languages, Visual Basic .NET is *line-oriented*. This means that where a line ends is significant—lines cannot end just anywhere. This is in contrast to other languages, such as C++, that are *free-format*. Free-format languages allow ending lines almost anywhere the programmer pleases, even in the middle of a statement (although not in the middle of a word).

Historical

Visual Basic .NET's line orientation is a byproduct of the past—because the BASIC language was originally an interpreted (rather than compiled) language, the interpreter needed to know when to start interpreting the next statement. Although Visual Basic .NET is not an interpreted language, it still retains this design point from its ancestors.

Except in the cases discussed later in the chapter, Visual Basic .NET does not allow more than one statement on a line and does not allow a statement to span more than one line. For example, although the follow program looks almost the same as the first `HelloWorld` program, it will not compile.

```
' This program will not compile!
Module
HelloWorld
  Sub Main
  (
  )
    Console.WriteLine("Hello, world!")
    Console.
      ReadLine
        ()
End Sub End Module
```

Compiling the preceding program will cause many different errors because Visual Basic .NET expects that an entire statement will appear on one line and that each statement will appear on its own line. The statement `Sub Main()` starts the `Main` subroutine, so the language expects that the entire statement will be together. Similarly, the `End Sub` statement ends the

`Main` subroutine, so the language expects that it will be the only statement on that line.

When you have a very long line of code, requiring that an entire statement be on one line can be painful. To help with this, a program can use *line continuations* to break a single statement across multiple lines. A line continuation allows a statement to be extended over one or more lines by placing an underscore (_) at the end of a line. This tells the compiler that the line continues on to the next line. It is important to notice that there has to be at least once space between the line continuation and anything that comes before it.

Design

There has to be one space before a line continuation because the underscore can also be part of a name. Without this rule, given a line that looks like x = y_, it would be unclear whether the underscore was part of the name y_ or a line continuation.

It is also possible to put more than one statement on a line by using a *statement separator*. A statement separator separates the statements on a line by placing a colon (:) between each statement. The one restriction on statement separators is that a subroutine or function declaration must always be the first statement on a line. For example, the following code is still not valid, because the `Sub Main` statement must be the first statement on a line.

```
' This program will not compile!
Module HelloWorld : Sub Main()
    Console.WriteLine("Hello, world!")
End Sub : End Module
```

The original example, though, could be made to compile using line continuations and statement separators.

```
Module _
HelloWorld
  Sub Main _
```

```
   ( _
   )
     Console.WriteLine("Hello, world!")
     Console. _
       ReadLine _
           ()
 End Sub : End Module
```

The line continuation characters keep the entire `Module` and `Sub` declaration statements together, while the statement separator separates the two `End` statements.

Comments

A *comment* is text that is intended solely for the programmer and not for the compiler. Comments can be used to provide descriptions of what code does or to serve as reminders of things that still need to be done. Comments in Visual Basic .NET are started by using the single quote character (`'`) anywhere on a line and continue from that point until the end of the line. The language ignores anything in a comment, so a comment may contain any text. For example:

```
  '
  ' This program prints the string "Hello, world!" to the output
  ' window.
  '


  '
  ' This contains the Main routine and does all the work.
  '
 Module HelloWorld
    '
    ' This is the main routine and prints out the string.
    '
    Public Sub Main()
      Console.WriteLine("Hello, world!")   ' Print the string
      Console.ReadLine()                   ' Wait for input
    End Sub   ' Main
 End Module   ' HelloWorld
```

Since everything after a comment begins is ignored, it is not possible to continue a comment across multiple lines. Comments that will not fit on one line must be broken into multiple lines with each line starting with a single quote, as in the preceding example. Comments cannot be placed after a line continuation.

```
' This program will not compile!
Module HelloWorld
    Sub Main( _              ' Invalid comment
      Args() As String _     ' Invalid comment
      )                      ' Valid comment
      Console.WriteLine("Hello, world!")
      End Sub
End Module
```

The second and third comments in this example are not valid comments, because they follow a line continuation. The last comment is valid because it does not.

Compatibility

In keeping with historical precedent, the word REM can also be used to start a comment, but its use is discouraged.

Declarations and Names

A Visual Basic .NET program contains *declarations*. A declaration is any statement that defines something new in a program, whether that new thing is a local variable, a method, a class, a namespace, and so on. When something new is declared in a program, it must be given a name. Names can be made up of any combination of letters, numbers, and the underscore character (_). Some examples of names follow.

```
Dim x As Integer
Dim _y, __z As Integer
Dim Choice1, Choice2, Choice3 As Integer
```

There are two restrictions on names in Visual Basic .NET: First, a name cannot begin with a number, and, second, a name that begins with an underscore must contain at least one other character. The second restriction allows the compiler to distinguish identifiers from line continuations. For example, the second local variable declaration in the following example is not valid in Visual Basic .NET.

```
Dim x As Integer
Dim _ As Integer    ' Error: _ is not a valid name
_ = 5
x = _
```

As can be seen from the example, if it were valid to have a name that was just an underscore, it would be extremely difficult to tell the name and a line continuation apart.

Some declarations, such as classes and namespaces, can contain other declarations. For example:

```
Module Test
   Sub Main()
      Dim x As Integer
   End Sub
End Module
```

In this example, the declaration of the module `Test` contains the declaration of the subroutine `Main`. The declaration of the subroutine `Main` contains the declaration of the local variable x. In general, declarations can only be referred to by name within the bounds of the containing declaration (including any nested declarations)—this defines the *scope* in which the name can be used. For example:

```
Namespace A
   Namespace B
      Class C
      End Class
   End Namespace
End Namespace

Module Test
   Sub Main()
      Dim x As C  ' Error: C is not found.
   End Sub
End Module
```

In this example, the scope of the class C is the containing namespace declaration B. Since the subroutine Main is not within the scope of class C's name, it can't refer to C.

In most cases, it is possible to refer to a name outside of its scope by *qualifying* the name with the name of its scope. This is done by putting a period and the name of the scope before the name you want. The name on the right side of the period then refers to a name that is within the scope of the declaration named on the left side of the period. For example:

```
Namespace A
   Namespace B
      Class C
      End Class
   End Namespace
End Namespace

Module Test
   Sub Main()
      Dim x As A.B.C
   End Sub
End Module
```

In this example, the subroutine Main is within namespace A's scope. The namespace C is qualified with the name of namespace B, which is further qualified with the namespace A, which is in scope. This allows Main to refer to the class C.

Two declarations in the same scope cannot use the same name. If they did, it might be impossible to determine which of the two declarations was being referred to. For example:

```
Module Test
   Sub Main()
      Dim x As Integer
      Dim x As Long      ' Invalid because x is already declared

      x = 5
   End Sub
End Module
```

In this case, there is no way to tell which local variable x is being assigned to. To avoid this kind of confusion, two declarations cannot use the same name (the one exception to this is method overloading, discussed in Chapter 10, Methods). Remember, however, that two declarations *can* use the same name if they are declared within separate scopes.

```
Module Test
  Sub Test()
    Dim x As Long
  End Sub

  Sub Main()
    Dim x As Integer
  End Sub
End Module
```

In this case, the two local variables named x are declared in different methods, so their names do not conflict.

Keep in mind that this is only a brief overview of how declarations and names work in Visual Basic .NET—there are exceptions that apply to certain kinds of declarations, and these special rules will be covered later in the book.

Forward References

When a Visual Basic .NET program is compiled, the entire source of the program is compiled together at the same time. This means that each source file can see the declarations made in all source files. Also, all the declarations within a file are processed at once, so there is no need for header files or forward references as in C or C++. This means that one declaration can refer to another declaration that occurs after it in a source file. For example, the following code compiles and runs fine, even though the method Add is declared after the method Multiply that calls it.

```
Function Multiply(ByVal x As Integer, ByVal y As Integer) As Integer
  Dim Result As Integer

  For Count As Integer = 1 to x
    Result = Add(Result, y)
  Next Count

  Return Result
End Function
```

```
Function Add(ByVal x As Integer, ByVal y As Integer) As Integer
   Return x + y
End Function
```

As a result, the organization of source code is entirely up to the programmer and is never dictated by the code itself. Where code goes in a program is completely a matter of programmer preference.

Accessibility

Every declaration in a Visual Basic .NET program has a particular access level associated with it. This access level determines the *accessibility* of the declaration by other parts of the code, or by other assemblies that might reference the compiled assembly. Accessibility is enforced not only by the compiler but also by the .NET Framework; it is part of the general security model of the Framework. Access levels for a member are specified by modifying a declaration with the desired access level.

The two simplest access levels are Public and Private. Public members can be accessed by anyone, without restriction, while Private members can only be accessed by the type that they are declared in. For example:

```
Class Employee
   Public Name As String
   Private Salary As Double
End Class

Module Test
   Sub Main()
     Dim c As Employee = New Employee()

     ' OK, Name is public
     c.Name = "John Doe"

     ' Invalid, Salary is private
     c.Salary = 100403.33
   End Sub
End Module
```

This example declared a class, Employee, that has two members: a Public field, Name, and a Private field, Salary. The Main subroutine can change the Name field because its Public access means anyone can access it. Main cannot change the Salary field, however, because that field is Private to the class.

The Friend access level allows access from within an assembly, but not outside of it. It is useful when writing objects that will go into a class library that will be used by other assemblies. Friend members can be used freely within the class library, but other assemblies will have no access to the members.

It is worth noting that accessibility applies to a declaration, not a particular instance of a type. So two Employee objects could access each other's Salary field.

```
Class Employee
  Public Name As String
  Private Salary As Double

  Public Sub CompareSalaries(ByVal Other As Employee)
    Console.Write(Name & " makes ")

    If Salary > Other.Salary Then
      Console.Write("more than ")
    Else If Salary < Other.Salary Then
      Console.Write("less than ")
    Else
      Console.Write("the same as ")
    End If

    Console.WriteLine(Other.Name)
  End Sub
End Class
```

One important thing to remember is that the access of any declaration may be constrained by the access of a declaration that contains it. For example, it is reasonable and valid to declare a Public field in a class that is declared to be Friend. Even though the field is Public, any access to the field has to come through the class, so the field's effective access level is Friend. The general rule of thumb is this: A member's access can never be greater than that of all its containers.

The .NET Framework

Programs written in Visual Basic .NET are designed to run on the .NET Framework (see Figure 2-1). Although a programmer does not need to understand everything about the Framework to be able to write programs for it, there are a few concepts that a programmer should understand because they affect the language and the behavior of some parts of the language.

As discussed briefly in the previous chapter, the output of a Visual Basic .NET compiler is an assembly that contains all of the program's code and metadata. However, this assembly is not a Windows executable in and of itself, because it contains IL instead of *x86* instructions that an Intel-compatible microprocessor can understand. For an assembly to be run, it must be loaded within the .NET Framework runtime environment and compiled from IL into actual *x86* instructions that can be run under Windows. This translation step, known as Just-In-Time (or JIT) compiling, allows the Framework to inspect the IL code for security and correctness before it is actually run.

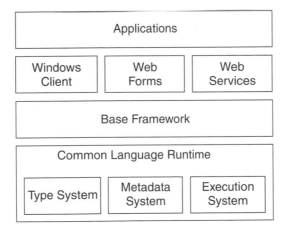

FIGURE 2-1: The .NET Framework

The Framework also provides a number of services to assemblies, such as automatic memory management, serialization, security, and interoperability with COM and Win32 APIs. This means that programmers do not have to write code to implement these services themselves.

Program Startup and Termination

The fact that the subroutine in the HelloWorld example in the previous chapter was named Main is not coincidental. After the Framework has loaded an assembly and translated the IL into *x86* instructions, it looks for a method named Main and starts executing the program with that method. The Main method is also known as the *entry point* of the program.

The entry point method can take several forms. In the simplest form, as in the HelloWorld example, it is just a subroutine that is called by the Framework and returns when the program is finished.

```
Module CommandLine
  Sub Main()
    . . .
  End Sub
End Module
```

Main can also be declared as a function that returns an Integer value. In that case, the value returned by Main will be passed out to the calling environment—for a console application, this sets the error level of the program when it is done. The method can also be declared to take a one-dimensional array of String as a parameter; at runtime, this array will be filled in by the Framework with the arguments, if any, passed in on the command line. The following example shows an application that prints the command-line arguments passed to the program and returns a value of 1.

```
Module CommandLine
  Function Main(ByVal Args() As String) As Integer
    For Each Arg As String In Args
      Console.WriteLine(Arg)
    Next Arg

    Return 1
  End Function
End Module
```

Entry points are only called for applications. Class libraries (DLLs) don't have explicit entry points, because they are loaded by applications and are never executed on their own.

Conclusion

This chapter has covered some of the basic aspects of the language and the .NET Framework as preparation for diving into the deeper details. From here, the discussion moves on to the fundamental types that all programs use, such as `Integer`.

Here are some style points to consider.

- Although the language is very relaxed in regard to casing, it is always a good idea to use correct casing because this increases the readability and understandability of code. The Visual Studio IDE will usually correct casing.
- In general, it is best to specify syntax even if it is optional. The Visual Studio IDE will usually insert optional syntax if it is omitted.
- In keeping with historical precedent, the word REM can also be used to start a comment, but its use is discouraged.

◼3◼
Fundamental Types

All information stored or used by a Visual Basic .NET program has a *type*. A type describes a piece of information to the .NET Framework, saying how it is used and stored. By assigning every piece of information a type, the language can enforce *type-safe programming*, which ensures that information is always interpreted in a correct manner, helping to reduce programming errors.

There are 11 fundamental types in Visual Basic .NET. All the fundamental types support *literals*, which are a textual representation of a particular value of a fundamental type. For example, the string 10.5 is a Double literal that represents the decimal value 10.5. The fundamental types are listed in Table 3-1.

Among the 11 fundamental types are seven numeric types. These numeric types split into three categories: integers of varying ranges (Byte, Short, Integer, and Long), floating-point numbers of varying ranges and precision (Single and Double), and a decimal number with a fixed range and precision (Decimal).

Boolean

The Boolean data type can store the two Boolean values "true" and "false." The Boolean data type is primarily used in conditional statements such as If or While, since the comparison operators (such as < or =) result in a

TABLE 3-1: Fundamental Types

Type	Description
Boolean	A Boolean (true/false) value
Byte	A 1-byte unsigned integer
Short	A 2-byte signed integer
Integer	A 4-byte signed integer
Long	An 8-byte signed integer
Decimal	A 16-byte scaled decimal number
Single	A 4-byte single precision floating-point number
Double	An 8-byte double precision floating-point number
Date	A time/date value
Char	A single Unicode character
String	A string of Unicode characters

Boolean value. For example, in the following function, the Negative local variable determines what is printed.

```
Dim a As Integer
Dim Negative As Boolean

a = 10 - 20
Negative = a < 0

If Negative Then
  Console.WriteLine("Less than zero.")
Else
  Console.WriteLine("Greater than or equal to zero.")
End If
```

The Boolean values "true" and "false" are represented by the literals True and False, respectively. The default value of Boolean is the literal False.

Integer Data Types

The integer data types store numbers with no fractional part. Because processing integers is simpler than processing numbers that have fractional parts, in most cases working with integer types will be faster than working with decimal numbers. The four integer types have different sizes and ranges.

- The Byte data type is one byte long and is the smallest of the integer data types. Its range is from 0 to 255, and it cannot represent negative numbers.
- The Short data type is two bytes long. Its range is from –32,768 to 32,767.
- The Integer data type is four bytes long. Its range is from –2,147,483,648 through 2,147,483,647.
- The Long data type is eight bytes long. Its range is from –9,223,372,036,854,775,808 through 9,223,372,036,854,775,807.

Advanced

Because of the way that signed integer types are represented in the .NET Framework, Short, Integer, and Long have a range that is one smaller on the positive side than it is on the negative side (i.e., the minimum value of Short is –32,768, but the maximum value is only 32,767)

Compatibility

The ranges of the Integer and Long types have been widened from previous versions, and a new type, Short, has been added. The range of Short is the same as the range of Integer in previous versions, and the range of Integer is equivalent to the range of Long in previous versions. When you are converting code from previous versions of Visual Basic, it is important to keep in mind this difference.

By default, most programs should use the `Integer` type to store integer numbers because it is the most natural integer size on the .NET Framework. For numbers that have a larger range than `Integer`, `Long` is an acceptable choice. The `Byte` and `Short` data types are less efficient on the Framework than `Integer` and `Long`, and so should not be used unless there are space concerns (such as may be the case with large arrays of integer values). The default value of the integer types is the literal `0`.

Advanced

`Byte` and `Short` tend to be less efficient at runtime because the Framework only represents numbers as 32-bit or 64-bit values. Thus, when you are performing operations on `Byte` and `Short` values, additional overflow checks must be explicitly performed to ensure that the resulting value stays within the range of the declared type. Nevertheless, their storage space savings may justify their use, especially in large arrays.

Integer Literals

Integer literals can be specified using one of three bases: decimal, octal, and hexadecimal. Decimal integer literals are decimal (base 10) numbers such as `10`, `43274`, and `34920492`. Octal integer literals are preceded by an ampersand (`&`) and the letter O, and are made up of a string of octal (base 8) digits, such as `&O30`, `&O4123`, and `&O7372`. Hexadecimal integer literals are preceded by an ampersand and the letter H, and are made up of a string of hexadecimal (base 16) digits—the numbers 0–9 and the letters A–F—such as `&H3A`, `&H49D`, and `&H4932`. The following shows some examples of integer literals.

```
Dim a As Byte
Dim b As Short
Dim c As Integer
Dim d As Long
```

```
a = 10
b = &O43S
c = 32767
d = &HFFFFFFFFFL
```

Decimal literals represent the decimal value of the literal, while octal and hexadecimal literals represent the binary value of the literal. In the preceding example, the hexadecimal literal `&HFFFFFFFFFL` is equal to the decimal literal `-1L`.

The type of an integer literal is always `Integer` unless it does not fit into the range of `Integer`. In that case, the type of the integer literal is `Long`.

Advanced

Integer literals are not signed. As a result, the expression `-10` is interpreted as the negation operator applied to the integer literal `10`. This has no consequence in most situations except when two particular values are being interpreted. The expression `−2147483648` is typed as `Long` instead of `Integer`, because the literal `2147483648` will not fit inside an `Integer` type (even though its negative will). Similarly, the expression `−9223372036854775808` will overflow because the literal `9223372036854775808` will not fit inside a `Long` type (even though its negative will).

An integer literal can also be explicitly typed by following the literal with a type character: S for `Short`, I for `Integer`, and L for `Long`. There is no type character for `Byte`, because it would be ambiguous when used with a hexadecimal literal (i.e., `&H1B`).

Style

The characters % and & can be used as type characters for `Integer` and `Long`, respectively, but their inclusion is for historical reasons, and their use is discouraged.

Floating-Point Data Types

The floating-point data types store numbers that can have fractional parts, and are most useful when you are dealing with values that are not integers. A floating-point number has three parts: a whole part (the part to the left of the decimal point), a fractional part (the part to the right of the decimal point) called the *mantissa*, and an *exponent*. The exponent indicates the power of ten to multiply the other two parts by to get the actual value of the floating-point number. For example, the floating-point literal `1.5E3` is equivalent to the floating-point literal `1500.0`. While the floating-point types can represent a large range (such as 1E+308), they have limited precision. This means that a sufficiently large or small value can keep only a certain number of significant digits. The `Double` type can preserve approximately 18 digits of precision, while the `Single` type can preserve only about 8 digits of precision. The default value of the floating-point types is the literal `0.0`.

Style

The `Double` type is the more natural floating-point size on the .NET Framework—the `Single` type should not be used unless explicitly needed.

The exact behaviors of the floating-point types are defined by the .NET Framework and are beyond the scope of this book. However, a few pitfalls are worth mentioning. Floating-point values differ from integer values in that they have special values such as positive and negative zero, positive and negative infinity, and NaN (Not a Number). This last value is the most interesting because the result of dividing a floating-point number by zero is NaN instead of an exception. In the following example, the code will run without error even though there is division by zero, and the variable a will end up with the value of NaN.

```
Dim a, b As Double

a = 1.5
b = 0.0
a = a / b
```

Compatibility

In previous versions of Visual Basic, the runtime environment would throw an exception if the result of a floating-point operation was NaN. This is no longer the case, so Visual Basic .NET programmers must always check the result of floating-point division to ensure that it is not NaN. The functions `Double.IsNaN` and `Single.IsNaN` can be used for this purpose.

Another thing to be aware of is that the .NET Framework may calculate floating-point operations at whatever precision the machine that the code is running on can support, and this may be a higher precision than `Double` or `Single` supports. As a result, comparing the results of floating-point operations may give unexpected results. Take the following example.

```
Dim a, b As Double

a = 1.0 / 3.0
b - 1.0 / 3.0

If a = b Then
  Console.WriteLine("equal")
Else
  Console.WriteLine("not equal")
End If
```

Depending on how the code is compiled by the JIT compiler at runtime, either result may be printed because one or both of the division operations may be calculated at a higher precision than the other.

Floating-Point Literals

Floating-point literals have same three parts as a floating-point value: a whole part, a mantissa, and an exponent. The whole part is just an integer literal and is followed by a decimal point. The decimal point is followed by the mantissa represented as an integer literal. An exponent can be specified by adding the character E to the end and then a signed integer literal specifying the exponent. The following shows some examples of floating-point literals.

```
Dim a As Single
Dim b, c, d As Double

a = 1.5F
b = 3E-30
c = 4R
d = 0.4
```

If a floating-point value specifies an exponent, it can choose to omit the mantissa. The type of a floating-point literal is always `Double`, unless it is explicitly typed using a type character: F for `Single` and R for `Double`.

Design

The choice of characters is somewhat strange because of a lack of suitable characters-S is already taken for Short and D is already taken for `Decimal`. F was chosen for `Single` because the type has historically been referred to as "float," while R was chosen for `Double` because the type has historically been referred to as "real."

An integer literal can also be turned into a floating-point literal by adding the floating-point type characters.

Style

The characters ! and # can be used as type characters for `Single` and `Double`, respectively, but their inclusion is for historical reasons, and their use is discouraged.

Decimal Data Type

The data type `Decimal` differs from the integer data types in that it can represent fractional values; it differs from the floating-point data types in that it is an exact representation of its value. Thus, `Decimal` is most useful in situations where fractional values are needed but exact precision is important, such as representing monetary values. Like floating-point numbers, Decimal has a whole part, a mantissa, and an exponent (also called its *scale*). The default value of the Decimal type is the literal 0.0D.

While Decimal has advantages in representation over floating-point types, it also has several drawbacks. It is significantly bigger than the floating-point types: While a Double variable takes up 8 bytes, a Decimal variable takes up 16 bytes—twice as much space. Also, most platforms do not have dedicated hardware support for Decimal operations, unlike the floating-point types, which are usually handled by a special floating-point processor. As a result, Decimal operations will be slower in most cases than floating-point operations.

Compatibility

Previous versions of Visual Basic supported both a Decimal and a Currency data type. The Currency data type also had a fixed precision but was only eight bytes. Because it had a smaller range than Decimal, it was dropped in Visual Basic .NET in favor of Decimal.

Decimal Literals

Decimal literals can be specified in the same way as floating-point literals, with the exception that they must be followed by the type character D.

Style

The character @ can be used as a type character for Decimal (in previous versions it was used for the Currency type), but its inclusion is for historical reasons, and its use is discouraged.

The following shows some examples of Decimal literals.

```
Dim a, b, c, d As Decimal

a = 1.5D
```

```
b = 3E-30D
c = 4D
d = 0.4D
```

Char and String Data Types

The Char and String data types are used to represent textual values. The Char data type represents a single character, while the String data type represents a string of characters. The characters stored in a Char or String variable are encoded using the Unicode UTF-16 encoding, which means that each character in a variable of type Char or String is encoded using a two-byte integer value defined by the Unicode 3.0 Specification. The numeric encoding is mostly important when dealing with characters that do not have actual text representations (such as the carriage return character) or that cannot be typed or viewed on a particular machine.

The default value of the Char data type is the value ChrW(0), also called the *null character*. The default value of the String data type is the literal Nothing, because String is a reference type (this is covered in more detail in Chapter 9, Classes and Structures). However, a String value of Nothing is considered to be the same as the literal "" by all the comparison operators as well as all the Visual Basic .NET runtime methods.

Character and String Literals

A string literal is just a series of characters surrounded by double quote (") characters. All characters between the beginning and ending double quotes are considered part of the literal. Two embedded double quote characters next to each other are interpreted as a single double quote character and do not end the literal. A character literal is just a string literal with one character in it, followed by the character "c." The following shows some examples of character and string literals.

```
Dim a, b, c As String
Dim d, e, f As Char

a = "The quick brown fox jumped over the lazy dog."
b = "This literal contains a ""quoted"" string."
c = "First line" & ChrW(&HD) & "Second line"
d = "a"c
```

```
e = """"c  ' This literal is the character "double quote"
f = ChrW(&H20AC)
```

The examples also use the `ChrW` function to represent characters that have no textual representation. In the example, the variable `c` contains a string with a carriage return in the middle of it, while the variable `f` contains the Euro character €.

Date Data Type

The `Date` data type represents a moment in time. The range of the `Date` data type is from midnight, January 1, 1, through one second before midnight (11:59:59 PM), December 31, 9999. The default calendar used for `Date` data types is the Gregorian calendar. The smallest unit of time that a `Date` variable can use to distinguish between two moments in time is 100 nanoseconds. It is important to remember that the `Date` data type does not encode the time zone of the day and time. Therefore, any calculations on `Date` variables that need to be sensitive to different time zones need to be handled explicitly using .NET Framework functions.

Date Literals

A date literal is a string that represents a particular day and time. A date literal begins and ends with a pound character (#). The date literal can be a date and a time value, a date value, or a time value. The date value is always represented in numerical month-day-year format, separated by either forward slashes (/) or dashes (-). If the date value is omitted, the default date of January 1, 1, is assumed. The time value is represented in numerical hour-minute-second format, separated by colons (:), followed by an AM or PM designator. If a time value is omitted, the default time of midnight is assumed. The following shows some examples of date literals.

```
Dim a, b, c As Date

a = #8/23/1970 3:40:32 AM#
b = #8/23/1970#
c = #3:40:32 AM#
```

The date value must be a valid day in the Gregorian calendar; to avoid ambiguities, the year must be specified with four digits if the year being represented is between the years 1 and 99.

Object Data Type

The `Object` data type is a special type in the .NET Framework type system in that, unlike other types, a variable typed as `Object` can have values of any type assigned to it. For example, the following is valid code.

```
Sub Main()
  Dim o1, o2, o3 As Object

  o1 = 5
  o2 = "abc"
  o3 = #8/23/70 4:30:23 AM#
End Sub
```

Why `Object` is such a special type is discussed in more detail in Chapter 13, Inheritance, but for now it is important to know only that an `Object` variable can hold any type, even reference types (which are discussed more in Chapter 9).

The default value of an `Object` variable is the literal `Nothing`, but `Nothing` is treated specially in the case of `Object`. When an `Object` variable containing `Nothing` is converted to another type, `Nothing` is converted to the default value of the target type. For example, the following code prints the number 0.

```
Sub Main()
  Dim o As Object
  Dim i As Integer

  i = 5
  i = o
  Console.WriteLine(i)
End Sub
```

The first assignment statement in the example assigns the value 5 to the variable `i`. The second statement assigns the value of the variable `o` to the variable `i`. Because `o` is initialized to `Nothing`, `Nothing` is converted to the default value of `Integer`, which is 0.

The Object type can be used in one of two ways. One way is to use the fact that Object can hold any kind of value to create very general code. For example, if you wanted to create a subroutine that accepted any kind of value and printed the type of that value, you could write the following:

```
Sub PrintType(ByVal o As Object)
  Console.WriteLine(o.GetType().ToString())
End Sub
```

Or you could write a general program to add 1 to any kind of numeric type.

```
Function AddOne(ByVal o As Object) As Object
  If TypeOf o Is Integer Then
    Return CInt(o) + 1
  ElseIf TypeOf o Is Double Then
    Return CDbl(o) + 1
  ' Handle the other types
  ...
  Else
    Throw New ArgumentException("Not a recognized value.")
  End If
End Function
```

A second way of using Object is to use it avoid worrying about what type the variables in a program are by typing everything as Object. When writing a Visual Basic .NET program in this way, the programmer is taking advantage of *loose typing*. Although all variables in a Visual Basic .NET program have a type, by typing all variables as Object, the programmer is leaving it entirely up to the compiler and the Framework to figure out what type things are at runtime and ensure correct behavior. While this can be a simpler way to write programs, it has drawbacks. Because the types of variables are not known to the compiler, more work has to be done at runtime to figure out what the correct behavior is. For example, in the following program, since the variables a and b are typed as Integer, the compiler knows that it is doing Integer addition. The variables c and d, however, are typed as Object, so the compiler does not necessarily know what type of addition is being done until runtime.

```
Dim a, b As Integer
Dim c, d As Object

a = 10
b = 20
```

```
a = a + b

c = 10
d = 20
c = c + d
```

Style

In general, programmers are encouraged to use *strong typing*—that is, to specify the exact type of all the variables declared in the program. Strong typing ensures that many logic errors are caught at compile time; it also produces faster and more efficient code. The Option Strict statement ensures that you use strong typing in your code.

Conversions

As discussed earlier in this chapter, every piece of information in a Visual Basic .NET program has a particular type. When you are assigning a value to a variable or performing some operation on two values, all the types involved in the operation must be the same. For example, it is not possible to store a String value into an Integer variable, because the two types are not the same. When you are working with many different types of information, however, it is often necessary to convert one type of information to another. While it is not possible to store a String value into an Integer variable, it *is* possible to take a String value and *convert* it into an Integer value (which can then be stored into an Integer variable).

By default, values in Visual Basic .NET will be converted from one type to another as needed. The compiler can do this because the types of all values and variables in Visual Basic .NET are always known and any needed conversions can be deduced from context. In the following example, the value in the String variable is implicitly converted to Integer when a is assigned to b.

```
Dim a As String
Dim b as Integer

a = "10"
b = a
```

It is also possible to explicitly convert a value from one type to another by using the conversion operators, listed in Table 3-2.

Style

Although they may appear to be functions, the conversion operators are an intrinsic part of the language. Because of that, using the conversion operators is much more efficient than calling the type conversion functions provided by the .NET Framework. The conversion operators should always be used unless there is a compelling reason not to do so.

TABLE 3-2: Conversion Operators

Operators	Description
CBool(<expr>)	Converts <expr> to Boolean
CByte(<expr>)	Converts <expr> to Byte
CShort(<expr>)	Converts <expr> to Short
CInt(<expr>)	Converts <expr> to Integer
CLng(<expr>)	Converts <expr> to Long
CDec(<expr>)	Converts <expr> to Decimal
CSng(<expr>)	Converts <expr> to Single
CDbl(<expr>)	Converts <expr> to Double
CDate(<expr>)	Converts <expr> to Date
CChar(<expr>)	Converts <expr> to Char
CStr(<expr>)	Converts <expr> to String
CObj(<expr>)	Converts <expr> to Object
CType(<expr>, <type>)	Converts <expr> to <type>
DirectCast(<expr>, <type>)	Converts <expr> to <type> without language-specific conversions

Each conversion operator takes a value of any type and attempts to convert it to the specified type. If the conversion cannot be accomplished, an exception will be thrown at runtime. The conversion operator CType is special in that the destination type is not part of the name of the operator; it is specified as part of the operation.

```
Dim a As String
Dim b as Integer

a = "10"
b = CInt(a)
b = CType(a, Integer)       Same as the previous statement
```

The usefulness of the CType operator will become more apparent later on in the book, when we start dealing with inheritance and interfaces. There is also a special conversion operator, DirectCast, which is useful specifically in inheritance situations. It will also be covered in Chapter 13.

Although the conversion operators are not required to convert from one type to another, using them is generally a good practice, especially when conversions may not succeed. The conversion operators call attention to the fact that a conversion is being performed. Sometimes explicit conversions may also be necessary because the type deduced is not correct. For example:

```
Dim a, b As Byte
Dim c as Short

a = 255
b = 1
c = a + b                    ' Runtime error: overflow
c = CShort(a) + CShort(b)  ' Succeeds
```

In the example, the expression a + b adds two Byte variables together. From this context, the result of the addition is assumed to be a Byte value—the compiler does not know beforehand that the addition will result in 256, which is not a valid Byte value. As a result, an error will occur even though the resulting type will fit into the ultimate destination (the variable c, which is typed as Short). The expression CShort(a) + CShort(b) will succeed, however, because the addition of a Short to a Short is assumed to result in a Short value. Since 256 is a valid Short value, the operation will succeed.

Widening and Narrowing Conversions

Conversions between some types are always guaranteed to succeed, while others are not. In the following example, the first conversion may fail if the Short variable contains a value that will not fit into a Byte variable, whereas the second conversion will always succeed because any value that fits into a Byte variable will fit into a Short variable.

```
Dim a As Byte
Dim b As Short

a = b
b = a
```

A conversion that is always guaranteed to succeed is called a *widening conversion* because the set of values that the destination type can hold is *wider* than the set of values that the source type can hold. In the preceding example, a conversion from Byte to Short is widening because every value of Byte is a valid value of Short as well. A conversion that might fail, however, is called a *narrowing conversion* because the set of values that the destination type can hold is *narrower* than the set of values that the source type can hold. Converting a Short value to Byte may or may not succeed, depending on whether the value is in the range of the Byte type.

As discussed in the previous section, explicit conversions between types are not required. However, this can lead programmers into trouble—it is easy when assigning from one variable to another to forget whether a conversion is being done and whether that conversion is widening or narrowing. If a widening conversion is taking place, there is nothing to worry about—the conversion is guaranteed to succeed at runtime. But if a narrowing conversion is taking place, the programmer must think about what happens if that conversion should fail. Not handling a conversion failure could cause a serious bug in the application. Therefore, it is always a good idea to do narrowing conversions explicitly by using the appropriate conversion operator.

To assist programmers in remembering to do so, the `Option Strict` statement can be placed at the beginning of a source file (or set as part of a project's options). One of the things that the `Option Strict` statement does is require narrowing conversions to be performed explicitly—if a narrowing conversion is done without a conversion operator, the compiler will give an error.

Style

Because it requires narrowing conversions to be stated explicitly, using `Option Strict` is highly recommended as good programming practice.

Supported Conversions

Visual Basic .NET supports the following conversions between the fundamental types.

- `Boolean`—`Boolean` values can be converted to and from all the numeric types (`Byte`, `Short`, `Integer`, `Long`, `Decimal`, `Single`, and `Double`). When a `Boolean` value is converted to a signed numeric type (i.e., all types except `Byte`), the value `True` converts into the value –1, and the value `False` converts into the value 0. For `Byte`, the value `True` converts into the value 255. All conversions to and from `Boolean` are considered narrowing.

Design

Although converting `Boolean` to and from the numeric types is not strictly narrowing, because there is no possibility of failure, the conversion is nonetheless considered narrowing because `Boolean` is not a numeric type.

- `Byte`, `Short`, `Integer`, `Long`, `Decimal`, `Single`, and `Double`—All the numeric types can be converted to and from one another. There is a progression of conversions that goes in general order of range:

Byte, Short, Integer, Long, Decimal, Single, and Double. Any type in the list widens to the types that come after it in the list and narrows to the types that come before it. One thing to note is that while the widening conversions are guaranteed to succeed because the range of every type is contained within all the types later in the list, the precision of values may not be entirely preserved. For example, the following code will print 4.9318203910293E+18.

```
Dim a As Long
Dim b As Double

a = 4931820391029301920
b = a
Console.WriteLine(b)
```

Although the Double variable was able to hold the value stored in the Long variable, it wasn't able to store it with the same precision as the Long variable. This is something to keep in mind when you are doing conversions from the integer or fixed-point numeric types to the floating-point types.

Advanced

Conversions from floating-point numbers to integer numbers use a method called *banker's rounding*. In banker's rounding, a floating-point number will be rounded to the nearest integer. If a floating-point number is equally close to the two integers on either side of it, it will be rounded to the closest *even* number. Thus, 4.5 will round to 4, while 5.5 will round to 6.

- String—String can be converted to and from the Boolean, numeric, and Date types. With the exception of Boolean (which is always converted to and from the English strings "true" and "false," case insensitively), all the conversions are done using the current UI culture of the .NET Framework. That is, while the value 10.5 will convert to the string "10.5" on a machine with a US English culture setting, it will convert to the string "10,5" on a machine with a

French culture setting, and vice versa. This is because in the US English culture the period is used as the decimal point, while the comma is used as the decimal point in the French culture (and many others). Also, when converting from `String`, currency values (also tied to the current culture setting) will be recognized and converted—so the string "$10.50" will convert to the `Double` value 10.5 if US English is the current culture.

Advanced

The current culture being used for conversions on a particular thread can be read or changed through the `System.Thread.CurrentCulture` and `System.Thread.CurrentUICulture` properties.

Conclusion

This chapter introduced the fundamental types that all programs make use of: numeric types, string types, Boolean types, and date/time types. It also discussed how to form literals of the fundamental types and how to convert a value from one type to another. The topics for the next chapter are more complex data types that are formed using the fundamental types: arrays and enumerations.

Here are some style points to consider.

- The ranges of the `Integer` and `Long` types have been widened from previous versions, and a new type, `Short`, has been added. The range of `Short` is the same as the range of `Integer` in previous versions, and the range of `Integer` is equivalent to the range of `Long` in previous versions. When you are converting code from previous versions of Visual Basic, it is important to keep in mind this difference.

- The characters % and & can be used as type characters for `Integer` and `Long`, respectively, but their inclusion is for historical reasons, and their use is discouraged.

- The `Double` type is the more natural floating-point size on the .NET Framework—the `Single` type should not be used unless explicitly needed.

- In previous versions of Visual Basic, the runtime environment would throw an exception if the result of a floating-point operation was NaN. This is no longer the case, so Visual Basic .NET programmers must always check the result of floating-point division to ensure that it is not NaN. The functions `Double.IsNaN` and `Single.IsNaN` can be used for this purpose.

- The characters ! and # can be used as type characters for `Single` and `Double`, respectively, but their inclusion is for historical reasons, and their use is discouraged.

- Previous versions of Visual Basic supported both a `Decimal` and a `Currency` data type. The `Currency` data type also had a fixed precision but was only eight bytes. Because it had a smaller range than `Decimal`, it was dropped in Visual Basic .NET in favor of `Decimal`.

- The character @ can be used as a type character for `Decimal` (in previous versions it was used for the `Currency` type), but its inclusion is for historical reasons, and its use is discouraged.

- In general, programmers are encouraged to use *strong typing*—that is, to specify the exact type of all the variables declared in the program. Strong typing ensures that many logic errors are caught at compile time; it also produces faster and more efficient code. The `Option Strict` statement ensures that you use strong typing in your code.

- Although they may appear to be functions, the conversion operators are an intrinsic part of the language. Because of that, using the conversion operators is much more efficient than calling the type conversion functions provided by the .NET Framework. The conversion operators should always be used unless there is a compelling reason not to do so.

- Because it requires narrowing conversions to be stated explicitly, using `Option Strict` is highly recommended as good programming practice.

■ 4 ■

Arrays and Enumerations

I n addition to the fundamental types such as `Integer` or `Double`, there
are two other simple types that programmers can use in their programs:
arrays and enumerations. Arrays are useful for storing multiple values of
a type, while enumerations are useful for giving friendly names to numeric
values.

Arrays

An *array* is a type that contains a set of variables of the same type that are
accessed by position rather than by name. The individual variables in the
array are called the *elements* of the array; the type of the variables is called
the *element type* of the array. A variable at a particular position in an array
is referenced by number, which is called the *index* of the element. For example, the following code creates a ten-element array of `Integer` and fills it
with the values 0 through 9.

```
Dim a() As Integer
Dim i As Integer

ReDim a(9)

For i = 0 To 9
  a(i) = i
Next i
```

The name of an array type is the element type of the array followed by a set of parentheses—for example, `Integer()`. In most cases, the parentheses can be placed on the variable name instead of the type name for emphasis, as in the previous example. The two declaration types are completely equivalent. The parentheses after the element type of an array indicate the number of dimensions in the array, also called the *rank* of the array. A one-dimensional array is like a list of variables, as illustrated in Figure 4-1. A two-dimensional array is like a matrix, as illustrated in Figure 4-2.

An array can have up to 32 dimensions. The rank of an array is represented by commas between the parentheses in the type name. The type `Integer()` has one dimension, the type `Integer(,)` has two dimensions, the type `Integer(,,)` has three dimensions, and so on. The following example creates a two-dimensional array of `Integer` and fills it with values.

1	2	3	4	5	6	7	8	9	10	Values
0	1	2	3	4	5	6	7	8	9	Index

FIGURE 4-1: A One-Dimensional Array

```
Dim a(,) As Integer
Dim x, y As Integer

ReDim a(9, 9)

For x = 0 To 9
  For y = 0 To 9
    a(x, y) = x * y
  Next y
Next x
```

ReDim and Erase Statements

Arrays must be created and given a size before they can be used. (This is because they are reference types, a topic covered in Chapter 9, Classes and Structures.) The `ReDim` statement can be used to allocate a new array with a particular set of dimension sizes.

Index	0	1	2	3	4	5	6	7	8	9
0	1	2	3	4	5	6	7	8	9	10
1	11	12	13	14	15	16	17	18	19	20
2	21	22	23	24	25	26	27	28	29	30
3	31	32	33	34	35	36	37	38	39	40
4	41	42	43	44	45	46	47	48	49	50
5	51	52	53	54	55	56	57	58	59	60
6	61	62	63	64	65	66	67	68	69	70
7	71	72	73	74	75	76	77	78	79	80
8	81	82	83	84	85	86	87	88	89	90
9	91	92	93	94	95	96	97	98	99	100

FIGURE 4-2: A Two-Dimensional Array

```
Dim a() As Integer
Dim b(,) As Double

ReDim a(9), b(3,4)
```

The length of a dimension in a ReDim statement is specified in terms of its upper bound. So the statement ReDim a(9, 9) creates an array of two dimensions with ten elements (0 through 9) in each dimension. The number of dimensions specified in a ReDim statement must be the same as the number of dimensions of the array type. When an array is dimensioned, each element in the array is initialized to the default value of the array element type. Multiple arrays may be dimensioned at one time, even if they have different element types and dimensions.

It is possible to use ReDim to change the size of the dimensions of an existing array. In that case, the values contained in the array are discarded unless the keyword Preserve is specified following the ReDim keyword. If Preserve is specified and the new array is bigger than the old array, the new elements are initialized to the default value of the array element type. If Preserve is specified and the new array is smaller than the old array, the elements that no longer fit are discarded. The following example will print the numbers 0 through 9 and then ten 0s.

```
Dim a() As Integer
Dim i As Integer

ReDim a(9)

For i = 0 To 9
  a(i) = i
Next i

ReDim Preserve a(19)

For i = 0 to 19
  Console.WriteLine(a(i))
Next i
```

Compatibility

The number of dimensions and/or the element type of the array could be changed as part of a ReDim statement in previous versions. This is no longer allowed because Framework arrays do not have this capability.

The Erase statement clears one or more arrays, resetting them to their original uninitialized state, and is the equivalent of assigning Nothing to the array variable. Because arrays take up space in memory, it is a good practice to erase arrays once they are no longer in use if the variable is going to exist for a long time.

```
Dim a(,) As Integer

ReDim a(32767, 32767)

' Manipulate the array
...

' Free the memory
Erase a

' Do some large amount of work
...
```

In a situation where a variable is going to exist for only a short time—say, a local variable in a small subroutine—it is not necessary to erase arrays.

Style

The `Erase` statement was the only way to clear an array in previous versions. Another way to clear an array in Visual Basic .NET is to set the array variable to `Nothing`. The two methods are exactly equivalent, and there is no advantage to one over the other.

Array Initializers

When you are declaring a variable of an array type, the variable can be initialized at the same time with an array of a particular size or with particular values. An array is initialized to a particular size at declaration time by providing the sizes of each dimension in the parentheses.

```
Dim a(,) As Integer
Dim b(3,3) As Integer

a = b
ReDim b(9,9)
```

In the example, the variable a is not initialized to anything—it starts out empty (i.e., initialized to the value `Nothing`). However, the variable b is initialized to a two-dimensional array with a length of 4 in both dimensions. As the rest of the example shows, initializing an array variable with an array of a particular length does not fix the size of the array in the variable. It is possible to redimension the variable later on, and it will take on the new size.

The actual values of an array can be specified by following the declaration with an equals sign and the values listed between curly brackets. When an array variable is initialized with a list of values, an explicit array size cannot be supplied—the size is derived implicitly from the size of the value list. The following example shows several arrays initialized to various sets of values.

```
Dim a() As Integer = { 1, 2, 3, 4, 5 }
Dim b() As String = { "one", "two", "three", "four", "five" }
Dim c(,) As Integer = { { 1, 2, 3 }, { 4, 5, 6 } }
```

As the preceding example shows, multidimensional arrays can be initialized by nesting the brackets. Each level of bracketing represents one dimension of the array, with the outermost level of bracketing representing the leftmost dimension and the innermost level of bracketing representing the rightmost dimension. In the example, the variable c is initialized with a two-by-three array. The number of elements at any particular level of the multidimensional array initializer must be the same length.

Arrays of Arrays

The element type of an array can be *any* type, including another array. An array whose element type is an array is indicated by adding another set of parentheses to the end of the type name. For example, the type name of a one-dimensional array of one-dimensional array of Integer is Integer()(). The important thing to keep in mind is that the element type of Integer()() is Integer()—thus, you have to first dimension each element of the outer array before you can assign an Integer value to an element of an inner array. In contrast, the element type of Integer(,) is Integer, which means you can always assign a value to an element in the array. Compare this example to the one in the previous section.

```
Dim a()() As Integer
Dim x, y As Integer

ReDim a(3)

For x = 0 To 3
  ReDim a(x)(x + 1)
  For y = 0 To x + 1
    a(x)(y) = x + y
  Next y
Next x
```

In the example, it is necessary to dimension each inner array that is an element of the outer array. Because arrays of arrays are usually asymmetrical, they are also known as *jagged arrays*. The array produced by the preceding example looks something like Figure 4-3.

Arrays of arrays are useful when an array has more than one dimension but the dimensions are not symmetrical. For example, imagine a soccer

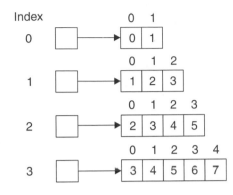

FIGURE 4-3: A Jagged Array

league with 12 teams that can be made up of 11 to 18 players. The names of all the members could be stored in a two-dimensional array of String (i.e., String(,)) whose dimensions are 12 by 18, but this would waste extra space if teams had fewer than 18 players. Instead, a one-dimensional array of the one-dimensional array of String (i.e., String()()) could be used. The dimension of the outer array would be 12, but the dimension of the inner array could be anywhere from 11 to 18. For example:

```
Dim Teams(12)() As Integer
Dim Team As Integer

For Team = 0 To 9
  Dim TeamSize As Integer
  Dim Member As Integer

  Console.WriteLine("How many players are on team " & Team & "?")
  TeamSize = CInt(Console.ReadLine())
  ReDim Teams(Team)(TeamSize - 1)

  For Member = 0 To TeamSize - 1
    Console.WriteLine("What is player " & Member & "'s name?")
    Teams(Team)(Member) = Console.ReadLine()
  Next Member
Next Team
```

Arrays of arrays may be nested to any level and may be of any dimension. For example, the type Integer()(,)(,,) is an array of two-dimensional arrays of three-dimensional arrays of Integer.

Advanced

Accessing the elements of a one-dimensional array is faster than accessing the elements of a multidimensional array on most versions of the .NET Framework. As a result, if performance is a consideration, it may be faster to use jagged arrays than regular multidimensional arrays.

Enumerations

An *enumeration* is a user-defined type that gives names to numeric values. For example, the following defines a new enumeration, `Colors`, that has values that represent the seven basic colors of the spectrum.

```
Enum Colors
    Red
    Orange
    Yellow
    Green
    Blue
    Indigo
    Violet
End Enum
```

The set of names in an enumeration can be used to refer to the numeric values. The names of the values are scoped to the enumeration itself, so enumeration values must always be qualified with the name of the type. For example:

```
Dim a As Colors

a = Colors.Red

If a = Colors.Blue Then
  Console.WriteLine("Blue")
End If
```

The values of the enumeration are scoped only to the type itself because you are likely to want to use the same names in different enumerations.

```
Enum Colors
   Red
   Orange
   Yellow
   Green
   Blue
   Indigo
   Violet
End Enum

Enum StopLightColors
   Red
   Yellow
   Green
End Enum
```

In the preceding example, if the values were not scoped to the enumerations, then `Red`, `Yellow`, and `Green` would be ambiguous.

Underlying Types

Because enumerations can only enumerate whole numbers, enumerations can only be based on the fundamental integer types (`Byte`, `Short`, `Integer`, or `Long`). The underlying type of an enumeration determines how many distinct values the enumeration can have. By default, the first value in an enumeration corresponds to the value 0, and each value after that represents one more than the one before it. In the `Colors` example earlier, the value of `Red` is 0, the value of `Orange` is 1, the value of `Yellow` is 2, and the value of `Violet` is 6.

The correspondence between an enumeration value and its underlying type can be explicitly set by assigning a value to the name in the enumeration declaration.

```
Enum Colors
   Red = 1
   Orange = 2
   Yellow = 4
   Green = 8
   Blue = 16
   Indigo = 32
   Violet = 64
End Enum
```

In this example, the `Colors` enumeration is defined such that each color value is a distinct binary value. This would allow combining the values of the `Colors` enumeration using the `And`, `Or`, and `Xor` bitwise operators.

Advanced

An enumeration whose values are distinct binary values is known as an enumeration of *flags*. Flag enumerations should have the attribute `System.FlagsAttribute` specified on them. This doesn't affect the language, but .NET Framework APIs such as `System.Enum.IsDefined` make use of it.

An enumeration value can be assigned any constant expression, even one involving another enumeration value—as long as the enumeration value's underlying value doesn't depend on itself.

```
Enum StopLightColors
   Red = Yellow  ' Invalid: Yellow's value depends on Red's value
   Green
   Yellow
End Enum
```

In this example, the enumeration value `Red` cannot have the same underlying value as the enumeration value `Yellow`, because `Yellow`'s underlying value depends on `Red`'s underlying value. Remember, if an enumeration member is not explicitly assigned a value, it will have the value of the previous enumeration member's underlying value plus one.

By default, an enumeration's underlying type is `Integer`. If another integral type size is needed, however, it can be specified in an `As` clause after the enumeration name.

```
Enum StopLightColors As Byte
   Red
   Green
   Yellow
End Enum
```

Conversions

Because all the names in an enumeration have a corresponding value in the enumeration's underlying type, an enumeration can always be converted to its underlying type, and the conversion is widening. The underlying type of an enumeration can also be converted to the enumeration, but because not all values of the underlying type may be represented in the enumeration, the conversion is narrowing. Enumerations can be converted from one to another. The conversion is narrowing or widening based on the underlying types. (So a `Long` enumeration conversion to an `Integer` enumeration would be narrowing.)

An enumeration can also be converted to any type its underlying type can convert to. For example, an enumeration with a `Long` underlying type can be converted to `Integer`. The conversion is either widening or narrowing depending on whether the conversion from the underlying type is widening or narrowing. (So a `Long` enumeration conversion to `Integer` would be narrowing.)

An enumeration value converted to `String` will result in the underlying value being converted to `String` (i.e., "0"). Similarly, converting a `String` to an enumeration requires the string to be the underlying value (i.e., "0") instead of the value's name (i.e., "Red"). The method `System.Enum.ToString`, however, will convert the value into the enumerated name (i.e., "Red"). The method `System.Enum.Parse` can be used to convert from an enumerated value name (i.e., "Red") back to the enumeration. For example:

```
Sub Main()
   Dim c As StopLightColors = StopLightColors.Red
   Dim s As String

   s = CStr(c)
   Console.WriteLine(s)   ' Prints out "0"

   ' Set c equal to StopLightColors.Green
   c = CType("1", StopLightColors)

   s = c.ToString()
   Console.WriteLine(s)   ' Prints out "Green"

   ' Set c equal to StopLightColors.Yellow
```

```
   c = Enum.Parse(GetType(StopLightColors), "Yellow")
End Sub
```

It's worth noting that the conversion from the underlying type of an enumeration to the enumeration exists even though the underlying type may be able to represent more values than the enumeration can. For example:

```
Enum StopLightColors
   Red
   Green
   Yellow
End Enum

Module Test
   Sub Main()
     Dim x As StopLightColors

     x = CType(42, StopLightColors)
   End Sub
End Module
```

It is valid to assign values to an enumeration variable that is not defined by the enumeration as long as they fit into the underlying type. This is allowed because, as noted in the previous section, some enumerations are used as flags.

```
Enum Colors
   Red = 1
   Orange = 2
   Yellow = 4
   Green = 8
   Blue = 16
   Indigo = 32
   Violet = 64
End Enum

Module Test
   Sub Main()
     Dim Green As Colors

     Green = Colors.Red And Colors.Yellow
   End Sub
End Module
```

In this situation, the colors can be combined to produce values that were not part of the original enumeration but that may be valid nonetheless.

Advanced

The shared method `System.Enum.IsDefined` can be used to determine at runtime whether a value is part of an enumeration or not. The `IsDefined` method takes the `System.Flags` attribute into consideration.

Conclusion

This chapter covers two types that are composed of other types: arrays and enumerations. Most programs make use of arrays and enumerations to store multiple values of the same type or to assign names to numeric values. Now that we have covered the basic types, the next chapter will discuss the operations that can be performed on these types.

Here are some style points to consider.

- The number of dimensions and/or the element type of the array could be changed as part of a `ReDim` statement in previous versions. This is no longer allowed because Framework arrays do not have this capability.
- The `Erase` statement was the only way to clear an array in previous versions. Another way to clear an array in Visual Basic .NET is to set the array variable to `Nothing`. The two methods are exactly equivalent, and there is no advantage to one over the other.

5

Operators

Information is not extremely useful if you can't do anything with it. *Operators* perform actions on values, producing a result. For example, the addition operator (+) takes two numbers and adds them together. An operator acts on values that are called the *operands*. An operator that acts on one operand is called a *unary operator,* while an operator that acts on two operands is called a *binary operator.* (A binary operator is called "binary" because it operates on two values.) This chapter discusses the operators defined in Visual Basic .NET.

Precedence

All operators in Visual Basic .NET have a certain *precedence* that determines in what order operations are performed if an expression has more than one operator. An operator with higher precedence than another operator will be evaluated first. Operators with equal precedence will be evaluated from left to right. (Thus, operators are *left-associative.*)

For example, the multiplication operator (*) has a higher precedence than the addition operator (+). Therefore, the result of the expression 2 * 4 + 2 is 10 and not 12. This is because the expression is evaluated as (2 * 4) + 2, not 2 * (4 + 2). The expression 2 * 4 / 2 is evaluated as (2 * 4) / 2 instead of 2 * (4 / 2) because the multiplication operator (*) has a precedence equal to the division operator (/).

Style

It is preferable to use parentheses to clarify how an operation is to be performed rather than relying on the precedence and associativity of operators. It is easy to forget the precedence order of the operators!

Table 5-1 lists the operators in order of precedence. Each box represents a different level of precedence, from highest to lowest. All operators at the same level have the same precedence.

TABLE 5-1: Operator Precedence

Precedence	Description
Exponentiation	x ^ y
Unary plus	+ x
Unary minus	– x
Multiplication	x * y
Division	x / y
Integer division	x \ y
Integer remainder	x Mod y
Addition	x + y
Subtraction	x – y
Concatenation	x & y
Shift	x << y
	x >> y
Equality	x = y
Inequality	x <> y
Less than	x < y

Greater than	x > y
Less than or equal to	x <= y
Greater than or equal to	x >= y
Type equality	TypeOf x Is y
Reference equality	x Is y
String matching	x Like y
Bitwise NOT	Not x
Bitwise AND	x And y
Logical AND	x AndAlso y
Bitwise OR	x Or y
Logical OR	x OrElse y
Bitwise XOR	x Xor y

Operator Resolution

With the exception of the comparison operators, the result type of an operation is the same as the type of the operation's operands. In other words, adding two Short values together will result in a Short value. If that expression happens to be 32767S + 32767S, the operation will result in an overflow, even though the value 65534 could fit into a wider type, like Integer.

When a binary operation involves two types that are not the same—for example, adding a Long and a Short together—the result type of the operation will be the wider of the two types—in this case, Long. This is because it is likely that the result of the operation will be a value that only fits into the wider of the two types. If the operator is being applied to a type for which it is not defined—for example, Not 10.5—then the result of the operation will be the type that is closest to the operand type and is defined for the operator—in this case, Long.

> ## Advanced
>
> The most common example of this rule is the division operator (/), which is only defined for the types `Single` and `Double`. Dividing two integers using the (/) operator will always result in a `Double`, even if the result is an integer value.

Because `String` is neither wider nor narrower than the numeric types, it is treated specially. The result type of numeric operations that include `String` is always the numeric type, not `String`. So the operation `1 + "2"` results in `3`, not the string `"12"`.

> ## Compatibility
>
> In previous versions, operations on `String` and the numeric types resulted in a `String` value, the exact opposite of what happens in Visual Basic .NET. The behavior was changed because many programmers did not expect `1 + "2"` to result in `"12"`.

When one of an operation's operands is typed as `Object`, the result type of the operation will be determined at runtime based on the types of the values and the value that results from the operation. Unlike operations on types other than `Object`, the result type of the operation will be widened if the result does not fit into the type of the operands.

```
Dim s1, s2, s3 As Short
Dim o As Object

s1 = 32767
s2 = 32767
s3 = s1 + s2                ' Overflow
o = CObj(s1) + CObj(s2)     ' Results in 65534
```

In this example, the first addition statement will result in an overflow because the result will not fit into a `Short` variable. However, the second statement at runtime will result in the `Integer` value `65534`.

Arithmetic Operators

The *arithmetic operators* are listed in Table 5-2. They are straightforward, with a few exceptions.

- The floating-point division operator (/) is always performed using floating-point values and always results in a floating-point value. The integer division operator (\), on the other hand, is always performed using integer values and always results in an integer value. Floating-point division is useful when the fractional part of a division operation is significant; integer division is useful when it is not.

Compatibility

Unlike in previous versions, dividing by zero with the floating-point division operator will produce the value NaN (Not a Number) instead of a division-by-zero exception. (Handling exceptions is covered in Chapter 7, Exceptions.)

- The integer remainder operator (Mod) calculates the integer remainder when the first operand is evenly divided by the second operand. In other words, x Mod y is equivalent to x - ((x \ y) * y).

TABLE 5-2: Arithmetic Operators

Class	Description
+	Addition
-	Subtraction and negation
*	Multiplication
/	Floating-point division
\	Integer division
Mod	Integer remainder
^	Exponentiation

- The exponentiation operator (^) calculates the value of the first operand raised to the power of the second operand.

The arithmetic operators are defined for all the numeric types and Boolean. The result type of an arithmetic operation depends on the type of the operands; in general, the result type of an operation between two different numeric types is the wider of the two types, since this type is most likely to be able to hold the result of the operation.

Comparison Operators

The *comparison operators* are used to compare two values. They take two operands of any type and result in a Boolean value as to whether the particular comparison is true or false. The comparison operators are listed in Table 5-3.

The Is and = operators each test for equality, but the Is operator tests reference equality, while the = operator tests value equality. Is can only be used on two references and determines whether the two references refer to the same location on the heap. The = operator, on the other hand, can only be used on the fundamental types and determines only whether the two values are the same, not whether they are stored at the same location. For example:

TABLE 5-3: Comparison Operators

Operators	Description
Is	Reference equality
=	Equality
<>	Inequality
<	Less than
>	Greater than
<=	Less than or equal to
>=	Greater than or equal to

```
Class cl
End Class

Module Test
  Sub Main()
    Dim x, y As Integer
    Dim a, b, c As cl

    a = New cl()
    b = a
    c = New cl()

    If a Is b Then
      Console.WriteLine("a and b are the same instance of cl.")
    End If

    If a Is c Then
      Console.WriteLine("a and c are the same instance of cl.")
    End If

    x = 5
    y = 5

    If x = y Then
      Console.WriteLine("x and y are equal.")
    End If
  End Sub
End Module
```

This example will print "a and b are the same instance of cl." because a and b each hold a reference to the same instance. Similarly, the example will print "x and y are equal." because they each hold the same value. (Reference types are covered in more detail in Chapter 9, Classes and Structures.)

When String values are compared, comparisons can be done either as *text comparisons* or as *binary comparisons*. A text comparison compares two strings using the culture of the current thread at runtime. The culture is used to compare each character and determine whether the two characters are the same according to the current culture. Thus, when a text comparison is done, it is possible that two characters with different Unicode values may nonetheless compare as equal if they are considered to be the same in the current culture. On the other hand, a binary comparison compares two strings according to whether each character has the same Unicode

code-point value. Binary comparisons will return the same value regardless of the culture of the current thread.

Advanced

The property `Thread.CurrentThread` can be used to get an object that represents the current thread of execution. The `CurrentCulture` property on the object can be used to get and set the current culture being used.

By default, string comparisons are done as binary comparisons. An `Option Compare` statement at the beginning of the file can change the default for that file. `Option Compare Binary` specifies that binary comparisons are to be used in the file, while `Option Compare Text` specifies text comparisons for the file.

Style

Text comparisons are significantly slower than binary comparisons because they require looking up information about the current culture. Unless culture-sensitive comparisons are needed, binary comparisons are recommended.

Logical and Bitwise Operators

When the operators `Not`, `And`, `Or`, and `Xor` are applied to `Boolean` values, they function as *logical operators*. That is, they perform the specified logical operation (NOT, AND, OR, or Exclusive OR) on the `Boolean` values. For example, the result of `True Or False` is `True`, and the result of `True Xor True` is `False`.

There are two additional logical operators: `AndAlso` and `OrElse`. `AndAlso` and `OrElse` are equivalent to `And` and `Or`, respectively, except that they can *short-circuit* their evaluation. This means that if the result of the operation can be determined only by evaluating the first operand, the second operand will not be evaluated. In the case of AndAlso, if the first operand evaluates to False, the second operand is not evaluated. In the case of OrElse, if the first operand evaluates to True, the second operand is not evaluated.

Short-circuiting is useful for two reasons. First, it can be used to produce more efficient code—if the second part of a logical operation is expensive to evaluate, not evaluating it can save execution time. Also, short-circuiting can be used to simplify statements, yet avoid runtime errors. For example, compare the two ways of calculating the result in the following code.

```
If x <> 0 Then
   If y \ x = 10 Then
      . . .
   End If
End If

If x <> 0 AndAlso y \ x = 10 Then
   . . .
End If
```

In the first case, two If statements are required because if x = 0, y \ x will throw a System.DivideByZeroException exception. In the second case, if x = 0, the second expression will not be evaluated and no error will occur.

When applied to the integer values, the operators Not, And, Or, and Xor function as *bitwise operators*, operating on the binary representation of the values. The bitwise operators execute the specific logical operation on each bit of the operand(s) to produce the result value: Not results in True if the bit is False, And results in True if both bits are True (see Figure 5-1), Or results in True if either bit is True, and Xor results in True if either bit is True, but not both.

The following are some examples of the result of the bitwise operators.

```
Dim a, b, c, d As Integer

a = Not 143      ' Result = -144
b = 312 And 43   ' Result = 40
c = 5823 Or 412  ' Result = 6079
d = 394 Xor 123  ' Result = 497
```

213 And 57 = 17

213	1	1	0	1	0	1	0	1

57	0	0	1	1	1	0	0	1

17	0	0	0	1	0	0	0	1

FIGURE 5-1: And Operation

Shift Operators

The shift operators (<< and >>) perform bitwise shifts on the binary representation of integer values. The << operator shifts the binary bits of a value left a specified number of places, while the >> operator shifts the binary bits of a value right a specified number of places (see Figure 5-2).

When a value is shifted left or right, bits that are shifted off the end of the value are discarded—bit shifting will never cause an overflow. When bits are shifted left, the low-order bits are always filled with zeros. When bits are shifted right, the high-order bit is filled with the same value, 1 or 0, that it already contains. This preserves the sign of Short, Integer, and Long values when bits are shifted right (see Figure 5-3).

It is possible to shift a value more places than the binary representation contains. In that case, the result will always be 0.

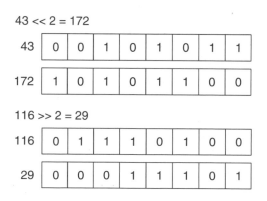

FIGURE 5-2: Left and Right Shifting

$-57s \gg 3 = -8s$

-57s	1	1	1	1	1	1	1	1	1	1	0	0	0	1	1	1

-8s	1	1	1	1	1	1	1	1	1	1	1	1	1	0	0	0

FIGURE 5-3: Right Shifting with Sign Preservation

String Operators

The string concatenation operator (&) takes two string operands and combines them into a single string. If either operand is not a string (or if they both are not strings), it will be converted to a string without requiring an explicit conversion, even if Option Strict is on. The result of a concatenation operation is a new string that represents the concatenation of the two operands.

> **Style**
>
> The + operator can also be used to concatenate strings. However, because of the possible confusion between concatenating strings ("1" + "2" = "12") and adding numbers (1 + "2" = 3), the & operator should always be used to concatenate strings.

One thing to remember is that because the concatenation operator returns an entirely new string, a series of concatenation operations may allocate quite a few new strings, which may have performance implications. When you are doing many concatenations, the type System.Text. StringBuilder can be used instead to make the concatenation faster.

```
Dim Count As Integer
Dim s As String
Dim sb As New Text.StringBuilder()

For Count = 1 To 10000
  s &= CStr(Count) & ","
Next Count
```

```
Console.WriteLine(s)

For Count = 1 To 10000
  sb.Append(CStr(Count))
  sb.Append(",")
Next Count

Console.WriteLine(s.ToString())
```

In this example, the second loop will be several times faster than the first.

The Like operator determines whether a string matches a given pattern. The first operand is the string being matched; the second operand is a string representing the pattern to match against. In the simplest case, where the pattern contains no special matching characters, the Like operator is equivalent to the = operator. However, the following character sequences have special meanings when used in a pattern.

- The character ? matches any character.
- The character * matches zero or more characters.
- The character # matches any numeric digit (0–9).
- A list of characters delimited by brackets ([ab...]) matches any character in the list.
- A list of character delimited by brackets and prefixed by an exclamation point ([!ab...]) matches any character not in the character list.

Two characters in a character list separated by a hyphen (-) specify a range of Unicode characters, starting with the first character and ending with the second character. If the second character is not later in the current thread's culture's sort order than the first character, a runtime error occurs. A hyphen that appears at the beginning or end of a character list specifies itself.

To match the special characters left bracket ([), question mark (?), pound (#), and asterisk (*), the particular character must be enclosed in brackets. The right bracket (]) cannot be used within a group to match itself, but it can be used outside a group as an individual character. The character sequence [] is considered to be the string literal "".

Some examples of the `Like` operator are the following.

```
Dim r As Boolean

r = "abc" Like "a?c"       ' Result: True
r = "abcdef" Like "a*f"    ' Result: True
r = "abc" Like "a[A-Z]c"   ' Result: False
r = "aBc" Like "a[A-Z]c"   ' Result: True
```

Character comparisons and ordering for character lists are dependent on the type of string comparisons being used. If binary comparisons are being used (i.e., `Option Compare Binary`), character comparisons and ordering are based on the numeric Unicode values. If text comparisons are being used (i.e., `Option Compare Text`), character comparisons and ordering are based on the current thread's culture.

Advanced

In some cultures, one character may represent two separate characters, and vice versa. For example, the character "æ" can be used to represent the characters "a" and "e" when they appear together, while the characters "^" and "O" can be used to represent the character "Ô". When text comparisons are used, the `Like` operator recognizes such cultural equivalences, and an occurrence of a single character in either a pattern or a string matches the equivalent two-character sequence in the other string. Similarly, a single character in a pattern enclosed in brackets (by itself, in a list, or in a range) matches the equivalent two-character sequence in the string, and vice versa.

Type Operators

The `TypeOf` operator determines whether a value is of a particular type or is derived from a particular type. This is particularly useful when you are dealing with values typed only as `Object`, or when working with types in an inheritance hierarchy. In the following example, a function that takes an `Object` value uses the `TypeOf` operator to determine the actual type of the value.

```
Function AddOne(ByVal o As Object) As Object
  If TypeOf o Is Integer Then
    Return CInt(o) + 1
  ElseIf TypeOf o Is Double Then
    Return CDbl(o) + 1
  ' Handle the other types
  ...
  Else
    Throw New ArgumentException("Not a recognized value.")
  End If
End Function
```

Advanced

Because it is not possible to derive from a value type (see Chapter 9), the TypeOf operator has no meaning for value types and is not allowed. (A value typed as a value type can never be anything but itself.) It is possible to test whether a value typed as Object is a value type, because a value type can always be converted to Object.

Style

Using TypeOf to determine the exact value of a type will be much faster at runtime than attempting to convert the value and handling a resulting exception.

The GetType operator returns an instance of the System.Type class that represents the specified type. The System.Type class is a .NET Framework reflection class that can be used to inspect a type and its members at runtime. It can also be used with other reflection classes to do things like create instances of the class dynamically.

```
Dim t As Type
Dim c As Collection

t = GetType(Collection)
c = Activator.CreateInstance(t)
```

This example dynamically creates an instance of the `Collection` class at runtime.

Constant Expressions

The result of some operations can be known at compile time —for example, the result of the operation `1 + 1` will always be the value 2, and the result of the operation `"a" & "b"` will always be the string `"ab"`. Operations that can be evaluated at compile time are called *constant expressions*. Constant expressions are more efficient than other types of expressions because the compiler can precompute them at compile time. There are also several places in the language that require constant expressions, such as field initializers.

Constant expressions can only contain literals and named constants. The runtime functions `Chr`, `Asc`, `ChrW`, and `AscW` (see Appendix A) are treated specially by the compiler and can be used in constant expressions, provided that their arguments are also constant expressions. Because string conversions depend on the current thread's culture at runtime, conversions to and from `String` cannot appear in constant expressions.

Advanced

Because the result of the `Chr` function also depends on the current runtime culture being used when the function is passed values greater than 128, `Chr` can only be used in constant expressions if the argument is 128 or less.

Conclusion

This chapter covered the operations that can be performed on the fundamental and user-defined types. The next chapter continues this discussion by covering the statements that can be used to act on types and operators.

Here are some points to consider.

- It is preferable to use parentheses to clarify how an operation is to be performed rather than relying on the precedence and associativity of operators. It is easy to forget the precedence order of the operators!

- In previous versions, operations on String and the numeric types resulted in a String value, the exact opposite of what happens in Visual Basic .NET. The behavior was changed because many programmers did not expect 1 + "2" to result in "12".

- Unlike in previous versions, dividing by zero with the floating-point division operator will produce the value NaN (Not a Number) instead of a division-by-zero exception. (Handling exceptions is covered in Chapter 7.)

- Text comparisons are significantly slower than binary comparisons because they require looking up information about the current culture. Unless culture-sensitive comparisons are needed, binary comparisons are recommended.

- The + operator can also be used to concatenate strings. However, because of the possible confusion between concatenating strings ("1" + "2" = "12") and adding numbers (1 + "2" = 3), the & operator should always be used to concatenate strings.

- Using TypeOf to determine the exact value of a type will be much faster at runtime than attempting to convert the value and handling a resulting exception.

6
Statements

Whereas operators perform operations on values, *statements* perform general actions. For example, the `For...Next` statement executes a set of statements some number of times. This chapter covers the set of Visual Basic .NET statements.

Local Declaration Statements

A local declaration statement declares a variable that can be used within a method. Local declarations can choose not to specify a type for the variable; if no type is specified, the type of the variable is assumed to be `Object`.

```
Dim x As Integer
Dim y                ' The type of the variable is Object
Dim z As Long
```

Style

In general, it is a good idea to explicitly declare the types of variables. Besides making it easy to see with a glance what type variables are, it produces faster code because the compiler can know at compile time what type a variable is. The `Option Strict` statement at the beginning of a source file requires that all variable declarations have an explicit type.

Multiple variables can be declared in one of two ways. If all the variables being declared are the same type, the names can be listed separated by commas, with the type specified at the end of the declaration. Otherwise, each local variable declaration must be separated by commas. The two forms can also be combined within the same statement.

```
Dim x, y As Integer
Dim a As Integer, b As Long
' c, d and e are of type Double; f and g are of type Single
Dim c, d, e As Double, f, g As Single
Dim h, i, j ' Types are all Object
```

Local variables are in scope only from the point of declaration to the end of the statement block in which they were declared. In the following example, the first reference to x is invalid because it attempts to refer to x before it is declared. The third reference to x is invalid because it attempts to refer to x outside the block in which it was declared.

```
Dim y As Integer

For y = 1 To 10
  x = 10   ' Error: x not declared yet
  Dim x As Integer
  x = 20
Next y

x = 30     ' Error: Can't refer to x outside of For loop
```

A local variable can be named using any valid name, provided that the name is not already used anywhere in the local variable's scope. Because locals are scoped to their containing block, this means two locals can be declared with the same name, provided that their scopes don't overlap. For example:

```
Dim y As Integer

If y > 0 Then
  Dim x As Integer
  x = y * 10
  Console.WriteLine(x)
End If

If y < 0 Then
```

```
    Dim x As Long
    Dim y As Long = 5  ' Error: y already declared in this scope
    x = y * 20
    Console.WriteLine(x)
  End If
```

In this example, the variable x can be declared in two places because the scopes of the two variables do not overlap. The declarations of the variable y, however, will cause an error because the scope of the y in the If statement overlaps the scope of the outer y.

Type Characters

It is also possible to declare the type of a variable by using a type character at the end of a name. The type characters are % for Integer, & for Long, ! for Single, # for Double, @ for Decimal, and $ for String. For example:

```
    Dim x%        ' Type is Integer
    Dim y@        ' Type is Decimal
    Dim z$        ' Type is String
```

Type characters can also be used when you are referring to a local variable, provided that the type character matches the type of the variable. In the following example, the reference to x is correct, while the reference to z will give an error because the types don't match.

```
    Dim x As Integer, z As String

    x% = 5
    z@ = 10              ' Error: Type character doesn't match type.
```

Compatibility

Type characters on variables are supported purely for historical reasons, and their use is discouraged.

Initializers

Local variables can have *initializers*, which give a local variable an initial value. Initializers are specified by following the local declaration with an equals sign (=) and the expression to assign to the variable. Multiple variables in a declaration can be initialized, but only if they have separate As clauses.

```
Dim x As Integer = 5
Dim y As String = Console.ReadLine()
Dim a As Integer = 6, b As Integer = 7
```

Initializers are equivalent to assignment statements (see the next main section) at the point of declaration. Every time execution reaches the local declaration statement, the variable is initialized.

```
Dim i As Integer

For i = 1 to 10
   Dim x As Integer = 5
   Console.WriteLine(x)
   x = i
Next i
```

In this example, the value 5 is printed ten times, because every time the declaration line is reached, the local is reinitialized with the value 5. The example is equivalent to this code.

```
Dim i As Integer

For i = 1 to 10
   Dim x As Integer
   x = 5
   Console.WriteLine(x)
   x = i
Next i
```

Constants

Local constants can also be declared; they use the same syntax as local variable declarations except that they use the keyword Const instead of Dim and must supply a constant expression initializer. Local constants can be used in the same way as local variables except that their value cannot be changed.

```
Dim i As Integer
Const Lower As Integer = 1
Const Upper As Integer = 10
```

```
For i = Lower to Upper
  Console.WriteLine(i)
Next i
```

Static Locals

Static locals are a special kind of local variable that retain their value across calls to the method. Normally, local variables are destroyed and lose their value when the method they are contained in exits. However, static locals are allocated in such a way that they are not destroyed when the method exits. For example, the following will print the numbers 1, 2, 3, 4, and 5 because the value of Number is preserved across calls.

```
Module Test
  Sub IncrementNumber()
    Static Number As Integer = 0

    Console.WriteLine(Number)
    Number += 1
  End Sub

  Sub Main()
    For i As Integer = 1 to 5
      IncrementNumber()
    Next i
  End Sub
End Module
```

A static local with an initializer is also special in that the initializer is only executed once, the first time that execution reaches the static declaration. In the preceding example, the static local Number is only initialized with the value 0 once.

Advanced

Static local initialization is done in a thread-safe way. If an exception occurs during initialization, the initialization will not be retried, and the static local will have the default value for the type.

Static locals in an instance method are stored in the containing instance, so each instance of a type will have its own set of static locals; static locals in a shared method are stored in the containing type, so all instances of the type will share the same static local. If variables shared across all instances are needed in an instance method, shared fields can be used.

The following example demonstrates the independent initialization of a static local variable in two instances of a class.

```
Class TestClass
  Function InstanceValue() As Integer
    Static Value As Integer = 0

    Value +=1
    Return Value
  End Function
End Class

Module Test
  Sub Main()
    Dim t1 As TestClass = New TestClass()
    Dim t2 As TestClass = New TestClass()

    Console.WriteLine(t1.InstanceValue())
    Console.WriteLine(t2.InstanceValue())
    Console.WriteLine(t1.InstanceValue())
  End Sub
End Module
```

This example prints the values 1, 1, and 2.

Implicit Locals

Local variables can also be declared *implicitly*; that is, the compiler can infer that a local was declared even if there is no explicit Dim statement. This can happen when the compiler encounters a name that has not been previously declared. Instead of giving an error, the compiler assumes that the name refers to an implicitly declared local variable with a type of Object.

```
Sub Test()
  For i = 1 to 10
    Console.WriteLine(i)
  Next i
End Sub
```

In this example, the variable i is not explicitly declared, so it is assumed to be a local of type Object. Implicit locals are always considered to be declared at the top of the subroutine or function, so they are always scoped to the entire method.

```
Sub Test()
  Dim y As Integer

  If y < 0 Then
    x = y * 20
    Console.WriteLine(x)
  End If

  x = 5
End Sub
```

In this case, the fact that x is first implicitly declared within an If block does not make it invalid for x to be accessed from outside the If block. If x had been explicitly declared within the If block, however, the reference would have been invalid.

The Option Explicit statement at the beginning of a source file requires that all variables be explicitly declared.

Style

It is highly recommended that Option Explicit always be specified. It is *very* easy to misspell a variable name and implicitly create a local by accident!

The following example illustrates this point.

```
Dim Cost As Integer

Cost = CInt(Console.ReadLine())

If Cots < 0 Then
  Console.WriteLine("Invalid cost")
Else
  Console.WriteLine("The cost is " & Cost)
End If
```

In this example, the local variable name Cost is misspelled as Cots in the If statement. With implicit variable declaration allowed, this will not give an error and will instead declare a variable named `Cots`. The resulting behavior will not be the one intended.

Assignment

The assignment statement assigns a value to a variable. The syntax is straightforward and should be familiar by now, given the examples used in the book so far. One thing that should be kept in mind is that, unlike some languages, such as C, the assignment operator is a statement and cannot be used within an expression—in an expression the equals sign means equality, not assignment. For example:

```
Dim x As Integer
Dim y As Boolean

x = 5
y = x = 5
```

In the example, the first statement assigns the value 5 to x. In the second statement, the first equals sign is assignment, while the second equals sign is equality. So the statement first calculates whether x is equal to 5 and then assigns the result (`True`) to the variable y.

Compatibility

Previous versions of Visual Basic made a distinction between value assignment (`Let`) and reference assignment (`Set`). `Let` and `Set` assignments are no longer supported, because the .NET Framework does not allow for the distinction.

When the result of an operation is assigned to a variable that is part of the operation, compound assignment operators can be used. For example:

```
Dim x As Integer = 10

x += 5     ' equivalent to x = x + 5
x *= 10    ' equivalent to x = x * 10
x \= 2     ' equivalent to x = x \ 2
```

When a compound assignment is performed, the left-hand side of the assignment (i.e., the variable being assigned to) is evaluated only once. In most cases, this makes no difference, but it does affect the situation where the variable being assigned to is an element of an array or an indexed property. In that case, the index values are evaluated only once.

```
Module Test
  Function a() As Integer
    Console.WriteLine("Got index")
    Return 0
  End Function

  Sub Main()
    Dim x(10, 10) As Integer

    x(a(), a()) += 5
  End Sub
End Module
```

In this example, the string "Got index" will be printed only twice—the function a will be invoked only twice, not four times. The values of each invocation will be stored and used to determine the value on the right-hand side of the assignment and the place to store the value on the left-hand side of the assignment.

With Statement

The With statement simplifies repeatedly accessing the members of a value. Within a With statement, an expression beginning with just a period or an exclamation point is interpreted as if the With expression preceded it. For example:

```
With TextBox1
  .TabIndex = 0
  .ForeColor = Color.Red
  .Text = "Red"
  .Show()
End With
```

The With expression is evaluated only once, at the beginning of the statement, so any changes to the underlying value of the With expression won't be applied until the With statement is reexecuted.

```
With TextBox1
  TextBox1 = New TextBox()
  .TabIndex = 0
  .ForeColor = Color.Red
  .Text = "Red"
  .Show()
End With
```

In this example, the original text box will be modified, even though the value in the `TextBox1` variable has been changed.

Conditional Statements

Conditional statements allow executing code depending on whether some situation is true or false. They are fundamental to the decision making processes within a program.

If Statement

The `If` statement is a simple conditional statement that executes code based on whether a condition is true or false. The expression in an `If` statement must to evaluate to a `Boolean` value—if the expression evaluates to `True`, the statements contained between the `If` statement and an `End If` statement are executed. If the expression evaluates to `False`, the statements are not executed.

```
If x > 0 Then
  Console.WriteLine("x is greater than zero.")
End If
```

The block can also contain a block that starts with the keyword `Else`. If the expression evaluates to `False`, the `Else` block will be executed instead of the `If` block.

```
If x > 0 Then
  Console.WriteLine("x is greater than zero.")
Else
  Console.WriteLine("x is less than or equal to zero.")
End If
```

It is also possible to chain `If` statements together by using the `ElseIf` keyword. The `If` statements will be evaluated in order from first to last. The first If statement to evaluate to True will be executed (or the Else block will be executed if there is one and no If statement evaluates to True).

```
If x > 0 Then
   Console.WriteLine("x is greater than zero.")
ElseIf x < 0 Then
   Console.WriteLine("x is less than zero.")
Else
   Console.WriteLine("x is zero.")
End If
```

An If statement can also be written entirely on one line—in that case, no End If is necessary. It is not possible to use an ElseIf in a line If statement, but Else can be used.

```
If x > 0 Then y = x
If y < 0 Then z = y Else z = 5
```

Note that all the statements that follow the Then or Else in a line if are considered part of the If statement. In the following example, nothing will be printed.

```
x = 0
If x > 0 Then x = x + 1 : Console.WriteLine("x is greater than zero.")
```

Select Statement

Often a decision needs to be made not on the basis of a simple true/false condition but by choosing between a set of different possibilities. The Select statement simplifies that process. A Select statement begins with the keywords Select Case and an expression that forms the basis of the following comparisons. The statement contains a set of Case statements that are tests for the Select expression. In its simplest form, a Case statement is just the Case keyword followed by an expression to compare the Select expression against. If the values are equal, the code between the Case statement and the next Case statement is evaluated. A Select statement is ended by an End Select statement.

```
Select Case x
   Case 0
     Console.WriteLine("x is zero")
   Case 1
```

```
    Console.WriteLine("x is one")
  Case 2
    Console.WriteLine("x is two")
  Case 3
    Console.WriteLine("x is three")
End Select
```

Any value that can be compared using the = operator can be used in a Select statement.

```
Select Case x
  Case "Red"
    Console.WriteLine("x is red")
  Case "Green"
    Console.WriteLine("x is green")
  Case "Blue"
    Console.WriteLine("x is blue")
End Select
```

The Case statements are compared in order from first to last—once a Case statement evaluates to True, no further comparisons are done. In the following example, the third case statement will never be executed.

```
Select Case x
  Case 0
    Console.WriteLine("x is zero")
  Case 1
    Console.WriteLine("x is one")
  Case 1
    Console.WriteLine("x is one, also")
End Select
```

Ranges of numeric values can be compared by specifying a value, followed by the To keyword and another value. If the Select expression is within that range, the Case statement will be executed.

```
Select Case x
  Case 0
    Console.WriteLine("x is zero")
  Case 1 To 5
    Console.WriteLine("x is one, two, three, four or five")
  Case 6 To 10
    Console.WriteLine("x is six, seven, eight, nine or ten")
End Select
```

If a comparison other than equality is needed, the `Case` keyword can be followed by the `Is` keyword, a comparison operator, and an expression. This causes the specified comparison to be performed. Also, a `Case Else` statement will be executed if none of the other `Case` statement evaluates to `True`. For example:

```
Select Case x
  Case Is < 0
    Console.WriteLine("x is less than zero")
  Case 0
    Console.WriteLine("x is zero")
  Case Else
    Console.WriteLine("x is greater than zero")
End Select
```

Finally, multiple cases can be combined by separating the `Case` expressions with commas. For example:

```
Select Case x
  Case 1, 3, 5, 7
    Console.WriteLine("x is prime")
  Case Is < 0, Is > 10
    Console.WriteLine("x is out of range")
  Case Else
    Console.WriteLine("x is not prime")
End Select
```

Looping Statements

Looping statements execute statements more than once.

For Statement

The `For` statement executes statements a set number of times. The statement begins with the keyword `For`, followed by a variable that will contain the value of the current iteration; this variable is called the *loop control variable*. The loop control variable is followed by the = assignment operator, the lower bound of the loop, the keyword `To`, and then the upper bound of the loop. A `For` loop statement is closed by a `Next` statement.

When a `For` statement begins, the lower bound is assigned to the loop control variable. All of the statements in the `For` loop are executed, and then the loop control variable is incremented by 1. If the loop control variable is greater than the upper bound, the loop ends. The following example prints the values 1 through 10.

```
Dim x As Integer

For x = 1 To 10
  Console.WriteLine("x = " & x)
Next x
```

For compactness, the loop control variable may be declared within the For statement itself; otherwise, the name must refer to a variable in an enclosing block. For example, the previous loop could have been written as follows.

```
For x As Integer = 1 To 10
  Console.WriteLine("x = " & x)
Next x
```

The Next statement may be followed by the name of the loop control variable of the For loop that the Next closes—the variable name must match the immediately containing For loop. A Next statement may also close multiple For loops by listing all the loop control variables in a comma-delimited list. In that case, the loop control variables close the For loops in order from left to right. For example:

```
Dim x, y, z As Integer

For x = 1 To 10
  For y = 1 To 10
    For z = 1 to 10
      Console.WriteLine(x + y + z)
Next z, y, x
```

Style

Closing more than one For loop with a single Next statement is generally discouraged, because it tends to be less readable.

For example, it is suggested that the previous example be written instead as follows.

```
Dim x, y, z As Integer

For x = 1 To 10
  For y = 1 To 10
    For z = 1 to 10
      Console.WriteLine(x + y + z)
    Next z
  Next y
Next x
```

A For loop may also specify how much each loop should increment the loop control variable. The default is 1, but the keyword Step and a value can be added after the upper bound to specify what the step should be. This allows any numeric value, including negative values. The following example prints the values 10 down to 1.

```
Dim x As Integer

For x = 10 To 1 Step -1
  Console.WriteLine("x = " & x)
Next
```

The loop control variable may be of any numeric type or of type Object. The bounds and the step value (if any) must be convertible to the type of the loop control variable. If the loop control variable's type is Object, the widest type of the values will be used as the type for the loop.

Advanced

The bounds and step values of a loop are only evaluated once, the first time that the loop executes. Any changes made to the values after the loop has been entered have no effect on the execution of the loop.

For Each Statement

The For Each statement loops through the elements in a *collection*. A collection can be any type that stores a set of values—an array is an example of a collection, and the class Collection is another one. The statement begins with the keywords For Each, followed by an expression that is used as the loop control variable. The loop control variable will contain the current element of the collection being iterated through. The loop control variable is followed by the keyword In and an expression that must be a collection type.

When a For Each loop begins, the loop control variable is initialized with the first element in the collection. After the statements in the loop are executed, the loop control variable is updated with the next item in the collection. If there are no more items in the collection, the loop ends. The following example fills an array with the numbers 1 through 10 and then prints them.

```
Dim x(10) As Integer
Dim y As Integer
Dim z As Integer

For y = 1 To 10
  x(y) = y
Next y

For Each z In x
   Console.WriteLine(z)
Next z
```

For compactness, the loop control variable may be declared within the For Each statement itself; otherwise, the name must refer to a variable in an enclosing block. For example, the previous loop could have been written as follows.

```
For Each z As Integer In x
   Console.WriteLine(z)
Next z
```

Because there is no place to put a conversion operator when the type of the loop control variable is not the same type as the collection type, a For Each statement will convert from the element type of the collection to the loop control variable without an error even if Option Strict is on. If a value cannot be converted, a runtime exception will occur.

Advanced

If the collection's enumerator type (see the Collection Types section) implements the `System.IDisposable` interface, the `For Each` statement will automatically call `Dispose` on the enumerator when the loop is complete.

While and Do Statements

The `While` and `Do` statements allow unbounded looping—both statements will continue looping until some user-defined condition evaluates to `True`. The `While` statement is the simpler of the two statements; it starts with the keyword `While` and an expression that is evaluated at the beginning of each loop. If the expression evaluates to `True`, the loop continues; if it evaluates to `False`, the loop ends. A `While` statement ends with an `End While` statement. The following example prints the values 1 through 10.

```
Dim x As Integer = 10

While x > 0
  Console.WriteLine("x = " & x)
  x -= 1
End While
```

A `Do` loop offers more flexibility in how and when the loop condition is tested. The `Do` statement takes one of two forms. One form begins with the keyword `Do`, followed by either `Until` or `While` and an expression, and ends with the `Loop` statement. In this form, the expression is evaluated at the beginning of the loop. If the keyword `Until` is specified, the loop continues if the expression evaluates to `False`; if the keyword `While` is specified, the loop continues if the expression evaluates to `True`.

```
Dim x As Integer = 10

Do While x > 0
  Console.WriteLine("x = " & x)
  x -= 1
Loop
```

```
Do Until x = 11
  Console.WriteLine("x = " & x)
  x += 1
Loop
```

The second form of Do loop moves the conditional expression to the Loop statement. In this form, the expression is evaluated at the end of the loop rather than the beginning.

```
Dim x As Integer = 10

Do
  Console.WriteLine("x = " & x)
  x -= 1
Loop While x > 0

Do
  Console.WriteLine("x = " & x)
  x += 1
Loop Until x = 11
```

In this example, each loop will always execute at least once, whereas the loops in the previous example may never execute if the condition is not satisfied.

Collection Types

Advanced

This section contains some advanced concepts. Beginning readers may want to skip it and revisit it after reading Chapter 13, Inheritance, and Chapter 14, Interfaces.

A *collection type* follows a design pattern that allows its members to be enumerated. Only collection types can be enumerated by a For Each statement. A collection type is any type that implements the interface System.IEnumerable or satisfies the following conditions.

- The type contains a method named GetEnumerator that returns a value of some type T.

- The enumerator type T contains a method named MoveNext that returns a `Boolean` value.
- The enumerator type T contains a read-only or read-write property named `Current`.

Just implementing the interface `IEnumerable` is sufficient to make a type a collection type, but a collection type that only implements `IEnumerable` suffers from the fact that `IEnumerable` uses the type `Object` as its element type. This means that every time a value is fetched from the collection, it must be converted to its actual type. By satisfying the three conditions listed earlier instead, a class can implement the collection methods in a strongly typed way. The following class is an example of a collection type that stores `Integer` values.

```
Class IntegerCollection
  Class IntegerEnumerator
    Private Collection As IntegerCollection
    Private Index As Integer = -1

    Public Sub New(ByVal Collection As IntegerCollection)
      Me.Collection = Collection
    End Sub

    Public Sub Reset()
      Index = -1
    End Sub

    Public Function MoveNext() As Boolean
      If Index < Collection.Length Then
        Index += 1
      End If

      Return (Index = Collection.Length)
    End Function

    Public ReadOnly Property Current() As Integer
      Get
        If Index = -1 OrElse Index = Collection.Length Then
          Throw New InvalidOperationException()
        End If

        Return Collection(Index)
      End Get
    End Property
```

```
    End Class

    Private Values() As Integer

    Public Sub New(ByVal Values() As Integer)
      Me.Values = Values
    End Sub

    Public ReadOnly Property Length() As Integer
      Get
        Return Values.Length
      End Get
    End Property

    Public Function GetEnumerator As IntegerEnumerator
      Return New IntegerEnumerator(Me)
    End Function
  End Class
```

Because many methods in the Framework take classes that implement IEnumerable, it is recommended that IEnumerable be implemented even if the strongly typed pattern is being used.

When a For Each loop executes, the collection's methods are called as follows: When the loop begins, GetEnumerator is called on the loop expression, and the returned enumerator is stored in a temporary variable. Then at the beginning of each loop, MoveNext is called on the enumerator. If the function returns False, the loop terminates. If the function returns True, the Current property is retrieved and assigned to the loop control variable; then the loop block executes. When the Next statement is reached, execution returns to the top of the loop.

Branching Statements

Branching statements allow transferring control from one location to another within a method.

Exit and Return Statements

The Exit statement allows exiting a particular kind of statement block. The Exit keyword is followed by the kind of block to be exited: Sub, Function, Property, Try, Select, Do, While, or For. If there is no containing block of the type specified, the compiler will give an error. Note that the statement will exit the containing block of the type specified, including any blocks that may be nested within that containing block.

```
For x As Integer = 1 To 10
  Dim y As Integer = x

  While y > 0
    y -= 1

    If y = 5 Then
      Exit For
    End If
  End While
Next x
```

In this example, when the `Exit For` is reached, execution will leave both the `While` loop *and* the `For` loop.

The `Return` statement returns control from a subroutine or a function, just as an `Exit Sub` or `Exit Function` statement does. In a function, however, the `Return` statement must supply an argument. This argument is returned as the value of the function. For example, the following function adds two numbers together and returns the result.

```
Function Add(ByVal x As Integer, ByVal y As Integer) As Integer
  Return x + y
End Function
```

Goto Statement and Labels

The `GoTo` statement transfers control to a specified label. A *label* is a name at the beginning of a line, followed by a colon.

```
Dim x, y As Integer

x = FetchValue()
If x < 0 Then Goto SkipDivision
y = 1 \ x

SkipDivision:
Return y
```

Compatibility

Numbers can also be used as labels, but this functionality is included for historical reasons and is not encouraged.

It is worth noting that whether a statement is a label or a method invocation may at times be ambiguous because they can look the same. Whenever there is any question, the statement is always assumed to be a label.

```
MsgBox("hello") : MsgBox("world!")   ' Two method calls
MsgBox:                              ' label
```

As a matter of style and good programming, use of the GoTo statement should be avoided unless absolutely needed. There are also several situations in which a GoTo statement is not allowed.

- A GoTo cannot branch into a With statement from outside the statement.
- A GoTo cannot branch into a For or For Each statement from outside the statement.
- A GoTo cannot branch into a SyncLock statement from outside the statement.
- A GoTo can only branch from a Catch statement into the Try block of the same statement.
- A GoTo can never branch out of a Finally statement.
- A GoTo can never branch into a Catch or Finally statement.

The first two restrictions deal with statements that do initialization at the beginning of the block; if the initialization were skipped, statements within the block would not work properly. The rest of the restrictions have to do with the way that the .NET Runtime handles exceptions (the Sync-Lock statement contains an implicit Try...Catch statement).

Compatibility

The GoSub statement and the computed forms of the GoTo and GoSub statements (On...GoTo and On...GoSub) are no longer supported.

Program Flow Statements

There are two statements that can control the overall program flow. The End statement causes program execution to end. This statement may not be used in class libraries (i.e., DLLs), because they are not executable. For example:

```
Module Test
  Sub Main()
    Dim x As Integer

    While True
      x = CInt(Console.ReadLine())
      If x = 0 Then
        End
      End If
    End While
  End Sub
End Module
```

Advanced

When an End statement is executed, the Finalize method on classes will be run before shutdown, but the Finally blocks of any currently executing Try statements will not be executed

The Stop statement also causes program execution to end, but will also transfer control to a debugger if one is present. Stop is primarily useful when you are developing a program that needs to run for some time before debugging begins. For example:

```
Module Test
  Sub Main()
    Dim x As Integer

    While x > 0
      x = CInt(Console.ReadLine())

      ' When x = -1, break into the debugger.
      If x = -1 Then
        Stop
      End If
    End While
  End Sub
End Module
```

Style

Because it is easy to forget to remove `Stop` statements from source code, setting breakpoints in the debugger is usually preferable to using `Stop` statements.

SyncLock

The .NET Framework allows programs to execute across multiple threads of execution. A full discussion of multithreading is beyond the scope of this book, but there is a statement that helps simplify writing multithreaded applications. The `SyncLock` statement can be used to prevent more than one thread of execution from entering the same block of code.

For example, the following code creates two threads to fill an array.

```
Imports System.Threading

Module Test
  Dim Array(10000) As Integer
  Dim CurrentIndex As Integer = 0

  Sub FillArray()
    For Number As Integer = 1 to 5000
      Array(CurrentIndex) = Number
      CurrentIndex += 1
    Next Number
  End Sub
```

```
    Sub Main()
        Dim t1 As Thread = New Thread(AddressOf FillArray)
        Dim t2 As Thread = New Thread(AddressOf FillArray)

        t1.Start()
        t2.Start()
    End Sub
End Module
```

The way this code is written, the array may or may not be completely filled when the program finishes executing. If thread 1 assigns a value into a particular index, it is possible that thread 2 will read the value of Cur- rentIndex before thread 1 has a chance to increment the value in the vari- able. Thus, thread 2 will then overwrite the value that thread 1 wrote, instead of using a new index.

The SyncLock statement uses an object as a signal to prevent more than one thread of execution from entering the protected block at a time. The preceding example can be rewritten as follows, using a SyncLock state- ment to prevent more than one thread from updating the array at one time.

```
Imports System.Threading

Module Test
    Dim Array(10000) As Integer
    Dim CurrentIndex As Integer = 0

    Sub FillArray()
        SyncLock Array.SyncRoot
            For Number As Integer = 1 to 5000
                Array(CurrentIndex) = Number
                CurrentIndex += 1
            Next Number
        End SyncLock
    End Sub

    Sub Main()
        Dim t1 As Thread = New Thread(AddressOf FillArray)
        Dim t2 As Thread = New Thread(AddressOf FillArray)

        t1.Start()
        t2.Start()
    End Sub
End Module
```

The argument to a SyncLock statement can be an instance of any reference type—in this example, the SyncLock statement uses the value returned by System.Array.SyncRoot as the signal. All SyncLock blocks that use the same instance will block each other, so care must be used when you are choosing what instance to use to block.

Advanced

Many collection classes like System.Array have SyncRoot properties that can be used with SyncLock to synchronize access to the collection.

Conclusion

Statements perform the main actions of a program, such as looping over statements. In the next chapter, we'll discuss how a program can handle errors and other exceptional situations in a program when they occur.

Here are some style points to consider.

- In general, it is a good idea to explicitly declare the types of variables. Besides making it easy to see with a glance what type variables are, it produces faster code because the compiler can know at compile time what type a variable is. The Option Strict statement at the beginning of a source file requires that all variable declarations have an explicit type.
- Type characters on variables are supported purely for historical reasons, and their use is discouraged.
- It is highly recommended that Option Explicit always be specified. It is *very* easy to misspell a variable name and implicitly create a local by accident!
- Closing more than one For loop with a single Next statement is generally discouraged, because it tends to be less readable.

- Numbers can also be used as labels, but this functionality is included for historical reasons and is not encouraged.

- The `GoSub` statement and the computed forms of the `GoTo` and `GoSub` statements (`On...GoTo` and `On...GoSub`) are no longer supported.

- Because it is easy to forget to remove `Stop` statements from source code, setting breakpoints in the debugger is usually preferable to using `Stop` statements.

7

Exceptions

In an ideal world, all programs would execute perfectly and always produce the correct value. In reality, however, bugs and other unexpected situations happen. These situations are dealt with in the .NET Framework through *exceptions*. An exception is an object that represents an unexpected or exceptional situation. An exception contains information that can be used to help understand what went wrong and where. When an error condition occurs in a program or in the Framework, a new exception object is created and *thrown*. Throwing an exception causes the program to stop executing and passes control to the .NET Framework, which looks for a specific kind of code, called an *exception handler*, which can *catch* the exception and handle it in some specific way.

Style

Exceptions should never just be ignored. Catching an exception and doing nothing but throwing away the exception is a very bad practice that is prone to causing serious bugs. Properly handling exceptions in a program is fundamental to proper execution of a program.

When an exception is thrown, the .NET Framework starts by looking for an exception handler in the method that threw the exception. If the current method has no handler to catch the exception, the Framework looks at the method that called the method that threw the exception. If that method has no handler, it then looks at the method that called the method that called the method that threw the exception, and so on. Eventually, the Framework reaches the `Main` method. If the `Main` method does not catch the exception, the exception is considered "unhandled," and the Framework will terminate the program and inform the user that an unhandled exception has occurred.

Style

Because looking for an exception handler incurs a fair amount of overhead (even if the exception handler is in the same method where the exception was thrown), exceptions should *only* be thrown in truly exceptional situations. Exceptions should not be used in place of returning a value from a function, for example, or communicating some value between two methods through reference parameters.

Throwing Exceptions

Exceptions can be thrown in one of two ways. The recommended way is to create a new exception object and throw it using the `Throw` statement. The following function throws an exception when the divisor passed in is zero.

```
Function Divide(ByVal x As Integer, ByVal y As Integer) As Integer
  If y = 0 Then
    Throw New ArgumentException("y", "Divisor cannot be zero.")
  End If

  Return x \ y
End Function
```

The argument to a `Throw` statement must be an instance of `System.Exception` or an instance of a type that is derived from the type `System.Exception` (see Chapter 13, Inheritance, for more on derived types). In general, it is important to throw the most specific exception possible to allow callers to handle only errors that they are prepared to deal with. Some of the more common exception types are listed in Table 7-1.

New exception types within an application can be created by defining new classes that inherit directly from `System.ApplicationException` or any type that inherits from `System.ApplicationException`.

TABLE 7-1: Common Exception Types

Types	Description
System.ApplicationException	An application-specific exception occurred.
System.ArgumentException	An argument is invalid.
System.ArgumentNullException	An argument is Nothing.
System.ArgumentOutOfRange-Exception	An argument was not within its valid range.
System.DivideByZeroException	An operation divided by zero.
System.DllNotFoundException	The Lib clause of a Declare statement was not found.
System.ExecutionEngine-Exception	The .NET Framework encountered an internal error.
System.InvalidCastException	A conversion from one type to another was not valid.
System.NotSupportedException	The method is not supported.
System.NullReferenceException	The program tried to use a Nothing value in an invalid way.
System.OutOfMemoryException	The program has run out of memory.
System.OverflowException	An operation overflowed.
System.Runtime.Interop-Services.COMException	An exception occurred while a COM object was being called.

Compatibility

Exceptions can also be thrown using the `Error` statement. The `Error` statement takes an error number as an argument instead of an exception object. This is a holdover from previous versions of the Visual Basic language, where exceptions were thrown by number instead of by type. In Visual Basic .NET, the error number is translated into the appropriate exception type, and then a new exception of that type is thrown. Use of the `Error` statement is strongly discouraged.

Structured Exception Handling

Structured exception handling is a style of exception handling in which exception handlers are defined for a specific block of code. A structured exception handling statement begins with the keyword `Try`. One or more `Catch` statements can follow the end of the statements in the `Try` block; each `Catch` statement handles a particular type of exception by specifying the keyword `Catch`, a variable to hold the exception, and the exception type to be caught. For example:

```
Dim x, y As Integer

Try
  x = CInt(Console.ReadLine())
  y = CInt(Console.ReadLine())
  Console.WriteLine(x \ y)
Catch e As OverflowException
  Console.WriteLine("Overflow")
Catch e As DivideByZeroException
  Console.WriteLine("Divide by zero")
Catch e As Exception
  Console.WriteLine(e.Message)
End Try
```

When an exception is thrown, each catch handler in the current `Try` statement is examined in order from first to last to determine whether the handler handles that kind of exception. If the type of the exception is the same as (or derived from) the handler exception type, the catch handler is executed. In the preceding example, if y was zero, the integer division operation x \ y would throw a System.DivideByZeroException exception. The system would check to see whether the first Catch block handled that type of exception. Since it doesn't, it would look at the second Catch block. Since the second Catch block handles that type of exception, it would execute the code that prints Divide by Zero.

Advanced

Because Catch blocks are checked from first to last, the more general exception types should come last. If Catch e As Exception had come first in the preceding example, none of the other Catch blocks would ever be used, because all exceptions derived from System.Exception!

A Try statement may also specify a Finally block. The statements in a Finally block will always be executed when execution leaves the Try block, no matter whether an exception occurred or not. Finally blocks are useful for ensuring that variables are cleaned up properly when an exception occurs.

```
Imports System.IO

Module Test
  Sub Main()
    Dim Output As FileStream = File.Open("output.txt", FileMode. _
Create)

    Try
      ' Write some values
      ...
    Finally
      ' Ensure the file is closed
      If Not Output Is Nothing Then
        Output.Close()
      End If
    End Try
  End Sub
End Module
```

> **■ NOTE**
> If an exception occurs in a `Finally` block, it won't be handled by its containing `Try` block. Instead, the exception will be handled by the next containing `Try` block, if any.

`Catch` blocks may also have conditional statements attached to them to provide additional conditions for handling an exception. This is done by adding the keyword `When` and a conditional expression that evaluates to a `Boolean` value. A `Catch` block can specify just a type (like `System.Exception`) or a `When` clause or both. For example:

```
Imports System.IO

Module Test
  Sub Main()
    Dim Output As FileStream = File.Open("output.txt", FileMode.Create)
    Dim Count As Byte

    Try
      ' Write some values
      For Count = 1 To 10
        Output.Write(Count)
      Next

      ...
    Catch e As Exception When Count < 10
      Console.WriteLine("Wrote only " & Count & " values.")
    Finally
      ' Ensure the file is closed
      Output.Close()
    End Try
  End Sub
End Module
```

Rethrowing Exceptions

It is sometime useful to catch an exception, handle the exception in some way, and then let the exception continue propagating, to be caught by another handler. The most straightforward way to do this is just to end the catch handler by throwing the exception again.

```
Try
    ...
Catch e As Exception
    ' Acknowledge that the exception was thrown
    Console.WriteLine("Exception: " & e.Message)

    ' Let the exception continue
    Throw e
End Try
```

The problem with this is that exceptions contain information about where they were thrown from. This information can be used by a debugger to show where an exception occurred or can be used by other catch handlers to provide diagnostics about program failure. When an exception is thrown, as in the preceding example, the .NET Framework marks the exception with the current location. Any existing location information already contained in the exception is overwritten. To avoid this problem, you can specify the Throw statement without an argument in a catch handler.

```
Try
    ...
Catch e As Exception
    ' Acknowledge that the exception was thrown
    Console.WriteLine("Exception: " & e.Message)

    ' Let the exception continue
    Throw
End Try
```

This causes the current exception to be rethrown, with all location information preserved.

Unstructured Exception Handling

In addition to structured exception handling, Visual Basic .NET supports another style of exception handling that is more compatible with the style of exception handling used in previous versions. This style is called *unstructured exception handling* because it does not explicitly specify which statements a particular handler might cover and is a much looser way of handling exceptions.

> ## Style
>
> Structured exception handling involves less overhead and is more precise than unstructured exception handling. Although there are no major technical disadvantages to using unstructured exception handling, the `Try...Catch` style of error handling is encouraged over `On Error`.

In a method that uses unstructured exception handling, one or more `On Error` statements establish the behavior when any exception occurs (it isn't possible to catch only certain types of exceptions using unstructured exception handling). An `On Error` statement can be followed by a `GoTo` statement that specifies where execution should be transferred to when an exception is caught. In the following example, the `On Error` statement specifies that execution should jump to the `HandleError` label when an exception occurs.

```
Dim x, y As Integer

On Error Goto HandleError

x = CInt(Console.ReadLine())
y = CInt(Console.ReadLine())
Console.WriteLine(x \ y)
Return

HandleError:

If TypeOf Err.GetException() Is OverflowException Then
  Console.WriteLine("Overflow")
Else If TypeOf Err.GetException() Is DivideByZeroException Then
  Console.WriteLine("Divide by zero")
Else
  Console.WriteLine(Err.GetException().Message)
End If
```

Unlike a `Try` statement, which applies only to the statements contained within it, an `On Error` statement establishes the exception handling behavior for the entire method. This is done every time the point of execution reaches the particular `On Error` statement. For example, by the time execution reaches the end of the following set of statements, the current exception behavior will be to go to the `First` label, because it was the last `On Error` statement to be executed.

```
Dim x, y As Integer

On Error Goto First

y = 0
x = 5

If y > 0 Then
   On Error Goto Second
End If

x = x \ y
Return

First:

Console.WriteLine("First handler")
Return

Second:

Console.WriteLine("Second handler")
Return
```

When execution enters a method that contains `On Error` statements, no handler is initially set up, and exceptions will not be caught in the method. Once an exception handler has been set, the statement `On Error Goto 0` will set the current exception handler back to nothing. Once an exception has been caught, the exception is available in the `Err` property in the `Microsoft.VisualBasic.Information` standard module. The `Err` property returns an instance of the `Microsoft.VisualBasic.ErrObject` class. (For more information on `Err` and `ErrObject`, see Appendix A.)

```
Dim x, y As Integer

On Error Goto Handler

y = 0
x = 5
x = x \ y
Return
```

```
Handler:

Console.WriteLine("Exception: " & Err.GetException().Message)
Return
```

The exception is stored in the property until the next exception occurs or until the method exits. The exception can be explicitly cleared by the statement On Error Goto -1.

Resume and Resume Next

One feature that unstructured error handling supports and that structured exception handling does not is resuming from exceptions. After an exception has occurred, the Resume or Resume Next statement will return execution to the statement that caused the exception or the statement following it, respectively. In the following example, when the divide-by-zero exception is thrown, the code will change the value of y to 1 and then reexecute the division.

```
Dim x, y As Integer

On Error Goto Handler

y = 0
x = 5
Return x \ y

Handler:

y = 1
Resume
```

It is important to note that Resume puts the execution point back at the *beginning* of the statement that caused the exception, not the exact point where an exception occurred. In the following example, if the method invocation b() causes an exception, the Resume statement will cause the method a() to be invoked again.

```
Dim x As Integer

On Error Goto Handler

x = a() + b()
```

```
Return

Handler:

Resume
```

The `On Error` statement can also be used in conjunction with the `Resume Next` statement. (The statement `On Error Resume` is not allowed, because it would be likely to result in an infinite loop of exceptions.) In general, it is extremely bad programming practice to use the `On Error Resume Next` statement except in very limited situations. Exceptions are thrown to indicate error conditions, and reflexively ignoring all exceptions could allow potentially serious bugs. For example:

```
On Error Resume Next

Dim x As FileStream = File.Open("output.txt", FileMode.Create)
x.WriteByte(10)
x.WriteByte(20)
x.Close()
```

In this example, if the file fails to open for some reason, all the method invocations that follow will fail as well. But the `On Error Resume Next` statement causes no exceptions to be raised, and the code will run with no complaint, even though its intended purpose has not been fulfilled.

Conclusion

Handling exceptions is a key part of any program, since programs must be equipped to deal with failure and unexpected situations. It is important not to neglect exception handling when you are writing a program! This chapter finishes the coverage of what goes on within methods; in our next chapter, we'll start discussing types by talking about modules, the simplest kind of user-defined type, as well as how types are organized.

Here are some style points to consider.

- Exceptions should never just be ignored. Catching an exception and doing nothing but throwing away the exception is a very bad practice that is prone to causing serious bugs. Properly handling exceptions in a program is fundamental to proper execution of a program.

- Because looking for an exception handler incurs a fair amount of overhead (even if the exception handler is in the same method where the exception was thrown), exceptions should *only* be thrown in truly exceptional situations. Exceptions should not be used in place of returning a value from a function, for example, or communicating some value between two methods through reference parameters.

- Exceptions can also be thrown using the `Error` statement. The `Error` statement takes an error number as an argument instead of an exception object. This is a holdover from previous versions of the Visual Basic language, where exceptions were thrown by number instead of by type. In Visual Basic .NET, the error number is translated into the appropriate exception type, and then a new exception of that type is thrown. Use of the `Error` statement is strongly discouraged.

- Structured exception handling involves less overhead and is more precise than unstructured exception handling. Although there are no major technical disadvantages to using unstructured exception handling, the `Try...Catch` style of error handling is encouraged over `On Error`.

8
Modules and Namespaces

While programs primarily consist of variables and executable code, they must also be organized in a way that is comprehensible to both the programmer and anyone else who might read the programmer's code. *Modules* are used to organize variables and methods into logical units, while *namespaces* are used to organize modules and types into higher-level groupings.

Modules

All fields and methods in a Visual Basic .NET program must be contained within a type. In the examples in previous chapters, the simplest type, a *module*, was used. Modules are just containers for fields and methods, and unlike types such as classes and structures, they are rarely referred to directly.

> **NOTE**
> Modules in Visual Basic .NET should not be confused with the .NET Framework's concept of "modules," which are compiled files that can be used to build assemblies made up of multiple files.

Normally, members of a container can only be used by qualifying them with the name of the container. However, because the name of a module is usually not important, the members of a module can be used without qualifying them with the module's name.

```
Module Test
  Sub Main()
    Console.WriteLine(Add(10, 20))
  End Sub
End Module

Module Math
  Function Add(ByVal x As Integer, ByVal y As Integer) As Integer
    Return x + y
  End Function
End Module
```

In this example, the `Math` module contains a function named `Add`, which the module `Test` can call without referring to `Math` at all. The module name can be omitted even if the name is being qualified with other names.

```
Module Test
  Sub Main()
    Console.WriteLine(Acme.Add(10, 20))
  End Sub
End Module

Namespace Acme
  Module Math
    Function Add(ByVal x As Integer, ByVal y As Integer) As Integer
      Return x + y
    End Function
  End Module
End Namespace
```

In this situation, the function `Add` is qualified by the namespace name `Acme`, but the module name `Math` is still omitted.

The one situation in which a module's name should be used is when two modules define members with the same name. For example:

```
Module Test
  Sub Main()
    Console.WriteLine(Add(10, 20))
  End Sub
End Module

Module IntegerMath
  Function Add(ByVal x As Integer, ByVal y As Integer) As Integer
```

```
      Return x + y
   End Function
End Module

Module LongMath
   Function Add(ByVal x As Long, ByVal y As Long) As Long
      Return x + y
   End Function
End Module
```

In this example, the call to Add is ambiguous—is the code intended to call IntegerMath.Add or LongMath.Add? It's not clear. To resolve the ambiguity, Add must be qualified with the name of the module that the method wants to call.

Advanced

When a program is compiled, modules are defined as types in the assembly. To the Framework, a module is equivalent to a class with a Private constructor and all Shared members.

Namespaces

A *namespace* is a name that is used to organize related types within an assembly or across assemblies. In most of the examples used in the book so far, not much organization has been needed because an example has typically declared only one or two types. However, consider the .NET Framework, which contains thousands upon thousands of types—finding a single type among all those types could be quite a chore, especially if you weren't sure what name you were looking for! Namespaces are used to organize and categorize the types in the .NET Framework to make it easier to find the types that might be needed in any particular situation. For example, all the types that are used to create forms are defined under the System.Windows.Forms namespace, while all the types that can be used to do disk I/O are defined in the System.IO namespace. As you can see from the examples just given, namespaces can contain other namespaces, allowing multiple levels of organization.

A new namespace is declared in Visual Basic .NET using a namespace declaration. Any type declaration within a namespace declaration becomes part of that namespace. For example, the following code declares the module `Test` within the `Testing` namespace.

```
Namespace Testing
   Module Test
      Sub Main()
      End Sub
   End Module
End Namespace
```

Namespace declarations can be nested within one another. The following example defines two modules: `Testing.Test` and `Testing.SubTest.Test`.

```
Namespace Testing
   Module Test
   ...
   End Module

   Namespace SubTest
      Module Test
      ...
      End Module
   End Namespace
End Namespace
```

Instead of nesting two namespace declarations within one another, it is also possible for brevity's sake to use a dot-separated name to refer to all the nested namespace declarations at once. The following two declarations define types in exactly the same namespace.

```
Namespace Testing.SubTest
   Module Test1
   ...
   End Module
End Namespace

Namespace Testing
   Namespace SubTest
      Module Test2
      ...
      End Module
   End Namespace
End Namespace
```

Namespaces are unlike any other kind of declaration in that they are *open-ended*. This means that the same namespace can be declared repeatedly, and each declaration adds members to the same namespace. For example, the following declarations add two modules to the same namespace; thus they can refer to one another without qualification.

```
Namespace Testing
  Module Test
    Sub Main()
      Console.WriteLine(Add(10, 20))
    End Sub
  End Module
End Namespace

Namespace Testing
  Module Math
    Function Add(ByVal x As Integer, ByVal y As Integer) As Integer
      Return x + y
    End Function
  End Module
End Namespace
```

> **■ NOTE**
>
> Because namespaces are open-ended, the accessibility level `Private` has no meaning in a namespace. Declarations in namespaces can only use the access levels `Public` and `Friend`.

Multiple assemblies can contribute types to a namespace. For example, all the class libraries in the .NET Framework contribute types to the `System` namespace (or to a subnamespace of the `System` namespace).

Style

Top-level namespaces are generally reserved for a particular company or broad category of functionality and should not be used when you are defining new types. For example, the top-level namespace `System` is reserved for types defined by the .NET Framework. Although it is possible to do so, new types should not be defined in the `System` namespace, to avoid confusion and to avoid name collisions when future versions of the Framework are released.

Fully Qualified Names

As discussed in Chapter 2, Basic Concepts, when a declaration occurs within a container, it is often necessary to use a qualified name (such as `System.Collection.ArrayList`) to refer to the declaration. The *fully qualified name* of a declaration is the name of the declaration qualified with all the namespaces and types that contain it. The fully qualified name of a declaration uniquely identifies it in the same way that a person's full name ("John Q. Smith") distinguishes them from others who may share the same first name or last name. The fully qualified name is useful when we are talking about declarations—for example, most references to Framework types in this book use the type's fully qualified name.

The following example gives some types and namespaces, and their fully qualified names in comments after the name.

```
Namespace A      ' Fully qualified name: A
   Class B       ' Fully qualified name: A.B
     Class C     ' Fully qualified name: A.B.C
     End Class
   End Class

   Namespace D.E ' Fully qualified name: A.D.E
     Class F     ' Fully qualified name: A.D.E.F
     End Class
   End Namespace
End Namespace
```

> ▪▫ **NOTE**
>
> Even though a module's name does not have to be used when you are referring to declarations in the module, the fully qualified name of those declarations still contain the module's name.

Within code, the fully qualified name of a declaration can almost always be used to refer to a type.

```
Namespace A
   Class B
   End Class
End Namespace

Namespace C
```

```
    Module Test
        Sub Main()
            Dim x As A.B
        End Sub
    End Module
End Namespace
```

The previous sentence was qualified with "almost always" because it is possible to "hide" the outermost namespace that a declaration is contained in, making it impossible to refer to the type by its fully qualified name.

```
Namespace A
    Class B
    End Class
End Namespace

Namespace C
    Class A
    End Class

    Module Test
        Sub Main()
            Dim x As A.B
        End Sub
    End Module
End Namespace
```

In this last example, when looking up the name A in the context of the subroutine Test, the compiler will first find the declaration for class C.A and assume that is what A is referring to. Since there is no member of C.A named B, the compiler will give an error.

Imports

Namespaces are very useful for organizing declarations, but as a practical matter, typing fully qualified names can get very tiresome. Having to type System in front of Console.WriteLine may be useful the first few times to understand where the type Console lives, but by the fiftieth or hundredth time (or thousandth time), you've probably gotten the point. To help this situation, a namespace or a type can be *imported* into a particular source file. Importing a namespace or type makes the members of that declaration available in that source file without qualification. For example:

```
Imports System

Module Test
  Sub Main()
    Console.WriteLine("Hello, world!")
  End Sub
End Module
```

The example imports the `System` namespace into the source file, so `Console` can be used without qualification.

▪ NOTE

The Visual Basic .NET compiler also allows imports to be defined at the project level, which are equivalent to `Imports` statements placed at the top of each source file in the project. For example, by default the `System` namespace is imported in all projects. This is why the examples in this book do not explicitly include an `Imports System` statement at the top of each example.

Advanced

The names in `Imports` statements are handled differently from other names—the names in an `Imports` statement must always be fully qualified names.

In general, only namespaces are really useful to import, but importing a class can be useful in the case of an enumeration.

```
Imports Colors

Enum Colors
  Red
  Green
  Blue
End Enum

Module Test
  Sub Main()
    Dim c As Colors = Red
```

```
      If c = Blue Then
         ...
      End If
   End Sub
End Module
```

If a name is imported through two separate imports, attempting to use the name will result in an ambiguity error. In the following example, the name `Test` is ambiguous between namespace A and namespace B.

```
Imports A
Imports B

Namespace A
   Class Test
   End Class
End Namespace

Namespace B
   Class Test
   End Class
End Namespace

Module TestModule
   Sub Main()
      Dim x As Test ' Error: Test is imported through A and B
   End Sub
End Module
```

To help resolve such ambiguities, an import can be assigned an *alias*. An alias is an alternate name given to the imported namespace or type and allows access to the members of the imported namespace or type through that alternate name. Using the previous example, we can resolve the ambiguity by assigning `A.Text` and `B.Text` aliases.

```
Imports ATest = A.Test
Imports BTest = B.Test

Namespace A
   Class Test
   End Class
End Namespace

Namespace B
   Class Test
```

```
    End Class
End Namespace

Module TestModule
  Sub Main()
    Dim x As Test   ' Error: Test is only imported through an alias
    Dim y As ATest
    Dim z As BTest
  End Sub
End Module
```

An import alias doesn't actually declare anything in the file, so it is possible to declare something else in the file with the same name as the import alias. However, the name of the alias must be unique in the top-level scope of the source file.

Preprocessing

Several special statements can be used in a source file to control compilation, even though they are not considered part of the code. These statements are called *preprocessing statements* because they are processed before the code is actually compiled. All preprocessing statements begin with the pound sign (#) at the beginning of a line.

Conditional Compilation Statements

The principle preprocessing statements are the *conditional compilation statements*, which allow code to be selectively compiled based on conditions external to the code. For example, you may wish to compile some code only if you are building an application for debugging purposes.

```
Module Test
  Sub Main()
#If DEBUG Then
    MsgBox("Application is starting!")
#End If
    Console.WriteLine("Hello, world!")
#If DEBUG Then
    MsgBox("Application is ending!")
#End If
  End Sub
End Module
```

In the preceding example, the two message boxes will appear only if the DEBUG conditional compilation constant is True. The #If statement has almost the same syntax as a regular If statement. For example:

```
Module Test
  Sub Main()
#If DEBUG Then
    MsgBox("Debug application")
#ElseIf RETAIL Then
    MsqBox("Retail application")
#Else
    MsgBox("Unknown type of application")
#End If
    Console.WriteLine("Hello, world!")
  End Sub
End Module
```

Conditional compilation constants are defined using #Const statements or through the Visual Studio environment. The #Const statement assigns a value to a conditional compilation constant. Conditional compilation constants are always typed as Object; it is not possible to specify a type in a #Const statement. For example:

```
#Const DEBUG = True

Module Test
  Sub Main()
#If DEBUG Then
    MsgBox("Debug application")
#ElseIf RETAIL Then
    MsgBox("Retail application")
#Else
    MsgBox("Unknown type of application")
#End If
    Console.WriteLine("Hello, world!")
  End Sub
End Module
```

Conditional compilation constants do not have to be defined before they can be used—the previous examples will compile even if DEBUG and RETAIL are never defined. The scope of a constant is from the #Const statement through the end of the file. If a constant is used before being defined, the value of the constant is Nothing. A conditional constant can be assigned to more than once.

```
#Const TEST = True

#If TEST Then
Module Test
  Sub Main()
    Console.WriteLine("Hello, world!")
  End Sub
End Module
#End If

#Const TEST = False
```

Region Statements

The other preprocessing statement is the #Region statement, which is used to mark text in the Visual Studio code editor but has no effect on compilation. A #Region statement can be followed by a string literal that describes the region. #Region statements are block statements that must be ended by #End Region statements. For example:

```
Module Test
#Region "The Main method of the application"
  Sub Main()
    Console.WriteLine("Hello, world!")
  End Sub
#End Region
End Module
```

#Region statements cannot appear within methods or property accessors and can only enclose valid blocks. In other words, #Region statements must span an entire block and cannot break in the middle.

```
Module Test
  ' Error: Invalid #Region statement
#Region "The Main method of the application"
  Sub Main()
    Console.WriteLine("Hello, world!")
#End Region
  End Sub
End Module
```

Conclusion

Modules are the simplest type and are useful for most simple programming needs. Namespaces are an essential tool for organizing types in a program and in the .NET Framework, and understanding how to work with them is important. In the next chapter, we will start talking about user-defined types—structures and classes—that can be used to develop programs that deal with more complex types of information than the fundamental types can hold.

A style point to consider is that top-level namespaces are generally reserved for a particular company or purpose and should not be used to define new types. For example, the top-level namespace System is reserved for types defined by the .NET Framework. Although it is possible to do so, new types should not be defined in the System namespace, to avoid confusion and to avoid name collisions when future versions of the Framework are released.

9

Classes and Structures

Until now, we've mostly talked about working with predefined types, such as Integer or String. However, it is often convenient to define new data types that represent more complex concepts than just numbers or strings. When we are writing an order-tracking program, for example, it may be convenient to define a type that represents a customer. The customer type would include information about each customer who has opened an order: the customer's name, the customer's address, the customer's phone number, and so on.

This chapter discusses classes and structures that can be used to define just these kinds of types.

Memory Management

Before we jump into classes and structures, however, it is necessary to take a step back for a moment and talk about memory. As discussed in Chapter 2, Basic Concepts, the .NET Framework provides many services to programmers, one of the most important of which is *memory management*. Because the Framework's method of managing memory on behalf of a program is central to how classes and structures work, it is worth spending a moment discussing how the Framework manages memory.

The Heap and the Stack

Information in a program can be stored in one of two places by the Framework: on the *stack* and on the *heap*. The stack is a pool of memory that can be used by local variables and method parameters; each time a method or property is executed, the Framework allocates space on the stack to store its locals and parameters. Since a method or property declares all its local variables and parameters at compile time, the amount of space allocated on the stack for a method or property is fixed at runtime and cannot change.

Programs that need to store a dynamic amount of information use the heap. The heap is a dynamic pool of memory that the Framework manages and makes available to programs to store information in at runtime. When a running program wishes to store a value on the heap, it gives the value to the Framework, which finds a place for the value on the heap, copies it there, and then gives back a *reference* to where the value was stored on the heap. Whenever the program wishes to access the value on the heap, then, it must use the reference to find the value (see Figure 9-1).

The lifetime of values stored on the stack versus those stored on the heap is different. The lifetime of values on the stack is tied to the method or property in which they are declared—for example, a local variable in a subroutine exists only as long as the subroutine is actually being executed;

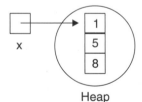

Heap

```
Class Test
    Public a As Integer
    Public b As Integer
    Public c As Integer
End Class
...
Dim x As Test = New Test()
x.a = 1
x.b = 5
x.c = 8
```

FIGURE 9-1: A Reference Type Variable and the Heap

once the subroutine is exited, the local variable disappears. The lifetime of values on the heap, on the other hand, is determined by whether any references to them exist. The Framework keeps track of all the references that it has handed out to a particular value on the heap. It then periodically checks to see which values on the heap no longer have any active references to them and frees up the space that those values are using. This process is called *garbage collection*. It is important to keep in mind that the lifetime of a value on the heap is under the control of the Framework and not the programmer. Even when the last reference to a value on the heap disappears, the value will not be discarded until the next time the Framework does a garbage collection. If there is a lot of free memory, the Framework may defer garbage collection for some time.

Compatibility

The Framework's method of memory management is very different from COM's method of memory management. Instead of garbage collection, COM uses a scheme called *reference counting* to track when values on the heap should be released. Reference counting requires a program, rather than the system, to keep track of how many references remain to a particular value. This has the advantage of allowing a program to free a value the moment the last reference to it is released. Reference counting is vulnerable to bugs (because of programs incorrectly tracking reference counts) and cannot handle circular references (i.e., object A has a reference to object B, which has a reference to object A).

Value Types and Structures

A *value type* is a type that stores its information directly in a variable or another type. The fundamental types `Integer`, `Double`, and `Date` are examples of value types, so for example, a local variable of type `Integer` that has the value 5 contains the value 5 itself rather than a reference to it, as in Figure 9-2. Similarly, an array of `Integer` values contains the values themselves rather than references to them, as in Figure 9-3.

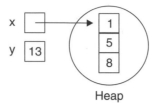

Heap

Dim y As Integer
y = 13

FIGURE 9-2: An Integer Variable

FIGURE 9-3: An Integer Array

Because value types are always stored directly in variables, they use memory efficiently. As shown earlier, an `Integer` local variable does not require any space on the heap, because the integer value can be stored directly on the stack. This also means that the storage for a value type never has to be allocated, because it's always part of something else. Because variables that hold value types directly contain their value, they must always *have* a value. The Framework initializes all value type variables to a "zero state," or their *default value*, when they are created. Thus, the value of an `Integer` variable that has not been assigned a value will be zero.

Structures are user-defined value types. For example, the following declares a new `Customer` structure that contains name, address, and phone number information about a customer.

```
Structure Customer
   Public Name As String
   Public Address As String
   Public PhoneNumber As String
End Structure
```

Because structures are value types, they do *not* have to be created before they can be used.

```
Dim x As Customer

' OK: structures do not have to be created
x.Name = "John Doe"
```

Reference Types and Classes

As discussed in the section on memory management, references to values on the heap can be stored in variables just as regular values can. A reference type is always stored on the heap. Thus, a variable of a reference type never contains its value directly—it always contains a *reference* to its value on the heap.

A *class* is a user-defined reference type. For example, the following declares a new Customer class that contains name, address, and phone number information about a customer.

```
Class Customer
   Public Name As String
   Public Address As String
   Public PhoneNumber As String
End Class
```

Before a reference type variable is assigned a reference, it contains a special reference called the *null reference*. The null reference represents a reference to nothing and is referred to, appropriately enough, by the keyword Nothing. Because classes are reference types, the initial value of a variable typed as a class will be Nothing. Before a reference type variable can be used, it first has to be assigned a reference to a value on the heap. The New operator creates a new instance of a class on the heap.

```
Dim x, y As Customer

' Error: x is Nothing
x.Name = "John Doe"

' OK: Creates a new instance of Customer
y = New Customer()
y.Name = "Jane Doe"
```

New can also be specified inline when a variable is declared. This is the equivalent of a variable initializer assigning a new expression. In the following example, the two declaration lines are completely equivalent.

```
Dim x As New Customer
Dim y As Customer = New Customer()
```

> **NOTE**
>
> Remember that initializers are run when execution reaches the declaration line. If the preceding lines were executed multiple times, the variables would be initialized multiple times. If the preceding lines were skipped, the variables would not be initialized.

Using a reference type variable at runtime that contains the null reference will result in a System.NullReferenceException exception. Reference type variables can be compared against Nothing using the Is operator to determine whether they contain a reference to the null reference. Assigning Nothing to a variable causes the reference it contains, if any, to be discarded. For example:

```
Module Test
  Sub SetName(ByVal c As Customer)
    ' Make sure c refers to something
    If c Is Nothing Then
      Console.WriteLine("c has no value.")
      Return
    End If

    c.Name = "John Doe"
  End Sub

  Sub Main()
    Dim c As New Customer()

    SetName(c)
    c = Nothing
  End Sub
End Module
```

Style

In general, it is best to set reference variables to Nothing as soon as you are finished with them so that the memory can be reclaimed by the garbage collector. However, a variable that reaches the end of its lifetime (for example, a local at the end of a subroutine) is automatically set to Nothing by the Framework and does not need to be set to Nothing.

When you assign a variable that contains a reference to another variable, the only thing that gets copied is the *reference*—not the value itself. This is important to remember, because it can have a big effect on the behavior of the variables. Take the following example.

```
Class b
   Public x As Integer
End Class

Module Test
   Sub Main()
      Dim a1, a2 As Integer
      Dim b1, b2 As b

      b1 = New b()

      a1 = 10
      b1.x = 10

      a2 = a1
      b2 = b1

      a1 = 20
      b1.x = 20

      Console.WriteLine(a2)
      Console.WriteLine(b2.x)
   End Sub
End Module
```

This program will print the values 10 and 20. This is because the variables a1 and a2 directly contain Integer values, while the variables b1 and b2 store their Integer values on the heap. When a1 is assigned to a2, this copies the value from a1 to a2. Thus, when a1 is changed, there is no effect on a2. But when b1 is assigned to b2, this copies the reference to the value from b1 to b2. When the value that b1 refers to is changed, the value that b2 refers to is changed as well because they both point to the same value.

Shared versus Instance

By default, all members of classes and structures are *instance members*. This means that all instances of a class or structure each have their own copy of the member. The following example will not print anything, because each Customer object has its own copy of the Name field. When the Name field of variable x is changed, it doesn't affect the Name field of variable y.

```
Class Customer
   Public Name As String
End Class

Module Test
   Sub Main()
      Dim x, y As Customer

      x = New Customer()
      y = New Customer()

      x.Name = "John Doe"

      If y.Name = x.Name Then
         Console.WriteLine("Equal")
      End If
   End Sub
End Module
```

Members declared with the Shared modifier, however, are *shared members*. Shared members are shared by *all* instances of the class or structure. That means that if one instance of a class or structure changes the value of a shared member, *all* other instances of the class or structure will see the new value. For example:

```
Class Customer
   Public Prefix As String
   Public Name As String
```

```
      Public Shared PrintPrefix As Boolean = True

      Sub PrintName()
        If PrintPrefix Then
          Console.Write(Prefix)
        End If

        Console.WriteLine(Name)
      End Sub
  End Class

Module Test
  Sub Main()
    Dim x, y As Customer

    x = New Customer()
    x.Prefix = "Mr."
    x.Name = "John Smith"

    Customer.PrintPrefix = False

    x.PrintName()   ' Prints 'John Smith'
  End Sub
End Module
```

In the preceding example, changing the shared `PrintPrefix` field changes the value for all instances of `Customer`, so the `PrintName` subroutine will not print the prefix.

Instance members can only be accessed through an instance of a type. Shared members, however, can be accessed either through an instance of a type or by using the type name itself. For example, one way to change `PrintPrefix` would be to say `Customer.PrintPrefix = False`, as it was in the preceding example. It would not be valid, however, to say `Customer.Name = "John Doe"`, because `Customer` is not an instance—it's a type. Because shared members can be called without an instance, they cannot refer to instance members.

Style

For clarity, shared members should always be accessed through the type name, not an instance.

Constructors

Sometimes it is desirable to do some initialization of a type when it is created. *Constructors* are methods that are run when an instance of a type is created, allowing for user-defined initialization. Constructors look exactly like regular methods (discussed in the next chapter) except that they have the special name New. For example:

```
Class Customer
  Public Name As String
  Public Address As String
  Public PhoneNumber As String

  Public Sub New(ByVal Name As String, ByVal Address As String)
    MyBase.New()
    Me.Name = Name
    Me.Address = Address
  End Sub
End Class

Module Test
  Sub Main()
    Dim Bob As Customer

    Bob = New Customer("Bob", "134 Main Street")
  End Sub
End Module
```

In this example, the Customer class defines a constructor that takes two parameters: a customer name and a customer address. It then initializes the Name and Address fields with these values. As shown in the example, arguments can be supplied in a New expression and are passed off to the constructor parameters. Like methods, constructors can be overloaded. If a class or structure doesn't define a constructor, the language will assume that the type has a constructor with no parameters that does nothing.

Unlike methods, constructors are not inherited—each class must declare its own constructor. To ensure that base classes have a chance to run their constructors, a constructor in a derived class automatically calls its base class constructor first. If there is no parameterless base constructor, the constructor must begin with a call to another constructor in the same class (Me.New(...)) or to another a constructor in the base class

(MyBase.New(...)). This ensures that each base class, all the way up to Object, has a chance to do proper initialization. For example:

```
Class Person
  Public Name As String

  Public Sub New(ByVal Name As String)
    MyBase.New()
    Me.Name = Name
  End Sub
End Class

Class Customer
  Inherits Person

  Public Address As String
  Public PhoneNumber As String

  Public Sub New(ByVal Name As String, ByVal Address As String)
    MyBase.New(Name)
    Me.Name = Name
    Me.Address = Address
  End Sub

  Public Sub New(ByVal Name As String, ByVal Address As String, _
    ByVal PhoneNumber As String)
    Me.New(Name, Address)
    Me.PhoneNumber = PhoneNumber
  End Sub
End Class
```

In this example, Customer provides two constructors: one that specifies a phone number and one that doesn't. The one that provides a phone number simply calls the one that doesn't to initialize the Name and Address fields before setting the PhoneNumber field.

Advanced

Field initializers are assigned immediately *after* the constructor call. This ensures that any values that they depend on from the base type are available.

Structure Constructors

Structures can have constructors too, even though structures never have to be allocated using New. Instead of creating a new instance on the heap, a structure constructor creates a new instance of the structure on the stack. This structure can then be assigned to a value type variable or passed as an argument to another function. For example:

```
Structure Point
   Public x, y As Integer

   Public Sub New(ByVal x As Integer, ByVal y As Integer)
     Me.x = x
     Me.y = y
   End Sub
End Structure

Module Test
   Sub PrintPoint(ByVal p As Point)
     Console.WriteLine(p.x & "," & p.y)
   End Sub

   Sub Main()
     Dim p1 As Point = New Point(10, 20)

     PrintPoint(New Point(20, 30))
   End Sub
End Module
```

In this example, the Point constructor simplifies the process of creating a new Point value. The first statement in Main assigns the Point value (10, 20) to the variable p1, while the second statement passes the Point value (20, 30) to the PrintPoint subroutine.

Unlike classes, structures cannot define a parameterless constructor. In the .NET Framework, a structure's parameterless constructor represents its default value. The following example initializes a Point variable with the default value of the Point type, (0,0).

```
Module Test
   Sub Main()
     Dim p1 As Point

     p1 = New Point()
   End Sub
End Module
```

Shared Constructors

Constructors are primarily used to initialize instances of types, but they can also be used to initialize shared information in a type. A shared constructor is declared the same way as a regular constructor except that it uses the `Shared` modifier, can have no parameters, and cannot be declared with an access level. The last two restrictions are due to the fact that a program never explicitly calls a shared constructor—the .NET Framework runtime will automatically call the shared constructor when necessary. For example:

```
Class Customer
  Public Prefix As String
  Public Name As String

  Shared PrintPrefix As Boolean

  Shared Sub New()
    PrintPrefix = True
  End Sub
End Class
```

Advanced

When shared constructors are run is determined by the .NET Framework, but the general rule of thumb is that the shared constructor will be run before anything that could depend on it can be accessed.

Nested Types

All types except for modules may be declared within another type. A type defined within another type is called a *nested type*. To refer to a nested type from outside the type it is declared in, you must qualify the type name with the outer type's name.

```
Class Customer
  Class FullAddress
    Public Street As String
    Public City As String
    Public State As String
```

```
        Public ZIP As Integer
    End Class

    Public Name As String
    Public Address As FullAddress
End Class
```

In this example, the address of a customer is stored in a `FullAddress` type that is declared within the `Customer` type. It could be used in the following way.

```
Dim Address As Customer.FullAddress
Dim Customer As Customer

Address = New Customer.FullAddress()
Address.Street = "134 Main Street"
Address.City = "Tulsa"
Address.State = "OK"
Address.ZIP = 19348

Customer = New Customer()
Customer.Name = "John Doe"
Customer.Address = Address
```

Nested types are most commonly used for helper types that are used only within a type.

Advanced

Nested types differ from inner types in languages such as Java. An instance of a nested type does not automatically contain an instance of its containing type.

Finalization and Resource Disposal

As discussed at the beginning of the chapter, when a value on the heap no longer has any active references to it, the .NET Framework will eventually garbage collect the value. At the point at which a value is garbage collected off the heap, it may be desirable to perform some action such as closing an open file. When a value is garbage collected, the Framework calls the method `Finalize` on the value. A class can override the implementation (see Chapter 13, Inheritance, for more information on overriding) and do whatever work it needs to do.

```
Imports System.IO

Class FileWriter
  Private Stream As FileStream

  ...

  Protected Overrides Sub Finalize()
    ' Close the stream
    Stream.Close()
  End Sub
End Class
```

Sometimes, however, it is not sufficient to wait for the garbage collector to clean up a reference type on the heap. In the preceding example, it is possible that the `FileWriter` class is heavily used. Setting a variable of type `FileWriter` to `Nothing` is not sufficient to cause the file to be closed, because the garbage collector may not run for some time, depending on available memory. If the garbage collector is not run often enough, the program may run out of file handles because too many instances of `FileWriter` are waiting to be finalized (and, therefore, still holding on to open files). In this case, it is desirable to free up the file resource as soon as the code that created the `FileWriter` class is finished with it.

The `System.IDisposable` interface can be implemented to indicate that a reference type contains precious resources that should be disposed as soon as they are no longer needed. (See Chapter 13 for more information on interfaces.) The `IDisposable` interface contains a single method named `Dispose`, whose responsibility is to dispose of any precious resources. For example:

```
Imports System.IO

Class FileWriter
  Implements IDisposable

  Public Stream As FileStream

  ...
```

```
    Sub Dispose() Implements IDisposable.Dispose
      If Not Stream Is Nothing Then
        Stream.Close()
        Stream = Nothing
      End If
    End Sub

    Sub New(ByVal FileName As String)
      Stream = New FileStream(FileName)
    End Sub
End Class

Module Test
  Sub Main()
    Dim Writer As FileWriter = New FileWriter("myfile.txt", _
      FileMode.Open)

    Try
      ...
    Finally
      Writer.Dispose()
    End Try
  End Sub
End Module
```

In this example, the `FileWriter` class implements the `IDisposable` interface, which allows the class's precious resources to be disposed of when they are no longer needed.

Style

`Dispose` should be written so it can be called multiple times, so that a programmer using the class does not have to keep track of whether `Dispose` has already been called.

Style

When using a disposable type, always put the call to `Dispose` in a `Finally` block. This ensures that even if an exception occurs while the class is being used, the class will still be disposed of.

Conclusion

Defining new classes and structures that represent complex data structures is a key aspect of any sufficiently complex program. Choosing between a class and a structure depends on the different ways that the types are allocated and used. Although the Framework handles many memory and resource management tasks, properly tracking and releasing memory and resources is still a consideration for programmers. Now that we have introduced user-defined types, the next chapter begins the discussion of type members with methods.

Here are some style points to consider.

- The Framework's method of memory management is very different from COM's method of memory management. Instead of garbage collection, COM uses a scheme called *reference counting* to track when values on the heap should be released. Reference counting requires a program, rather than the system, to keep track of how many references remain to a particular value. This has the advantage of allowing a program to free a value the moment the last reference to it is released. Reference counting is vulnerable to bugs (because of programs incorrectly tracking reference counts) and cannot handle circular references (i.e., object A has a reference to object B, which has a reference to object A).

- In general, it is best to set reference variables to Nothing as soon as you are finished with them so that the memory can be reclaimed by the garbage collector. However, a variable that reaches the end of its lifetime (for example, a local at the end of a subroutine) is automatically set to Nothing by the Framework and does not need to be set to Nothing.

- For clarity, shared members should always be accessed through the type name, not an instance.

- Dispose should be written so it can be called multiple times, so that a programmer using the class does not have to keep track of whether Dispose has already been called.

- When using a disposable type, always put the call to `Dispose` in a `Finally` block. This ensures that even if an exception occurs while the class is being used, the class will still be disposed of.

■ 10 ■
Methods

A *method* is a collection of executable statements used to accomplish some task. Methods are the primary way to take action in a program.

Subroutines and Functions

A method is either a *function* or a *subroutine.* A subroutine performs some action and returns. For example:

```
Sub Main()
  Console.WriteLine("Hello, world!")
End Sub
```

A *function,* on the other hand, calculates a value that is returned to the caller when the function ends. When a function is declared, it specifies the type of the value that it returns in much the same way that a variable specifies its type. For example, the following function calculates the sum of two numbers and returns the result.

```
Function Add(ByVal x As Integer, ByVal y As Integer) As Integer
  Return x + y
End Function
```

If the type of a function is omitted, the type is assumed to be `Object`. The `Option Strict` statement at the beginning of a source file requires that all variable declarations have an explicit type.

Values can be returned from functions in one of two ways. One way is by using the `Return` statement, as discussed in Chapter 6, Statements. Alternatively, every function implicitly declares a local variable with the same name as the function itself to hold the return value of the function. This variable is called the *function return variable*. The previous example could have been written as follows.

```
Function Add(ByVal x As Integer, ByVal y As Integer) As Integer
  Add = x + y
End Function
```

When the function exits, the value stored in the `Add` function return variable is returned as the value of the function.

Parameters

Callers can pass values into methods through *parameters*. Parameters are declared in parentheses after the name of a method. Each parameter is declared like a local variable, with a name and, optionally, a type supplied. Multiple parameters are separated by commas. The following examples show functions declared with parameters.

```
Function Square(ByVal Number As Integer) As Integer
  Return Number * Number
End Function

Function Multiply(ByVal x As Integer, ByVal y As Integer) As Integer
  Return x * y
End Function
```

Style

A method declaration with no parameters can choose to omit the parentheses, but they are suggested for emphasis and readability.

There are two types of parameters: value parameters and reference parameters. A *value parameter* is equivalent to a local variable initialized by the caller. Parameters are value parameters by default; prefixing a parameter with the keyword ByVal explicitly makes the parameter a value parameter.

Compatibility

In previous versions of Visual Basic, parameters were reference parameters by default. The default changed in Visual Basic .NET because the overhead of reference parameters made them less desirable as the default type of parameter.

A *reference parameter* is special in that it is not a variable at all—instead, it is a *reference* to the variable that was passed in by the caller. Reference parameters are declared by prefixing the parameter with the keyword ByRef. When a value is read from or assigned to a reference parameter, the program actually reads or assigns the value that is contained in the variable that was passed in by the caller. Thus, the caller will see any changes made in the variable when the function returns, and vice versa. For example:

```
Function Multiply(ByVal x As Integer, ByVal y As Integer, _
          ByRef OperationOverflowed As Boolean) As Integer
  Try
    Multiply = x * y
  Catch e As OverflowException
    OperationOverflowed = True
  End Try
End Function

Sub Main()
  Dim Overflowed As Boolean
  Dim Result As Integer

  Result = Multiply(10, 20, Overflowed)

  If Overflowed Then
    Console.WriteLine("Overflow")
  Else
    Console.WriteLine(Result)
  End If
End Sub
```

In this example, the parameter OperationOverflowed is a reference parameter. Instead of just holding the value passed in from the variable Overflow in the subroutine Main, it represents the variable Overflow itself. So when a value is assigned to the parameter OperationOverflowed, the value is actually stored in the variable Overflow. In all other regards, though, OperationOverflowed looks like a normal variable. It's just that its storage is provided by the caller. Reference parameters are mainly used when a method needs to return more than one value.

Optional Parameters and Parameter Arrays

Sometimes a parameter to a method will have a common value that most callers will use. For example, the following method has a parameter, New-Line, that will usually be passed the value False.

```
Sub PrintList(ByVal Number As Integer, ByVal NewLine as Boolean)
  If NewLine Then
    Console.WriteLine(Number)
  Else
    Console.Write(Number & ",")
  End If
End Sub

Sub Main()
  PrintList(10, False)
  PrintList(20, False)
  PrintList(30, False)
  PrintList(40, True)
End Sub
```

In this situation, it would be convenient to have the PrintList method assume that the value of the parameter NewLine is False unless the caller said otherwise.

Optional parameters allow specifying the default value for the parameter if the caller does not specify a value explicitly. Optional parameters are parameters with the Optional keyword in front of them and a default value assigned to them after the declaration (just like a local variable initializer). Optional parameters must always be declared after nonoptional parameters. The preceding example can be rewritten as follows, making the NewLine parameter optional, with a default value of False. Thus, only the method call that wishes to use a different value for the parameter must specify it.

```
Sub PrintList(ByVal Number As Integer, _
         Optional ByVal NewLine as Boolean = False)
  If NewLine Then
    Console.WriteLine(Number)
  Else
    Console.Write(Number & ",")
  End If
End Sub

Sub Main()
  PrintList(10)
  PrintList(20)
  PrintList(30)
  PrintList(40, True)
End Sub
```

The default value of an optional parameter must be a constant value. This is because the optional value is substituted for the omitted argument at compile time rather than runtime.

Compatibility

Previous versions of Visual Basic supported optional `Variant` parameters without default values. Visual Basic .NET no longer supports declaring such parameters, but does still support calling COM methods that have such parameters.

There are also situations where a method can take a variable number of parameters. In the `PrintList` example used earlier, it would be more convenient if the caller could supply one or more of the numbers to print in a single call. The problem, of course, is that it is not always possible to know ahead of time how many parameters the method might be called with. *Parameter arrays* can be used instead to represent a variable number of parameters to a method.

A parameter array is declared by putting the `ParamArray` keyword in front of a parameter typed as a one-dimensional array. The parameter array must be the last parameter in the parameter list. When the method is called, any extra arguments at the end of the argument that do not match other parameters to the method are collected into an array, and the array is passed into the parameter array. The type of the array specifies what type each extra parameter will be converted to. For example, `PrintList` could be rewritten to take a parameter array of `Integer` values.

```
Sub PrintList(ByVal Header As String, _
              ByVal ParamArray Numbers() As Integer)
  Console.Write(Header & ": ")
  For Index As Integer = 0 To Numbers.Length - 2
    Console.Write(Numbers(Index) & ",")
  Next Index

  Console.WriteLine(Numbers(Numbers.Length - 1))
End Sub

Sub Main()
  PrintList("Numbers", 10, 20, 30, 40)
End Sub
```

In this example, the first parameter to `PrintList`, the string "Numbers," is matched to the parameter `Header`. All the rest of the numbers are gathered into an `Integer` array and passed to the method as a whole.

It is also possible to pass an array to a parameter array, in which case the array represents the array that would have been passed to the parameter by the compiler. This is mostly useful when one method with a parameter array wishes to call another method that takes a parameter array.

```
Sub PrintNumberList(ByVal ParamArray Numbers() As Integer)
  For Index As Integer = 0 To Numbers.Length - 2
    Console.Write(Numbers(Index) & ",")
  Next Index

  Console.WriteLine(Numbers(Numbers.Length - 1))
End Sub

Sub PrintList(ByVal Header As String, _
        ByVal ParamArray Numbers() As Integer)
  Console.Write(Header & ": ")
  PrintNumberList(Numbers)
End Sub
```

```
Sub Main()
  PrintList("Numbers", 10, 20, 30, 40)
End Sub
```

In this example, the method `PrintList` passes the parameter array `Numbers` to the `Numbers` parameter of the `PrintNumberList` method as a whole array.

> ### ▪▪ NOTE
>
> Not all .NET Framework languages support optional parameters. Languages such as Visual C# .NET require all parameters to be explicitly supplied, even if they are declared as optional in Visual Basic .NET.

Method Invocation

As many of the examples so far have shown, a method is invoked by supplying the name of the method and then a list of values in parentheses. The values in the parentheses are called the *arguments* to the method call. Each argument in the argument list is matched with the parameter that is in the same position in the parameter list: The first argument matches the first parameter, the second argument matches the second parameter, and so on. The type of each argument must be convertible to the type of the parameter. Once all the arguments have been matched to parameters, any remaining arguments are matched against a parameter array argument if there is one. The type of each argument must be convertible to the element type of the parameter array.

An argument list can omit optional arguments if it likes, as discussed in the previous section. In that case, the default value is supplied in place of the missing argument. Optional arguments can be omitted either implicitly or explicitly. For example:

```
Sub Main()
  MsgBox("Hello, world!")         ' Omits the last two arguments
  MsgBox("Hello, world!", , "My App")  ' Omits the middle argument
End Sub
```

In the first case, the last two arguments of `MsgBox` are implicitly omitted. In the second case, the second argument of `MsgBox` is explicitly left blank and will be filled in by the default value of the parameter.

Advanced

The values that optional parameters are initialized with are compiled into the caller's invocation of the method rather than being filled in by the method itself. This means that if a class library changes the default value of an optional parameter, any applications that have already been compiled against that class library won't pick up the new default value until they are recompiled as well.

Arguments and Reference Parameters

As discussed in a previous section, reference parameters are special in that they refer directly to the argument variable that is passed in. But what if the argument being passed in isn't a variable? For example:

```
Function Multiply(ByVal x As Integer, ByVal y As Integer, _
          ByRef OperationOverflowed As Boolean) As Integer
  Try
    Multiply = x * y
  Catch e As OverflowException
    OperationOverflowed = True
  End Try
End Function

Sub Main()
  Dim Result As Integer

  Result = Multiply(10, 20, True)
  Console.WriteLine(Result)
End Sub
```

The constant value `True` is being passed in to the reference parameter `OperationOverflowed`, but because `True` is not a variable, the reference parameter has nowhere to point to. In this kind of case, a reference parameter behaves just like a value parameter. Assigning to the reference parameter does not do anything special.

If an argument variable's type exactly matches the type of a reference parameter, the reference parameter contains a reference directly to the argument variable. This type of reference parameter passing is called *true byref*. However, if the type of the argument variable and the type of the reference parameter do not exactly match, it is not possible for the reference parameter to hold a direct reference to the argument variable. Instead, the value of the argument variable is copied into a temporary variable that matches the reference parameter type, and the reference parameter gets a reference to the temporary variable. When the method returns, the value in the temporary variable is copied back into the argument variable. This type of reference parameter passing is called *copy-in/copy-out*.

The differences between true byref and copy-in/copy-out can be quite subtle. For example:

```
Module Test
  Dim IntVal As Integer = 10
  Dim DoubleVal As Double = 20

  Sub PrintValues()
    Console.WriteLine(IntVal & ":" & DoubleVal)
  End Sub

  Sub ModifyValue(ByRef Value As Integer)
    Value = 30
    PrintValues()
  End Sub

  Sub Main()
    ModifyValue(IntVal)
    ModifyValue(DoubleVal)
    PrintValues()
  End Sub
End Module
```

This example will print the following.

```
30 : 20
30 : 20
30 : 30
```

The first call to `ModifyValue` passes an actual reference to the `IntVal` field because the type of the argument matches the type of the parameter.

Thus, when the reference variable `Value` is modified, the field `IntVal` is modified. However, the second call to `ModifyValue` cannot pass `Double-Val` as a true byref, because its type does not match the parameter type. Instead, a temporary variable is passed copy-in/copy-out. Thus, when the reference variable `Value` is modified, only the temporary variable is modified, not the field `DoubleVal`. After the method returns, however, the value is copied out, so `DoubleVal` is modified.

Named Arguments

When you are calling a method with many arguments, especially optional arguments, it is sometimes convenient to refer to parameters by name instead of position. In this example, the second argument to `MsgBox` is omitted because it does not matter what its value is.

```
Sub Main()
  MsgBox("Hello, world!", , "My App")
End Sub
```

However, instead of supplying a blank argument, the method invocation could have referred to the `Title` argument by name.

```
Sub Main()
  MsgBox("Hello, world!", Title := "My App")
End Sub
```

Arguments that refer to the name of the parameter they match to are called *named arguments*. Arguments that match to a parameter solely by position are called *positional arguments*. Named arguments must come after all the positional arguments in the argument list and are matched against the name of the parameter in the method being called.

Late Binding

Normally, only methods that exist on an object at compile time can be invoked. In the following example, a compile error will occur on the call to the method `AddOrder` because the class `Customer` does not contain such a method.

```
Class Customer
  Dim Name As String
```

```
    End Class

    Class Order
      ...
    End Class

    Module Test
      Sub Main()
        Dim c As Customer = New Customer()

        ' Error: No such method.
        c.AddOrder(New Order())
      End Sub
    End Module
```

Sometimes, however, it is necessary to call a method even though it may not exist (or may not be known to exist) at compile time. This occurs most commonly when you are dealing with COM components that do not expose type information, but it could also occur when you are writing methods that take general `Object` parameters. When you are making a method call on a value that is typed as `Object`, all type checking—including whether the method even exists—is deferred until runtime. (The only exceptions to this rule are the methods that are explicitly defined on `Object`, such as `GetHashCode`.) This style of method invocation is called *late binding*, because the actual method is not bound until runtime. For example, the following method takes a value typed as `Object` and calls the method `AddOrder` on it.

```
    Class Order
      ...
    End Class

    Module Test
      Sub AddOrder(ByVal o As Object)
        o.AddOrder(New Order())
      End Sub
    End Module
```

In this example, the `AddOrder` method must only exist on the actual type that is passed in to the method at runtime. If no such method exists, or if the method does not take an `Order` as an argument, a runtime exception will occur.

Conditional Methods

As discussed in Chapter 8, Modules and Namespaces, conditional compilation can be used to compile code into a program only under certain circumstances. For example, it is common to have two different build configurations: release, which is the final program intended to be released to the public, and debug, which is the program with extra code included to help track down bugs. Here is an example of how this might work.

```
Function Divide(ByVal x As Integer, ByVal y As Integer) As Integer
#If DEBUG Then
  Debug.Assert(y > 0, "Should never divide by zero.")
#End If
  Return x \ y
End Function
```

In this example, the Divide function asserts that the divisor is not zero. If a caller passes in a divisor that is zero, the Assert function will pop up a dialog that contains the message "Should never divide by zero." The Assert call is put in a conditional compilation block so that the check is not present in the release version, only in the debug version.

Including such debugging code in a program is good programming style, but using conditional compilation to accomplish it can become burdensome in some cases. Besides the fact that adding conditional compilation directives requires more typing, it can also make code hard to read. To assist this, methods can be marked as being *conditional methods*. A conditional method is called normally, but the call is compiled into the program only if a conditional compilation constant evaluates to True. The method System.Diagnostics.Debug.Assert is such a method. Debug.Assert will be compiled into a program only if the conditional compilation constant DEBUG evaluates to True. Otherwise, the call is ignored. So the preceding example can just be written as follows.

```
Function Divide(ByVal x As Integer, ByVal y As Integer) As Integer
  Debug.Assert(y > 0, "Should never divide by zero.")
  Return x \ y
End Function
```

Conditional methods are defined by adding the System.Diagnostics.ConditionalAttribute attribute to a method. The argument of the attribute is the conditional compilation constant to evaluate. The attribute may be applied multiple times to a method—if any of the conditional compilation constants evaluate to True, the call will be compiled. For example:

```
<Conditional("DEBUG"), Conditional("TEST")> _
Sub PrintTestMessage(ByVal Message As String)
  Console.WriteLine(Message)
End Sub
```

In this example, the conditional method PrintTestMessage will be called only if DEBUG or TEST evaluates to True.

Overloading

In general, a type cannot contain more than one member with the same name. For example, if a module contained a field named Cost and a method named Cost, it would be difficult or impossible for the compiler (and even more difficult to someone reading the code) to figure out which one was being referenced at any one time. However, when you are dealing with methods, sometimes a caller may want to supply some parameters but not others, or may want to supply different types of arguments at different times. Optional parameters can be used to deal with the first situation, but using optional parameters can result in methods with long parameter lists that require named arguments to be used effectively. Parameters declared as Object can be used to deal with the second situation; this requires the overhead of casting values back and forth from Object and the loss of strong typing when calling the method.

Another way of dealing with this situation is to use overloading. *Overloading* is the ability to define more than one method in a class with the same name. Hence, the method name is *overloaded* with multiple meanings. Each method overloaded on a particular name must have a unique set of parameter types to distinguish it from other methods. For example:

```
Module Test
  Sub Print(ByVal i As Integer)
    Console.WriteLine("Integer: " & i)
  End Sub

  Sub Print(ByVal d As Double)
    Console.WriteLine("Double: " & d)
  End Sub

  Sub Print(ByVal s As String)
    Console.WriteLine("String: " & s)
  End Sub

  Sub Main()
    Print(10)       ' Prints "Integer: 10"
    Print(40.40)    ' Prints "Double: 40.40"
    Print("abc")    ' Prints "String: abc"
  End Sub
End Module
```

In this example, the name `Print` is overloaded with three methods, each of which takes a different type and prints something different.

Declaring overloaded methods requires no special syntax—just reusing a previously used name is sufficient. Overloaded methods must all be *distinct* from one another. Two methods are distinct if the types in their parameter lists are distinct—that is, they are not exactly the same types in exactly the same order. Overloading depends on the parameter types because the types of the arguments supplied to a method call are the only things that the compiler can use when deciding which of the overloaded methods it needs to call. For example, the following methods cannot be overloaded.

```
Module Test
  Sub Print(ByVal x As Integer)
    ...
  End Sub

  ' Error: Invalid overload.
```

```
   Sub Print(ByRef y As Integer)
      ...
   End Sub
End Module
```

These two methods cannot overload each other because each takes an `Integer` parameter. The fact that the parameters have different names or that one parameter is `ByRef` and another is `ByVal` is irrelevant when you are deciding whether two methods can be overloaded.

Similarly, the return type of functions is irrelevant when you are determining whether two methods can overload each other. The following two methods cannot overload one another, because their parameter lists are the same (i.e., empty) even though they return different types. In the following example, the function `GetValue` is incorrectly overloaded because the two functions have the same (empty) parameter list and only differ by return type. Functions cannot be overloaded on return types, because there would be many situations in which calls would be ambiguous. In the following example, the call to `GetValue` in `Main` cannot be resolved, because it is not clear whether the `Integer` or `Double` function should be called, since both convert to `Object`.

```
Module Test
   Function GetValue() As Integer
      ...
   End Function

   ' Error: Invalid overload.
   Function GetValue() As Double
      ...
   End Function

   Sub Main()
      Dim o As Object

      o = GetValue()
   End Sub
End Module
```

The first example in this section showed the use of overloading to handle different kinds of types. The following shows the use of overloading to deal with parameters that may or may not be supplied by a caller. Contrast this with the example in the section on optional parameters earlier in this chapter.

```
Sub PrintList(ByVal Number As Integer, ByVal NewLine as Boolean)
  If NewLine Then
    Console.WriteLine(Number)
  Else
    Console.Write(Number & ",")
  End If
End Sub

Sub PrintList(ByVal Number As Integer)
  PrintList(Number, False)
End Sub

Sub Main()
  PrintList(10)
  PrintList(20)
  PrintList(30)
  PrintList(40, True)
End Sub
```

Style

Overloading is preferred over using `Object` to handle parameters that can accept more than one type, because it allows arguments to be strongly typed. Overloading is also preferred over using optional parameters, because it often is easier to call.

Overload Resolution

When a compiler encounters a call to a method that has several overloads, it must choose between the overloaded methods. In some situations, choosing may be very easy because of the number and types of the arguments supplied.

```
Module Test
  Sub Print(ByVal i As Single)
    Console.WriteLine("Single: " & i)
  End Sub

  Sub Print(ByVal d As Double)
    Console.WriteLine("Double: " & d)
  End Sub
```

```
    Sub Print(ByVal t As Date)
        Console.WriteLine("Date: " & t)
    End Sub

    Sub Print()
        Console.WriteLine()
    End Sub

    Sub Main()
        Print()
        Print(#8/23/70#)
        Print(10D)
    End Sub
End Module
```

In the case of the first two calls to `Print`, the correct overload to use is obvious—the first call has no arguments, so it can only call the parameterless `Print` method; the second call has a `Date` argument that has no conversion to `Single` or `Double`, so it can only call the `Print` method that takes a `Date`. But the third call is more difficult because its argument is `Decimal`, and `Decimal` converts to both `Single` and `Double`. How does the language choose between the two overloads? The following steps describe how the call is resolved. If after any step only one method remains under consideration, that method is called.

1. All methods are eliminated that cannot be called because of a mismatch in the number of arguments and parameters, or because one of the arguments is of a type that has no conversion to the type matching parameter.
2. All methods are eliminated that require a narrowing conversion between an argument type and a parameter type.
3. All methods are examined to determine the "most specific" method of the available methods to call.

Method A is considered *more specific* than method B if the type of each of A's parameters either is the same type as B's corresponding parameter or has a widening conversion to the type of B's corresponding parameter. If the language encounters two methods where neither method is more specific than the other, it gives up and gives an ambiguity error.

Advanced

If overload resolution fails only because one or more methods were eliminated because of a narrowing conversion to `Object`, the overload resolution will be deferred until runtime by making the method invocation late-bound. As with regular late binding, specifying `Option Strict` at the top of a file prevents the call from being made late-bound.

The overload resolution rules may seem obscure, but the overall intent is simpler than it sounds. In general, the rules are designed to choose an overload that most closely matches the given argument list. In the preceding example, the language will choose to call the `Print` method that takes a `Single` for the `Print(10D)` call, because `Single` is closer to `Decimal` than `Double` is. (`Single` is closer to `Double` because it has a widening conversion to `Double`, whereas `Double` has a narrowing conversion to `Single`.) When choosing between overloads, however, the language can only choose between widening conversions because those are the only ones that are guaranteed to succeed. For example:

```
Module Test
  Sub Print(ByVal i As Integer)
    Console.WriteLine("Integer: " & i)
  End Sub

  Sub Print(ByVal s As Short)
  Console.WriteLine("Short: " & s)
  End Sub

  Sub Main()
    Dim x As Long = CLng(Console.ReadLine())
    Print(x)
  End Sub
End Module
```

In this example, the argument x is of type `Long`, which narrows to both `Integer` and `Short`. It is not clear from context which method should be called—`Short` is the more specific of the two methods, but it is possible that the value input may not fit into a `Short`. The value input may not fit into an `Integer` either, for that matter. Rather than try to pick a winner and be wrong some of the time, the language simply gives an error and require the developer to choose which overload they want to call by inserting a conversion. For example, changing the line to `Print(CInt(x))` would make it clear which overload to call.

Declare Statements

Although the .NET Framework provides an extensive library of classes, there are still times when it is necessary to call methods that exist outside the .NET Framework, such as Win32 APIs. Because methods external to the Framework do not have metadata associated with them, the Framework does not automatically understand how to call them. Instead, when a developer wants to call an external method, the method must first be described using a `Declare` statement. A `Declare` statement looks very much like a normal method declaration, with a few additions and no method body (since the implementation of the method is external to the Framework).

The first difference between a `Declare` statement and a regular method is that the method declaration is prefixed by the keyword `Declare`. Then, the name of the method in a `Declare` statement is followed by a *library clause* that tells the .NET Framework the name of the DLL where it can find the external method. The library clause begins with the word `Lib` followed by the name of the DLL (for example, `"user32.dll"`). If the extension is left off of the name in the library clause, ".DLL" is assumed. The following example shows a `Declare` statement for the external method `GetWindowsDirectoryA`, defined in the DLL `kernel32.dll`.

```
Module Test
  Declare Function GetWindowsDirectoryA Lib "kernel32" _
    (ByVal Buffer As String, ByVal Size As Integer) As Integer

  Sub Main()
    Dim s As String
    Dim Count As Integer

    s = Space(256)     ' Fill the string with spaces
    Count = GetWindowsDirectoryA(s, s.Length)

    If Count < 256 Then
```

```
        Console.WriteLine(s)
      End If
    End Sub
End Module
```

■ NOTE

Many external methods call the Win32 API `SetLastError` to give an error code if the method fails. This value can be retrieved using the `System.Runtime.InteropServices.Marshal.GetLastWin32-Error` method.

Sometimes the name of an external method may conflict with an existing method or a type member in a program, or it may be desirable to use a different name than the one used by the external method. In that case, the library clause may be followed by an *alias clause* that gives the true external method name. If you add an alias, the name of the `Declare` statement is not required to match the external method name. In the following example, the `GetWindowsDirectoryA` external method is renamed to `GetWindowsDirectory`.

```
Module Test
  Declare Function GetWindowsDirectory Lib "kernel32" _
    Alias "GetWindowsDirectoryA" _
    (ByVal Buffer As String, ByVal Size As Integer) As Integer

  Sub Main()
    Dim s As String
    Dim Count As Integer

    s = Space(256)    ' Fill the string with spaces
    Count = GetWindowsDirectory(s, s.Length)

    If Count < 256 Then
      Console.WriteLine(s)
    End If
  End Sub
End Module
```

Advanced

The alias clause can be a DLL ordinal value instead of a name if the external method is not exposed by name. The ordinal value is represented with a leading @ (i.e., `Alias "@10"`).

Advanced

`Declare` statements are equivalent to placing the `System.Interop-Services.DllImportAttribute` on a `Shared` method. In general, `Declare` statements are preferred for readability, but there are a few advanced settings available in the attribute that cannot be set through a `Declare` statement.

Character Translation

Although the .NET Framework always uses the Unicode standard when encoding text characters, many external methods use the older ANSI standard. When calling an external method that takes a string argument, the Framework needs to know whether it needs to translate the string from Unicode to ANSI and back. If the wrong kind of translation is done, the external method will not be able to correctly understand the passed-in string, and unexpected things may happen.

If the external method being called uses the Unicode standard for strings, the `Declare` keyword should be followed by the `Unicode` keyword. If the external method being called uses the ANSI standard for strings, the `Declare` keyword should be followed by the `Ansi` keyword. For example:

```
Module Test
  Declare Unicode Function GetWindowsDirectoryW Lib "kernel32" _
    (ByVal Buffer As String, ByVal Size As Integer) As Integer

  Declare Ansi Function GetWindowsDirectoryA Lib "kernel32" _
    (ByVal Buffer As String, ByVal Size As Integer) As Integer
```

```
Sub Main()
    ...
End Sub
End Module
```

The `GetWindowsDirectory` method, like many Win32 APIs, actually has two different versions: an ANSI version and a Unicode version. In the preceding example, the `GetWindowsDirectoryW` declaration will call the Unicode version, while the `GetWindowsDirectoryA` declaration will call the ANSI version.

Although sometimes it is necessary to explicitly specify the character set to use when calling an external method, commonly the .NET Framework can infer the correct character set based on context. This is called using the "auto" character set and is the default if `Unicode` or `Ansi` isn't specified (although the `Auto` keyword can be supplied for clarity). When the auto character set is used, the Framework first decides whether the operating system it is running on is a native ANSI system (for example, Windows 98) or a native Unicode system (for example, Windows XP). If the operating system is ANSI, the Framework first looks for the method using the given `Declare` name or alias. If it is unable to find the method, it then appends an "A" to the end of the name and tries again. If the operating system is Unicode, the Framework first appends a "W" to the end of the name and looks for the method. If it is unable to find the API, it then looks up the name as it was originally given. This algorithm tends to choose the correct character set for the correct platform.

String Parameters

Advanced

The mechanics of passing `String` values to external methods is an advanced topic, and you don't need to understand it to use `Declare` statements.

External methods and the .NET Framework treat `String` parameters differently. In the Framework, when a string variable is passed to a parameter declared as `ByVal String`, the original variable is not modified if the string is changed. In the following example, the `Main` method will still print the string "Original".

```
Module Test
  Sub Modify(ByVal s As String)
    s = "New"
  End Sub

  Sub Main()
    Dim s As String = "Original"

    Modify(s)
    Console.WriteLine(s)
  End Sub
End Module
```

In external methods, however, when a string variable is passed to the equivalent of a `ByVal String` (usually, `char *`), the string variable is still modifiable. As a result, many external methods that take a `ByVal String` modify the string with the expectation that the caller will see the result.

To make this work, when passing a string variable to an external method parameter that is declared `ByVal String`, Visual Basic .NET treats the argument in a special way. Instead of just passing the value of the string variable in by value, the string variable will be passed by reference using copy-in/copy-out. For example:

```
Module Test
  Declare Function GetWindowsDirectoryA Lib "kernel32" _
    (ByVal Buffer As String, ByVal Size As Integer) As Integer

  Sub Main()
    Dim s As String = Space(1024)
    Dim ReturnedChars As Integer

    ReturnedChars = GetWindowsDirectoryA(s, 1024)
  End Sub
End Module
```

In this example, even though the `Buffer` parameter is defined as being a value parameter, the `GetWindowsDirectoryA` method can still modify the string. When the modified string is passed out of the external method, the new string will be copied back into the local variable `s`.

To suppress this behavior in situations where changes to String parameters do not need to be reflected back, the System.InteropServices.MarshalAsAttribute can be applied to the parameter with an argument of System.InteropServices.UnmanagedType.LPStr or System.InteropServices.UnmanagedType.LPWStr, depending on whether the method is ANSI or Unicode, respectively.

```
Imports System.Runtime.InteropServices

Module Test
  Declare Function GetWindowsDirectoryA Lib "kernel32" _
    (<MarshalAs(UnmanagedType.LPStr)> ByVal Buffer As String, _
    ByVal Size As Integer) As Integer

  Sub Main()
    Dim s As String = Space(1024)
    Dim ReturnedChars As Integer

    ReturnedChars = GetWindowsDirectoryA(s, 1024)
  End Sub
End Module
```

In this example, the value of s will never change because all changes made to the string in GetWindowsDirectoryA are thrown away upon returning from the method.

It is worth noting that when an external method is repeatedly called in this way, it may be more efficient to use an instance of System.Text.StringBuilder to make the call. The StringBuilder class is designed specifically to be modifiable, so there is no need to do any copying on the way in or the way out of the method. For example:

```
Imports System.Text

Module Test
  Declare Function GetWindowsDirectoryA Lib "kernel32" _
    (ByVal Buffer As StringBuilder, ByVal Size As Integer) As Integer

  Sub Main()
    Dim s As StringBuilder = New StringBuilder(1024)
    Dim ReturnedChars As Integer

    ReturnedChars = GetWindowsDirectoryA(s, 1024)
  End Sub
End Module
```

In this case, `Buffer` is directly modifiable by `GetWindowsDirectoryA`, so no string copying is done, making the call more efficient.

Conclusion

Methods are the workhorses of the language, containing most of the executable code of a program. `Declare` statements allow calling code that is external to the Framework. Now that we have covered executable statements, the next chapter talks about fields, which are variables that can be stored within types, and properties, which are a cross between methods and fields.

Here are some style points to consider.

- A method declaration with no parameters can choose to omit the parentheses, but they are suggested for emphasis and readability.
- In previous versions of Visual Basic, parameters were reference parameters by default. The default changed in Visual Basic .NET because the overhead of reference parameters made them less desirable as the default type of parameter.
- Previous versions of Visual Basic supported optional `Variant` parameters without default values. Visual Basic .NET no longer supports declaring such parameters, but does still support calling COM methods that have such parameters.
- Late binding should only be used when absolutely necessary. Deferring type checking until runtime is more prone to errors and limits the ability of Visual Studio to provide Intellisense. Specifying `Option Strict` at the top of a file disallows late binding within that file.
- Overloading is preferred over using `Object` to handle parameters that can accept more than one type, because it allows arguments to be strongly typed. Overloading is also preferred over using optional parameters, because it often is easier to call.

■ 11 ■
Fields and Properties

The previous chapter discussed executable statements (methods) as type members, so now it is worth talking about variables as type members. Like local variables, which are locations to store information in methods, fields and properties are locations that store information in classes or structures.

Fields

A *field* is a variable that lives in a class or a structure instead of inside a method. Fields are declared in exactly the same way that local variables are declared.

```
Module Test
  Dim x As Integer
  Dim y As Long = 5
  Dim z(5) As Integer
End Module
```

Instance fields live as long as the class or structure that contains them lives, while shared fields live for the length of the program's execution. Fields declared in modules are equivalent to shared fields, since modules live for the entire length of the program. The following example uses a field to keep track of how many lines have been read from the console.

```
Module Test
  Dim LineCount As Integer = 0
  Const MaxLines As Integer = 30

  Sub Main()
    Dim Line As String = Console.ReadLine()

    While (Line <> "") AndAlso (LineCount < MaxLines)
      Line = Console.ReadLine()
      LineCount += 1
    End While

    Console.WriteLine("Read in " & LineCount & " lines.")
  End Sub
End Module
```

The example also shows the use of constant fields, which are equivalent to constant locals.

Read-Only Fields

Constants provide a useful way to represent values that do not change, but they are limited by the fact that they can only be initialized by a constant expression. Therefore, constants cannot be initialized by the result of a function call or by the result of an object instantiation expression. In some situations, though, a value will be constant throughout a program, but the value cannot be expressed in a constant expression. In the following example, the field MyAddress might not change throughout the entire program, but because it requires an instance to be constructed, the field cannot be declared as a constant field.

```
Structure Address
  Public Street, City, State, ZIP As String

  Sub New(ByVal Street As String, ByVal City As String, _
    ByVal State As String, ByVal ZIP As String)
    Me.Street = Street
    Me.City = City
    Me.State = State
    Me.ZIP = ZIP
  End Sub
End Structure
```

```
Module Test
  Public MyAddress As Address = _
    New Address("120 Main Street", "Durham", "NC", "27706")

  Sub Main()
    ...
  End Sub
End Module
```

An alternative to declaring a constant field, however, is to declare a *read-only field*. Read-only fields can only be assigned a value once, when the class or structure is being initialized, and then are read-only afterward. The previous module could have been written as follows instead.

```
Module Test
  Public ReadOnly MyAddress As Address = _
    New Address("120 Main Street", "Durham", "NC", "27706")

  Sub Main()
    ...
  End Sub
End Module
```

In this example, the read-only field MyAddress is initialized with a new instance when the module is initialized. Once the module has been initialized, the MyAddress field cannot be changed. Read-only fields can only be assigned to by an initializer or within the constructor for a type.

Read-only fields can also be used when you are declaring fields that should not change over the lifetime of an instance of an object. In the preceding example, it may be that once an Address structure has been created, the fields in the structure should never change. This could be enforced by declaring the structure with read-only fields.

```
Structure Address
  Public ReadOnly Street, City, State, ZIP As String

  Sub New(ByVal Street As String, ByVal City As String, _
    ByVal State As String, ByVal ZIP As String)
    Me.Street = Street
    Me.City = City
    Me.State = State
    Me.ZIP = ZIP
  End Sub
End Structure
```

> ### Advanced
>
> A type whose fields are all read-only is called an *immutable type* because once an instance of the type has been created, the value contained within it cannot change.

Properties

It is sometimes desirable to expose information as if it were a field on a type, even though the information may be calculated from multiple variables rather than stored in a single variable. For example, an `Order` class that contains `Quantity` and `Cost` fields may want to expose the total amount of the order. This can be done as a function, but it would be ideal if the information could be exposed as if it were a field.

```
Class Order
  Public Cost As Double
  Public Quantity As Integer

  Public Function Total() As Double
      Return Cost * Quantity
  End Function
End Class

Module Test
  Sub Main()
    Dim Order As Order = New Order()

    Order.Cost = 34.32
    Order.Quantity = 5

    Console.WriteLine(Order.Total())
  End Sub
End Module
```

Properties are type members that *behave* as if they were fields but that *work* like methods. In the preceding example, instead of exposing the order total as a function, we can use a property.

```
Class Order
  Public Cost As Double
  Public Quantity As Integer
```

```
    Public ReadOnly Property Total() As Double
      Get
        Return Cost * Quantity
      End Get
    End Property
  End Class

Module Test
  Sub Main()
    Dim Order As Order = New Order()

    Order.Cost = 34.32
    Order.Quantity = 5

    Console.WriteLine(Order.Total)
  End Sub
End Module
```

Like a field, every property has a type that defines what kind of information it accepts or returns. The property also defines methods called *accessors* that are used to access the value of the property. The Get accessor of a property reads the value of the property, while the Set accessor writes the value of the property. The accessor methods can contain any code necessary to accomplish the particular operation. For example, a property can be used to validate the value being assigned to a field.

```
Class Order
  Private _Cost As Double

  Public Property Cost() As Double
    Get
      Return _Cost
    End Get

    Set (ByVal Value As Double)
      If Value <= 0 Then
        Throw New ArgumentException("Cost cannot be zero or less.")
      End If

      _Cost = Value
    End Set
  End Property

  Public Quantity As Integer
End Class
```

In this example, the _Cost field is kept private and only exposed through a public property. The property Get accessor just returns the field's value, but the property's Set accessor validates that the property is not being assigned a value of zero or less.

Style

When a programmer creates a Private field to store the information for a Public property, a common naming convention is to use the property name with a leading underscore. For example, a Public property named Total would be stored in a Private field named _Total.

A Set accessor is followed by a parameter that represents the value being assigned to the property. Only one parameter is allowed in the parameter list, and the type must match the type of the property itself. If a property omits a Set accessor, the property is read-only and cannot be assigned to. Read-only properties must additionally be declared with the ReadOnly modifier. If a property omits a Get accessor, the property is write-only and cannot be assigned to. Write-only properties must additionally be declared with the WriteOnly modifier. For example:

```
Class Order
  Private _Cost As Double

  Public WriteOnly Property Cost() As Double
    Set (ByVal Value As Double)
      If Value <= 0 Then
        Throw New ArgumentException("Cost cannot be zero or less.")
      End If

      _Cost = Value
    End Set
  End Property
End Class

Module Test
  Sub Main()
    Dim Order As Order = New Order()

    ' OK, property has a setter
    Order.Cost = 10
```

```
    ' Error, property is write-only
    Console.WriteLine(Order.Cost)
  End Sub
End Module
```

Design

The `ReadOnly` and `WriteOnly` modifiers are required on the property declaration so that properties can be declared in situations where no accessors are allowed, such as `MustOverride` properties and properties in interfaces.

Advanced

When a property returns a structure, the fields of the value cannot be directly changed. This is because the property returns the value of the property directly, so changing the fields of that value would not affect the value stored in the property.

To illustrate the advanced point, consider this example.

```
Structure Order
  Public Cost As Double
  Public Quantity As Integer
End Structure

Class Customer
  Private _Order As Order

  Public Property Order() As Order
    Get
      Return _Order
    End Get

    Set (Value As Order)
      _Order = Value
    End Set
  End Property
End Class
```

```
Module Test
   Sub ChangeOrderCost(ByVal c As Customer)
      ' Error: The value of Cost cannot be changed directly
      c.Order.Cost = 10.34

      ' OK: The value of Cost is not changed directly
      Dim o As Order = c.Order
      o.Cost = 10.34
      c.Order = o
   End Sub
End Module
```

In this example, the expression c.Order returns the actual Order itself because Order is a structure. If c.Order.Cost = 10.34 were allowed to work, it would only change the Cost field of the Order value that was returned from the property, not the actual _Order field of the Customer class. The second part of the ChangeOrderCost subroutine shows how to change the Cost field of the Customer's Order field. Copying the value back into the Order property updates the _Order field of the Customer class.

Indexed Properties

Properties can also take parameters; such properties are called *indexed properties* because when they are used, they are indexed in the same manner that arrays are. For example, the following code defines an OrderCollection object that functions the same as an array of Order objects.

```
Class Order
   Public Cost As Double
   Public Quantity As Integer
End Class

Class OrderCollection
   Private _Orders(10) As Order

   Public Property Orders(ByVal Index As Integer) As Order
      Get
         If _Orders(Index) Is Nothing Then
            _Orders(Index) = New Order()
         End If

         Return _Orders(Index)
      End Get

      Set (Value As Order)
         _Orders(Index) = Value
```

```
      End Set
    End Property
End Class

Module Test
  Sub Main()
    Dim OrderCollection As New OrderCollection()

    OrderCollection.Orders(5).Cost = 10.34
    Console.WriteLine(OrderCollection.Orders(5).Cost)
  End Sub
End Module
```

The parameter list of a property works exactly the same as the parameter list of a function, with the exception that property parameters cannot be declared ByRef.

Compatibility

Previous versions of Visual Basic allowed indexed property parameters to be reference parameters. This is now disallowed because the .NET Framework does not allow indexed properties to modify index arguments.

Properties can be overloaded based on their parameter lists, though not on their type. This is the same as for methods, which can only be overloaded on their parameter list and not their return type. For example:

```
Class Customer
  Public Name As String
End Class

Class CustomerCollection
  Private _Customers(10) As Customer

  Public ReadOnly Property Customer(ByVal Index As Integer) As _
Customer
    Get
      If _Customers(Index) Is Nothing Then
        _Customers(Index) = New Customer()
      End If

      Return _Customers(Index)
    End Get
  End Property
```

```
Public ReadOnly Property Customer(ByVal Name As String) As Customer
  Get
    For Each CurrentCustomer As Customer In _Customers
      If CurrentCustomer.Name = Name Then
        Return CurrentCustomer
      End If
    Next CurrentCustomer

    Throw New ArgumentException("No customer by that name.")
  End Get
End Property
End Class

Module Test
  Sub Main()
    Dim Customers As New CustomerCollection()

    Console.WriteLine(Customers.Customer(5).Name)
    Console.WriteLine(Customers.Customer("Harry").Name)
  End Sub
End Module
```

In the example, the `Customers` indexed property is overloaded on both `Integer` and `String`. This allows indexing the property by using either a numerical index or a customer name.

Like methods, indexed properties can be called late bound if the type of the variable being indexed is `Object`. For example, the following code defers checking for indexed properties until runtime.

```
Module Test
  Sub Main()
    Dim o As Object = New OrderCollection()

    o.Orders(5).Cost = 10.34
    Console.WriteLine(o.Orders(5).Cost)
  End Sub
End Module
```

Style

Late binding should only be used when absolutely necessary. Deferring type checking until runtime is more prone to errors and limits the ability of Visual Studio to provide Intellisense. Specifying `Option Strict` at the top of a file disallows late binding within that file.

Default Properties

An indexed property can be declared as the *default property* of a type. This allows the type to be indexed as if it were the default property. In the following example, when the index is applied to the Customers variable, it is equivalent to applying the index to the default property of the Customer-Collection class.

```
Class Customer
  Public Name As String
End Class

Class CustomerCollection
  Private _Customers(10) As Customer

  Public Default Property Customer(ByVal Index As Integer) As Customer
    Get
      If _Customers(Index) Is Nothing Then
        _Customers(Index) = New Customer()
      End If

      Return _Customers(Index)
    End Get

    Set (Value As Customer)
      _Customers(Index) = Value
    End Set
  End Property
End Class

Module Test
  Sub Main()
    Dim Customers As New CustomerCollection()

    ' Customers(5).Name is equivalent to Customers.Customer(5).Name
    Customers(5).Name = "John Doe"
    Console.WriteLine(Customers(5).Name)
  End Sub
End Module
```

In this example, the index expression 5 is applied directly to the Customers variable. The compiler knows to interpret Customers(5) as Customers.Customer(5) instead. Default properties *must* have index parameters.

Compatibility

Previous versions of Visual Basic allowed defining default properties without parameters because the language distinguished between value assignment (`Let`) and reference assignment (`Set`). Without this distinction, it would be impossible to assign to a variable of a type with a parameterless default property because there would be no way to tell whether the assignment was to the variable or to the default property. Default parameterless properties on COM objects can still be accessed by adding parentheses after the value (i.e., `obj ()` will call the default parameterless property, if any, of the variable `obj`).

Dictionary Lookup

A class with a default property that is indexed by a single `String` parameter can be accessed in a shorthand way by using the *dictionary lookup operator*. This operator (also called the *bang operator* because it uses an exclamation point) takes the identifier that follows it and uses it as the parameter to the default indexed property. For example:

```
Class Customer
  Public Name As String
End Class

Class CustomerCollection
  Private _Customers(10) As Customer

  Public ReadOnly Default Property Customer(ByVal Name As String) _
     As Customer
    Get
      For Each CurrentCustomer As Customer In _Customers
        If CurrentCustomer.Name = Name Then
          Return CurrentCustomer
        End If
      Next CurrentCustomer

      Throw New ArgumentException("No customer by that name.")
    End Get
  End Property
End Class
```

```
Module Test
   Sub Main()
      Dim Customers As New CustomerCollection()

      ' Using a regular indexed property
      Console.WriteLine(Customers("Harry").Name)

      ' Using the dictionary lookup operator
      Console.WriteLine(Customers!Harry.Name)
   End Sub
End Module
```

In this example, the second `WriteLine` statement is equivalent to the first—the string `Harry` after the exclamation point is passed to the default property as a string.

The dictionary lookup operation can also be used in a `With` statement.

```
Module Test
   Sub Main()
      Dim Customers As New CustomerCollection()

      With Customers
         Console.WriteLine(!Harry.Name)
         Console.WriteLine(!John.Name)
         Console.WriteLine(!Tom.Name)
      End With
   End Sub
End Module
```

Conclusion

Fields provide storage for information within classes and structures. Properties allow calculated information to be exposed as if they were fields and enable validation of information as it is assigned to a field. The next chapter discusses events, which are a way for types to provide notifications to other types. It also discusses delegates, which are references to methods.

Here are some style points to consider.

- When a programmer creates a `Private` field to store the information for a `Public` property, a common naming convention is to use the property name with a leading underscore. For example, a

`Public` property named `Total` would be stored in a `Private` field named `_Total`.

- Previous versions of Visual Basic allowed indexed property parameters to be reference parameters. This is now disallowed because the .NET Framework does not allow indexed properties to modify index arguments.

- Previous versions of Visual Basic allowed defining default properties without parameters because the language distinguished between value assignment (`Let`) and reference assignment (`Set`). Without this distinction, it would be impossible to assign to a variable of a type with a parameterless default property because there would be no way to tell whether the assignment was to the variable or to the default property. Default parameterless properties on COM objects can still be accessed by adding parentheses after the value (i.e., `obj()` will call the default parameterless property, if any, of the variable `obj`).

12

Events and Delegates

A frequent design pattern in Windows programs is to write code that is triggered when a specific situation occurs (such as clicking a button) and then reacts to the event in some way. For example, when the menu item Exit is selected, the application might shut itself down, or when a button called Refresh is clicked, the application might refresh the data it is showing on the screen. This style of programming is called *event-driven programming* because the action in a program is driven by reacting to events. In event-driven programming, a type declares the events that it exposes. Then when an event occurs, the type *raises* the event and other types *handle* the event.

There are two ways of handling an event: declaratively and dynamically. Both are covered in this chapter.

Defining and Raising Events

A type declares an event in much the same way that it declares a subroutine.

```
Class Button
    Private X, Y As Integer

    Public Event Click()
    Public Event Moved(ByVal X As Integer, ByVal Y As Integer)
End Class
```

In this example, the `Button` class declares two events: a `Click` event that will be raised when the button is pressed and a `Moved` event that will be fired when the button is moved somewhere else on the screen. The `Moved` event has two parameters that represent the coordinates of where the button is being moved to. These parameters will be passed to any method that handles the event.

An event is raised by using the `RaiseEvent` statement, which has much the same syntax as a method invocation.

```
Sub Move(ByVal X As Integer, ByVal Y As Integer)
  Me.X = X
  Me.Y = Y

  ' Notify other types that we have moved.
  RaiseEvent Moved(X, Y)
End Sub
```

This example moves the button to a new location and then raises the `Moved` event, passing in the new coordinates of the button.

One thing to keep in mind about events is that they are *multicast*; this means that an event can be handled by more than one handler. In the following example, the same `Click` event is handled by two separate types.

```
Class Form1
  Public WithEvents Button1 As Button

  Sub Clicked() Handles Button1.Click
    ...
  End Sub
End Class

Class Form2
  Public WithEvents Button2 As Button

  Sub Clicked() Handles Button2.Click
    ...
  End Sub
End Class

Module Test
  Sub Main()
    Dim f1 As Form1 = New Form1()
    Dim f2 As Form2 = New Form2()
    Dim b As Button = New Button()
```

```
        f1.Button1 = b
        f2.Button2 = b
    End Sub
End Module
```

Because both `f1` and `f2` handle the `Click` event for the same instance of the `Button` class, when that button is clicked, both `Form1.Clicked` and `Form2.Clicked` will be called. The order in which the event handlers are called is determined by the .NET Framework at runtime.

Declarative Event Handling

Of the two ways of handling events, declarative event handling is simpler because it allows you to declare what events you handle, and the compiler takes care of the rest for you. For example, the following class has a `Button` field that has a `Click` event.

```
Class Form1
   Public Button1 As Button
End Class
```

To handle the `Click` event, the first thing that has to happen is that the `Button1` field must be declared as something that can raise events. This is done by adding the `WithEvents` modifier to the beginning of the declaration.

```
Class Form1
   Public WithEvents Button1 As Button
End Class
```

The `WithEvents` modifier can only be specified on fields whose type is a reference type that actually raises events. Also, the `WithEvents` modifier can only be specified on fields in classes, not in structures.

Advanced

Adding the `WithEvents` modifier to a field changes its behavior when the field is passed to reference parameters. Because the containing class needs to track when the value of a field is changed, the field will be passed using copy-in/copy-out rather than true byref, even if the type exactly matches the type of the parameter.

Now that `Button1` has been declared as raising events, a method can be declared that handles an event that `Button1` raises. In this case, a subroutine named `Button1_Click` is declared with no parameters to handle the `Click` event. The declaration includes a `Handles` clause that references the particular event of `Button1` that is handled.

```
Class Form1
  Public WithEvents Button1 As Button

  Public Sub Button1_Click() Handles Button1.Click
    MsgBox("Button1 was clicked!")
  End Sub
End Class
```

The variable specified in a `Handles` clause must always be a `With-Events` variable in the class, and the parameters of the event must exactly match the parameters of a method that handles it. A particular method can choose to handle multiple events by listing them all in the `Handles` clause.

```
Class Form1
  Public WithEvents Button1 As Button
  Public WithEvents Button2 As Button

  Public Sub Button_Click() Handles Button1.Click, Button2.Click
    MsgBox("A button was clicked!")
  End Sub
End Class
```

A derived class may also handle events raised by its base class by specifying the keyword `MyBase` instead of a `WithEvents` variable name. For example:

```
Class BaseForm
  Event Click()
End Class

Class DerivedForm
  Inherits BaseForm

  Sub Clicked() Handles MyBase.Click
    ...
  End Sub
End Class
```

In the declarative event model, events are always handled for the instance that is stored in the `WithEvents` variable. When a new value is assigned to a `WithEvents` variable, the type stops handling events from the instance currently stored in the variable and starts handling events from the new instance being stored into the variable. For example:

```
Class Form1
  Public WithEvents Button1 As Button

  Public Sub Button1_Moved(ByVal X As Integer, ByVal Y As Integer) _
    Handles Button1.Moved
    MsgBox("Button1 was moved!")
  End Sub

  Public Sub Test()
    Dim Temp As Button

    Button1 = New Button()
    Button1.Move(10, 10)

    Temp = Button1
    Button1 = New Button()
    Temp.Move(20,20)
  End Sub
End Class
```

In this example, the message "`Button1 was moved!`" will appear only once rather than twice. When a new button is assigned to `Button1` a second time, all the handlers automatically stop handling events from the existing instance, now only stored in `Temp`, and start handling events from the new instance. So when `Move` is called on `Temp`, the `Form1` class is no longer handling the `Moved` event for that particular instance, and `Button1_Moved` is not called.

Handling Events Dynamically

Sometimes it is impossible or undesirable to handle events declaratively. For example, `Shared` events cannot be handled declaratively, because no field can be declared using the `WithEvents` keyword. Or a class may wish to handle a particular event for only a short period of time without adding the overhead of creating a new field. There are two statements,

AddHandler and RemoveHandler, that allow a program to dynamically start and stop handling events.

The AddHandler and RemoveHandler statements each take two operands: an event and an event handler. The first operand, the event, specifies the event to be handled and the instance that will raise it; the statements do not require a WithEvents variable, so they are more flexible than declarative event handling. The event handler is specified by putting the keyword AddressOf in front of the name of the handler. (The meaning and use of AddressOf is explained in more detail later in the chapter.) For example, AddHandler and RemoveHandler can be used as follows.

```
Class Form1
  Public Buttons As ArrayList = New ArrayList()

  Public Sub CreateButton()
    Dim NewButton As Button = New Button()

    AddHandler NewButton.Click, AddressOf Me.Button_Click
    Buttons.Add(NewButton)
  End Sub

  Public Sub DeleteAllButtons()
    For Each Button As Button in Buttons
      RemoveHandler Button.Click, AddressOf Me.Button_Click
    Next Button

    Buttons.Clear()
  End Sub

  Public Sub Button_Click()
    MsgBox("Button1 was clicked!")
  End Sub
End Class
```

In this example, the method CreateButton dynamically creates a button on the form. Since CreateButton can create an arbitrary number of buttons on the form, there is no way to know how many WithEvents fields you might need (and adding a Handles clause for all of them would be unwieldy!). Instead, when a new button is created, CreateButton dynamically hooks up the Button_Click method to the Click event of the new button. When DeleteAllButtons goes to destroy all the buttons, it is important to stop listening to Click events from the buttons. The

`RemoveHandler` statement removes the class from the list of those handling the button's `Click` event.

> ### ■ NOTE
> Remember that `RemoveHandler` only removes the handler for the particular instance that qualifies the event handler. If two instances of `Form1` were handling the `Click` event on the same button, a `Remove-Handler` statement could remove only one of the two handlers at a time.

Delegates

Events are built on top of *delegates*, which are types that represent references to methods. A delegate is declared just like a subroutine or a function.

```
Delegate Sub SubroutineDelegate(ByVal x As Integer, ByVal y As Integer)
Delegate Function FunctionDelegate() As Integer
```

A variable whose type is a delegate type can then contain a reference to any method in any type that has the exact same set of parameters and the same return type. For example, the following code creates a new instance of a `SubroutineDelegate` that refers to the method `Button.Move`.

```
Class Button
   Public Sub Move(ByVal x As Integer, ByVal y As Integer)
      ...
   End Sub
End Class

Module Test
   Sub Main()
      Dim s As SubroutineDelegate
      Dim b As Button = New Button()

      s = New SubroutineDelegate(AddressOf b.Move)
   End Sub
End Module
```

Once a delegate has been constructed, it can be passed around like any normal value. It can also be invoked just as a subroutine or function is invoked. When the delegate is invoked, it calls the method that the delegate refers to. In the following example, the delegate s is invoked and calls the method Button.Move.

```
Module Test
  Sub Main()
    Dim s As SubroutineDelegate
    Dim b As Button = New Button()

    s = New SubroutineDelegate(AddressOf b.Move)
    s(10, 20)
  End Sub
End Module
```

The power of delegates is that they do not represent a reference to a particular method in a particular class, but instead represent a reference to a method with some general signature. Any method that matches the signature of the delegate can be referred to by that delegate. For example, the following function modifies the elements of an Integer array based on a custom modification function that's passed in as a delegate.

```
Module Test
  ' Delegate performs some action on the value.
  Delegate Function ModifyDelegate(ByVal Value As Integer) As Integer

  Sub ModifyArray(ByVal a() As Integer, ByVal Modify As ModifyDelegate)
    For Index As Integer = 0 To a.Length() - 1
      a(Index) = Modify(a(Index))
    Next Index
  End Sub

  ' Adds one to its argument
  Function AddOne(ByVal i As Integer) As Integer
    Return i + 1
  End Function

  ' Divides its argument by two
  Function DivideByTwo(ByVal i As Integer) As Integer
    Return i \ 2
  End Function

  Sub Main()
    Dim a(9) As Integer

    ' Add one to each element of the array
    ModifyArray(a, AddressOf AddOne)
```

```
        ' Divide each element of the array by two
        ModifyArray(a, AddressOf DivideByTwo)
    End Sub
End Module
```

Because a delegate is a reference type, it must be created before it can be used. All delegate types have the same kind of constructor, which takes a single parameter. The argument to the constructor must be an `AddressOf` expression. The `AddressOf` operator takes either a shared method or an instance method qualified with an instance and produces a reference to that particular method. This reference is then stored in the delegate. For example:

```
Class Class1
    Public Sub S1(ByVal x As Integer, ByVal y As Integer)
        MsgBox(x)
    End Sub

    Public Shared Sub S2(ByVal x As Integer, ByVal y As Integer)
        MsgBox(x)
    End Sub

    Public Function F() As Integer
        Return 10
    End Function
End Class

Module Test
    Sub Main()
        Dim s1, s2 As SubroutineDelegate
        Dim f As FunctionDelegate
        Dim t As Class1 = New Class1()

        s1 = New SubroutineDelegate(AddressOf t.S1)
        s2 = New SubroutineDelegate(AddressOf Class1.S2)
        f = New FunctionDelegate(AddressOf t.F)
    End Sub
End Module
```

Notice in the example that the shared method `S2` was qualified with the class name—in the case of shared methods, no instance is required to construct a delegate. If, however, the code had tried to say `AddressOf Class1.S1`, a compile-time error would have occurred because an instance is required for instance methods.

As long as the type of delegate can reasonably be inferred from the surrounding context, an `AddressOf` expression can be used in place of the full delegate construction syntax. So the following code:

```
s1 = New SubroutineDelegate(AddressOf t.S1)
s2 = New SubroutineDelegate(AddressOf Class1.S2)
f = New FunctionDelegate(AddressOf t.F)
```

could have been written as follows:

```
s1 = AddressOf t.S1
s2 = AddressOf Class1.S2
f = AddressOf t.F
```

This is an example of a place where the type of the delegate cannot be inferred.

```
Dim o As Object

' Error: Delegate type cannot be inferred.
o = AddressOf Class1.S2
```

In this case, the exact type of the delegate that needs to be constructed is not clear, because the value is being assigned to `Object`. This would produce a compile-time error.

Delegates are *multicast*, which means that a single delegate can contain a reference to more than one method. The methods can be completely different, as long as they have exactly the same set of parameters and the same return type. A delegate can refer to more than one method when it is combined with another delegate using the `System.Delegate.Combine` method. For example:

```
Class Button
  Public Sub Move(ByVal x As Integer, ByVal y As Integer)
    . . .
  End Sub
End Class

Class Form
  Public Sub Move(ByVal x As Integer, ByVal y As Integer)
    . . .
  End Sub
End Class
```

```
Module Test
   Sub Main()
      Dim s1, s2 As SubroutineDelegate
      Dim b As Button = New Button()
      Dim f As Form = New Form()

      s1 = AddressOf b.Move
      s2 = AddressOf f.Move
      s1 = CType(System.Delegate.Combine(s1, s2), SubroutineDelegate)
      s1(10,20)
   End Sub
End Module
```

In this example, the delegate s1 ends up referring to both Button.Move and Form.Move. When the delegate is invoked, both methods are called, one after the other. The order in which the delegates are invoked is defined by the .NET Framework and cannot be relied upon.

Once delegates have been combined, the method System.Delegate. Remove can be used to break them apart. The following example only calls Button.Move because the reference to Form.Move has been removed from the delegate s1.

```
Module Test
   Sub Main()
      Dim s1, s2 As SubroutineDelegate
      Dim b As Button = New Button()
      Dim f As Form = New Form()

      s1 = AddressOf b.Move
      s2 = AddressOf f.Move
      s1 = CType(System.Delegate.Combine(s1, s2), SubroutineDelegate)
      s1 = CType(System.Delegate.Remove(s1, s2), SubroutineDelegate)
      s1(10,20)
   End Sub
End Module
```

Asynchronous Invocation

When a delegate is invoked normally, it is invoked *synchronously*. This means that while the delegate is being invoked, the method that invoked the delegate sits and waits for the delegate to finish. However, delegates can also be invoked *asynchronously*. That is, the delegate can be invoked in such a way that the method that invoked the delegate can continue executing while the delegate is being invoked. Asynchronous delegate invocation is accomplished through use of multiple threads of execution, a topic that is beyond the scope of this book. However, a quick discussion of how asynchronous delegate invocation works may be worthwhile.

Every delegate type contains two methods called BeginInvoke and EndInvoke that allow the delegate to be called asynchronously. The parameters to BeginInvoke are the parameters to the delegate itself, a callback delegate to invoke when the delegate is finished executing, and an argument that should be passed in to the callback delegate. BeginInvoke returns an instance of an object that implements System.IAsyncResult, which can be used to monitor the progress of the delegate call. Thus, a delegate declared as follows:

```
Delegate Function CalculateDelegate(ByRef Iterations As Integer) _
    As Integer
```

would have a BeginInvoke call that looked like this.

```
Function BeginInvoke(ByVal Iterations As Integer, _
                     ByVal DelegateCallback As AsyncCallback, _
                     ByVal DelegateAsyncState As Object) As
                     IAsyncResult
```

When you call BeginInvoke, the .NET Framework queues the delegate in the thread pool. When a thread in the thread pool becomes available, the delegate is executed on that thread and runs until the delegate returns. When the delegate returns, the result of the delegate, if any, is stored in the object returned from BeginInvoke.

When the delegate call has completed, or if the code invoking the delegate wishes to block until the delegate call completes, EndInvoke is called on the delegate. EndInvoke takes the IAsyncResult from the BeginInvoke call as an argument and returns the value from the delegate call, if any. It also takes parameters for all the ByRef parameters in the delegate call—this allows the delegate the chance to pass back the reference parameters. Thus, the EndInvoke method for the CalculateDelegate example would look like this.

```
Function EndInvoke(ByRef Iterations As Integer, _
                   ByVal DelegateAsyncResult As IAsyncResult) As _
                   Integer
```

The following code shows an example of using `BeginInvoke` and `EndInvoke` to invoke a method asynchronously.

```vb
Module Test
  Function Calculate(ByRef Iterations As Integer) As Integer
    Dim Result As Integer = 0

    For Number As Integer = 1 To Iterations
      Result += Number
    Next Number

    Return Result
  End Function

  Delegate Function CalculateDelegate(ByRef Iterations As Integer) _
    As Integer

  Sub Main()
    Dim d As CalculateDelegate = AddressOf Calculate
    Dim AsyncResult As IAsyncResult
    Dim Result As Integer
    Dim Iterations As Integer = 10000

    AsyncResult = d.BeginInvoke(Iterations, Nothing, Nothing)

    Console.WriteLine("Waiting for the result...")

    Result = d.EndInvoke(Iterations, AsyncResult)

    Console.WriteLine("The result is " & Result & ".")
  End Sub
End Module
```

Delegates and Event Implementation

Advanced

How events are implemented in Visual Basic .NET using delegates is an advanced topic. It is not necessary to understand the implementation if you only wish to *use* events or delegates. Readers who are not interested in this topic can feel free to skip to the chapter's conclusion.

Hidden behind the event syntax described in this chapter is a fair amount of plumbing. Events are not as simple as they look—underneath the covers, an event is really just a delegate. (This is why this chapter covers both events and delegates.) For example, the following code:

```
Class Button
  Event Moved(ByVal X As Integer, ByVal Y As Integer)

  Sub Move(ByVal X As Integer, ByVal Y As Integer)
    RaiseEvent Moved(X, Y)
  End Sub
End Class
```

at an implementation level looks more like this.

```
Class Button
  Public Delegate Sub ClickEventHandler()

  Private ClickEvent As ClickEventHandler

  Public Sub add_Click(ByVal NewHandler As ClickEventHandler)
    ClickEvent = CType(System.Delegate.Combine(ClickEvent, _
      NewHandler), ClickEventHandler)
  End Sub

  Public Sub remove_Click(ByVal OldHandler As ClickEventHandler)
    ClickEvent = CType(System.Delegate.Remove(ClickEvent,
    OldHandler), _
            ClickEventHandler)
  End Sub

  Public Sub Click()
    Dim TempClickDelegate As ClickEventHandler

    TempClickDelegate = ClickEvent
    If Not TempClickDelegate Is Nothing Then
      TempClickDelegate()
    End If
  End Sub
End Class
```

It's worthwhile going through this code step-by-step. The first step in declaring an event is to define a delegate that has the same signature as the event. When you are declaring an event, the compiler declares a nested delegate type named XEventHandler for an event named X. It is also possible to use a preexisting delegate type when you are declaring an event by using an alternate event syntax.

```
Class Button
   Event Click As EventHandler
End Class
```

In this case, the event does not declare its own delegate type—instead, it uses the `System.EventHandler` delegate type as its delegate type. This means it has the same signature as if the declaration had been as follows.

```
Class Button
   Event Click(ByVal sender As Object, ByVal e As EventArgs)
End Class
```

Note that the delegate type used in the alternate syntax must be a subroutine—declaring events with return types is not supported.

The delegate is used to hold references to all the methods that are handling a particular event. When another class wants to handle the `Click` event, it creates a delegate that refers to its handler and then passes the delegate to the `add_Click` method. The `add_Click` method combines the passed-in delegate with the other delegates already handling the event, if any. When another class wants to stop handling the `Click` event, it creates another delegate that refers to its handler and then passes the delegate to the `remove_Click` method. The `remove_Click` method removes the delegate from the list of delegates handling the event.

When a class raises an event, it must first check to make sure that the delegate is not `Nothing`. If the delegate is `Nothing`, no one is handling the event and no work needs to be done. If the delegate is not `Nothing`, the delegate is invoked with the provided parameters. This causes each handler to be called with the specified parameters.

Advanced

The value of `ClickEvent` is read into a temporary variable before it is invoked, to prevent a race condition in a multithreaded application. If this weren't done, it might be possible for the last handler to be removed from the delegate between the check for `Nothing` and the delegate being invoked, causing a runtime exception.

This covers the event declaration side, but what of the event handling side? AddHandler and RemoveHandler turn into direct calls to the add and remove methods of the event. But declarative event handling turns out to be quite a bit more complex. For example, the following code:

```
Class Form1
  Public WithEvents Button1 As Button

  Public Sub Button1_Click() Handles Button1.Click
    MsgBox("Button1 was clicked!")
  End Sub
End Class
```

at an implementation level looks more like this.

```
Class Form1
  Private _Button1 As Button

  Public Property Button1() As Button
    Get
      Return _Button1
    End Get

    Set (ByVal Value As Button)
      If Not _Button1 Is Nothing Then
        RemoveHandler _Button1.Click, AddressOf Button1_Click
      End If

      _Button1 = Value

      If Not _Button1 Is Nothing Then
        AddHandler _Button1.Click, AddressOf Button1_Click
      End If
    End Set
  End Property

  Public Sub Button1_Click()
    MsgBox("Button1 was clicked!")
  End Sub
End Class
```

At the implementation level, a WithEvents field is a property that knows how to hook up all the event handlers for that field. When a value is assigned to the property, the Set accessor first removes the event handlers from the existing delegate stored in the property. It then changes the value of the property and adds the event handlers to the new instance.

Declaratively handling events in a base class is a little different because there is no field to hook up to. Instead, the instance that raises events is always the instance of the class itself. So the following code:

```
Class Base
  Public Event Click(ByVal x As Integer, ByVal y As Integer)
End Class

Class Derived
  Inherits Base

  Public Sub Clicked(ByVal x As Integer, ByVal y As Integer) _
    Handles MyBase.Click
    MsgBox("Derived was clicked!")
  End Sub
End Class
```

at an implementation level looks more like this.

```
Class Derived
  Inherits Base

  Public Sub New()
    AddHandler Me.Click, AddressOf Me.Clicked
  End Sub

  Public Sub Clicked(ByVal x As Integer, ByVal y As Integer)
    MsgBox("Derived was clicked!")
  End Sub
End Class
```

When the class is constructed, all it needs to do is add a handler to the base event. It never needs to stop handling the event, because that will happen automatically when the class is finalized.

Conclusion

Event-driven programming is a key part of the Windows programming model, so events have an important role in Visual Basic .NET programming. Delegates, which are used by events, provide a general way to refer to methods in a dynamic way. Now that we have covered all the kinds of type members, the next chapter jumps into the topic of inheritance, which can be used to reuse type members between similar types.

13

Inheritance

Often, types in a program share the same characteristics. For example, a program may contain types that represent a customer and an employee.

```
Class Customer
    Public Name As String
    Public Address As String
    Public City As String
    Public State As String
    Public ZIP As String

    Public CustomerID As Integer
End Class

Class Employee
    Public Name As String
    Public Address As String
    Public City As String
    Public State As String
    Public ZIP As String

    Public Salary As Integer
End Class
```

In this situation, both the Customer and Employee classes contain a number of identical fields. This is because the two classes each describe a person, and a person has certain characteristics, such as a name and address, that exist independent of whether or not they are a customer or an employee.

This commonality between the Customer type and the Employee type can be expressed through *inheritance*. Instead of repeating the same information in both types, you can create a class called Person that contains the common characteristics of a person.

```
Class Person
  Public Name As String
  Public Address As String
  Public City As String
  Public State As String
  Public ZIP As String
End Class
```

The class Person represents all the characteristics of a person that exist independent of whether the person is a customer or an employee. Once the Person class is defined, the Customer and Employee classes can *inherit* all the members of the Person class. This means that the classes have to define only the members that are unique to each class.

```
Class Customer
  Inherits Person

   Public CustomerID As Integer
End Class

Class Employee
  Inherits Person

   Public Salary As Integer
End Class
```

When one class inherits members from another class, the inheriting class *derives* from the other type. The type being derived from is called the *base type*. A type inherits all the members that the base type defines, including methods and events. So the Employee and Customer classes still have fields named Name, Address, City, State, ZIP, and Phone, even though they don't explicitly declare them, because they inherit them from Person. For example, the classes can be used as follows.

```
Module Test
  Sub Main()
    Dim c As Customer = New Customer()
    c.Name = "John Smith"
```

```
        Dim e As Employee = New Employee()
        e.Name = "Jane Doe"
    End Sub
End Module
```

Advanced

Visual Basic .NET supports only *single inheritance*, which means that a class can derive from only one base type.

A class that derives from another class can in turn be derived from by another class. For example, Employee can be further specialized by classes such as Manager and Programmer.

```
Class Programmer
    Inherits Employee

    Public Project As String
End Class

Class Manager
    Inherits Employee

    Public Programmers() As Programmer
End Class
```

In this example, the Programmer class contains the members defined in its immediate base class, Employee, as well the members defined in Employee's base class, Person. Related types can be viewed as a hierarchy with a tree structure, as in Figure 13-1.

Obviously, a type cannot directly or indirectly inherit from itself. Also, notice that the type Object is at the top of the inheritance hierarchy. If a class does not explicitly inherit from another class, it inherits from Object by default. Thus, Object is always the common root of all inheritance hierarchies. Also notice that in this type hierarchy, the most general types are at the top of the tree. As you move down the hierarchy, the classes at each level become more specialized and specific. Inheritance is a very powerful way of expressing the relationships between types.

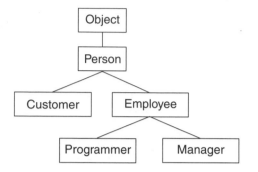

FIGURE 13-1: An Inheritance Hierarchy

Protected Accessibility

An important thing to keep in mind about inheritance and accessibility is that a derived class does not have access to its base classes' `Private` members. Private members can be accessed only by the immediate type in which they're defined. *Protected* members, however, can be accessed within an inheritance hierarchy. The `Protected` access level restricts access to a member to only the class itself, but it extends access to all derived classes as well. For example:

```
Class User
  Private SSN As String
  Protected Password As String
End Class

Class Guest
  Inherits User

  Sub New()
    ' Error: SSN is private to User
    SSN = "123-45-7890"

    ' OK: Password is protected and can be accessed
    Password = "password"
  End Sub
End Class
```

The class `Guest` can access the `Password` field inherited from its base class because it is `Protected`. However, it cannot access the `SSN` field, because it is `Private`.

When a class accesses a `Protected` member, the access must take place through an instance of that class or a more derived class. It cannot take place through a base class. For example, the following code is incorrect.

```
Class User
  Protected Name As String
  Private SSN As String
  Protected Password As String
End Class

Class Guest
  Inherits User

  Shared Sub ChangeName(ByVal u As User, ByVal Name As String)
    ' Error: Access to Name in User cannot go through
    ' base class User
    u.Name = Name
  End Sub
End Class
```

This rule may seem strange, but it is necessary to prevent unexpected access to `Protected` members. Without the rule, it would be possible to gain access to a `Protected` member of another type simply by deriving from a common base class.

```
Class User
  Protected Name As String
  Private SSN As String
  Protected Password As String
End Class

Class Administrator
  Inherits User
End Class

Class Guest
  Inherits User

  Public Sub PrintAdministratorPassword(ByVal u As User)
    ' Error: Access to Password in User cannot go through
    ' base class User
    Console.WriteLine(u.Password)
  End Sub
End Class
```

In this example, Guest cannot access Administrator's protected field Password—it can only access the Password field of instances of Guest.

> **▪ NOTE**
>
> Protected and Friend access levels can also be combined—the Protected Friend access level is the union of the two access levels.

Conversions

When a class derives from another class, it automatically inherits all the members of the base class. As a result, a derived class can always be safely converted to one of its base classes. For example:

```
Class Person
  Public Name As String
  Public Address As String
  Public City As String
  Public State As String
  Public ZIP As String
End Class

Class Employee
  Inherits Person

  Public Salary As Integer
End Class

Module Test
  Sub Main()
    Dim p As Person = New Employee()
    p.Name = "John Doe"
  End Sub
End Module
```

In this example, the Framework can allow an instance of Customer to be assigned to a variable of type Person because it knows that a Customer is also a Person. Thus, a Customer can be treated like a Person, and the fields that Customer inherits from Person can be changed. If the preceding example had tried to access fields that were specific to Customer or Employee, however, an error would be given because when an instance is viewed as as a Person, only the members defined by Person can be used, as the following example illustrates.

```
Module Test
  Sub Main()
    Dim p As Person

    p = New Customer()

    ' Error: CustomerID is not a member of Person
    p.CustomerID = 10

    p = New Employee()

    ' Error: Salary is not a member of Person
    p.Salary = 34923.23
  End Sub
End Module
```

Conversely, an instance of a base class can be converted to a derived class, but the conversion is not always guaranteed to succeed. A variable typed as Person could contain an instance of the Employee class, but it could also contain an instance of some other type.

```
Module Test
  Sub Main()
    Dim p As Person = New Employee()
    ' Error: Can't convert Employee to Customer
    Dim c As Customer = CType(p, Customer)
  End Sub
End Module
```

The Customer class also inherits from Person, so it can be converted to Person. However, the instance stored in the variable is still a Customer; as such, it cannot be treated as an instance of the Employee class. In this case, the Framework will throw a System.InvalidCastException exception at runtime when the conversion is executed.

The important principle to keep in mind is that when you create an instance of a class, it always stays that type, no matter what it is converted to. A Customer class converted to Person is still a Customer, even if the additional fields that Customer adds to the Person class are not visible. The power of inheritance is that it allows code to be written that works on the most general type in a hierarchy, which means that code can be written very broadly. For example, a method that takes a Person and prints the name and address of that Person can take a Customer or an Employee, instead of having to write separate methods for Customer and Employee.

```
Module Test
  Sub PrintAddress(ByVal p As Person)
    Console.WriteLine(p.Name)
    Console.WriteLine(p.Address)
    Console.WriteLine(p.City & ", " & p.State & " " & p.ZIP)
  End Sub

  Sub Main()
    Dim c As Customer
    Dim e As Employee

    PrintAddress(c)
    PrintAddress(e)
  End Sub
End Module
```

Array Covariance

Inheritance conversions extend to arrays as well. In general, an array of a particular type cannot be converted to any other type, because the array storage is allocated based on the type of the array. For example, it is not possible to covert a one-dimensional array of `Integer` to a one-dimensional array of `Long`, because `Integer` and `Long` do not have the same size. Thus, an array of ten `Integer` values could not hold ten `Long` values within the same space. However, because classes are reference types, the size of an array that holds ten `Customer` instances is the same size as an array that holds ten `Employee` instances. Thus, an array of a reference type may be converted to an array of another reference type, provided that the element types themselves convert to one another. For example:

```
Module Test
  Sub Main()
    Dim Customers(9) As Customer
    Dim People() As Person

    For Index As Integer = 0 To 9
      Customers(Index) = New Customer()
    Next Index

    People = Customers

    For Index As Integer = 0 To 9
      People(Index).Name = "John Doe"
    Next Index
  End Sub
End Module
```

The one-dimensional array of `Customer` can be converted to a one-dimensional array of `Person` because a `Customer` can be converted to a `Person`.

This conversion behavior of arrays is called *covariance*. Covariance is useful in the same way that inheritance is.

```
Module Test
  Sub SetCityState(ByVal People() As Person, ByVal City As String, _
                   ByVal State As String)
    For Each Person As Person In People
      Person.City = City
      Person.State = State
    Next Person
  End Sub

  Sub Main()
    Dim Employees(9) As Employee

    ...

    SetCityState(Employees, "Akron", "OH")
  End Sub
End Module
```

In this example, the base class `Person` provides a method that will set the `City` and `State` fields for an array of `Person` instances. The `Main` method can pass an array of `Employee` instances to the method because an array of `Employee` can be converted to an array of `Person`. One important thing to note, though, is that even though the array has been converted to an array of `Person`, it still can only hold `Employee` instances. Thus, an attempt to assign any other type into the array will cause a `System.InvalidCastException` exception. For example:

```
Module Test
  Sub FillArray(ByVal People() As Person)
    For Index As Integer = 0 To People.Length -1
      People(Index) = New Person()
    Next Index
  End Sub

  Sub Main()
    Dim Employees(9) As Employee

    FillArray(Employees)
  End Sub
End Module
```

This example will throw an exception because the array being passed in to `FillArray` is an array of `Employee`, not `Person`, so only `Employee` instances can be stored in the array.

The .NET Framework Type Hierarchy

As previously discussed, if a class does not have an explicitly stated base class, its base class is `Object`. This means that all classes ultimately derive from `Object`. Indeed, *all* types in the Framework type system—even the fundamental types, structures, enumerations, delegates, and arrays—derive from `Object` through special base classes that cannot otherwise be inherited from (see Figure 13-2). Structures and the predefined types derive from the type `System.ValueType`. Enumerations derive from the type `System.Enum`. Delegates derive from the type `System.Delegate`. Arrays derive from the type `System.Array`. And all these types inherit from `Object`.

What this means is that *any* type in the type system can be converted to `Object`. This makes `Object` a *universal type*. A method that takes `Object` can accept any type, while a field typed as `Object` can store any type.

Compatibility

The `Object` type combines the capabilities that used to be split between the `Object` type and the `Variant` type in previous versions of Visual Basic.

One interesting aspect of this design is that `Object` is a reference type. This raises the question: How can structures and fundamental types like `Integer` and `Double`, all of which are value types, inherit from a reference type? More specifically, how can a value type like `Integer` be converted to its base class, `Object`, when `Object` is a reference type? The Framework solves this conundrum through a process called *boxing*. When a value type is converted to `Object`, the Framework *copies* the value stored in the value type to the heap and returns a reference to the value. This process is called *boxing* the value type (see Figure 13-3). The reference can then be used to access the boxed value on the heap.

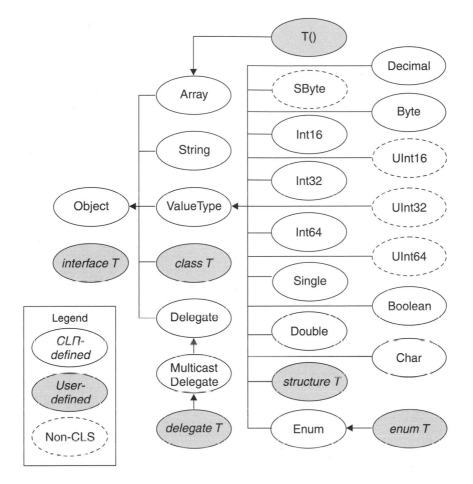

FIGURE 13-2: The .NET Framework Type Hierarchy

When a reference to a boxed value type is converted back to the value type, the Framework copies the value stored on the heap back into the variable. This process is called *unboxing* a boxed value type (see Figure 13-4).

The following code shows an example of boxing and unboxing an Integer.

```
Module Test
  Sub Main()
    Dim o As Object
    Dim i As Integer

    i = 5
    o = i  ' Copies the value to the heap
```

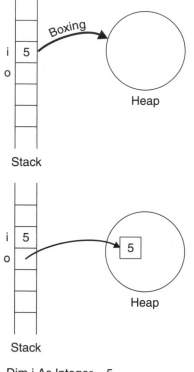

```
Dim i As Integer = 5
Dim o As Object
o = i
```

FIGURE 13-3: Boxing an Integer Value

```
    Console.WriteLine(o)
    i = CInt(o)   ' Copies the value back from the heap
    Console.WriteLine(i)
  End Sub
End Module
```

DirectCast

In general, a boxed value type can only be unboxed back to its specific type. For example, the following code will throw an exception because a boxed value of structure X cannot be unboxed into a variable typed as structure Y.

```
Structure X
  Public Value As Integer
End Structure
```

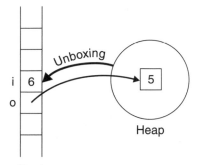

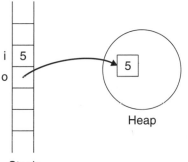

```
Dim i As Integer = 6
Dim o As Object = 5
i = o
```

FIGURE 13-4: Unboxing an Integer Value

```vbnet
Structure Y
  Public Value As Integer
End Structure

Module Test
  Sub Main()
    Dim o As Object
    Dim x As X
    Dim y As Y

    ' Box the value of x
    o = x

    ' Error: Cannot unbox a value of type X into a variable of type Y
    y = CType(o, Y)
  End Sub
End Module
```

The exceptions to this rule are the fundamental types: It is possible to unbox a boxed fundamental type into any other fundamental type that it has a conversion to. For example, the following code is valid because the Integer value in x can be unboxed into the Long variable y.

```
Module Test
  Sub Main()
    Dim o As Object
    Dim x As Integer = 5
    Dim y As Long

    ' Box the value of x
    o = x

    ' OK: Can unbox the Integer value into a Long variable
    y = CLng(o)
  End Sub
End Module
```

This can be very useful, but it comes at a price. When any value is converted from Object, the program must check at runtime to see whether the value is a boxed fundamental type so that it can apply the special unboxing behavior described in the previous paragraph. These checks add a little bit of overhead to the conversion, which normally is not significant. However, if it is known ahead of time that the conversion type exactly matches the boxed type, there may be some advantage to avoiding the overhead. For example, when lots of conversions are being performed, the overhead could become significant.

The DirectCast operator works just like the CType operator, except that it does not allow unboxing a boxed value type into anything but its original type—even if the boxed value type is a fundamental type. The advantage, though, is that the overhead of checking for the fundamental types is avoided. For example, in the following code the second conversion will be more efficient than the first.

```
Module Test
  Sub Main()
    Dim o As Object
    Dim x As Integer = 5
    Dim y, z As Integer
    Dim a As Long
```

```
      ' Box the value of x
      o = x

      ' Normal conversion
      y = CInt(o)

      ' More efficient conversion
      z = DirectCast(o, Integer)

      ' Error: Types do not match
      a = DirectCast(o, Long)
    End Sub
End Module
```

The last conversion emphasizes the fact that `DirectCast` can only unbox boxed values to their original type. So, unlike in the previous example, o cannot be unboxed into a `Long` variable.

Style

Unless code is particularly performance sensitive and doing a lot of unboxing, `CType` is more general than `DirectCast` and is preferred.

Overriding

Defining an inheritance hierarchy is all about defining the types in a system from most general to most specific. With inheritance, however, a derived type can only *add* new members to those it inherits from its base type. Sometimes, though, a derived type may want to *change* the behavior of members that it inherits from a base type. For example, the base class `Person` may define a `Print` method that prints information about the class.

```
Class Person
    Public Name As String
    Public Address As String
    Public City As String
    Public State As String
    Public ZIP As String

    Sub Print()
        Console.WriteLine(Name)
```

```
      Console.WriteLine(Address)
      Console.WriteLine(City & ", " & State & " " & ZIP)
    End Sub
End Class

Class Employee
  Inherits Person

  Public Salary As Integer
End Class
```

In this example, though, calling the method `Employee.Print` will only print the name and address of an employee, not the employee's salary. There is no way, using inheritance, to change the inherited implementation of `Person.Print`.

Changing the implementation of derived methods is possible, however, through *overriding*. A base class can declare that a particular method or methods are `Overridable`, which means that a derived class can replace the implementation that the base class provides. For example:

```
Class Person
  Public Name As String
  Public Address As String
  Public City As String
  Public State As String
  Public ZIP As String

  Overridable Sub Print()
    Console.WriteLine(Name)
    Console.WriteLine(Address)
    Console.WriteLine(City & ", " & State & " " & ZIP)
  End Sub
End Class

Class Employee
  Inherits Person

  Overrides Sub Print()
    Console.WriteLine(Name)
    Console.WriteLine(Address)
    Console.WriteLine(City & ", " & State & " " & ZIP)
    Console.WriteLine("Salary = " & Salary)
  End Sub

  Public Salary As Integer
End Class
```

In this example, the `Employee` class overrides `Person`'s implementation of the `Print` method with its own version of the `Print` method that prints the salary as well as the employee's name and address.

One interesting thing to note is that when a type overrides a base type's member, that override applies to *all* instances of the type, no matter what their stated type is. In other words, `Employee`'s implementation of `Print` is the one that will be called on an `Employee` instance, *even if it is typed as a Person*. The following example:

```
Module Test
  Sub Main()
    Dim e As Employee = New Employee()
    Dim p As Person

    e.Name = "John Doe"
    e.Address = "123 Main St."
    e.City = "Toledo"
    e.State = "OH"
    e.ZIP = "48312"
    e.Salary = 43912

    p = e
    p.Print()
  End Sub
End Module
```

will print this:

```
John Doe
123 Main St.
Toledo, OH 48312
Salary = 43912
```

even though the type of the variable that `Print` is being called on is `Person` instead of `Employee`.

Properties can also be overridden. The following is an example of overriding a property.

```
Class Order
  Public Cost As Double
  Public Quantity As Integer

  Public Overridable ReadOnly Property Total() As Double
    Get
      Return Cost * Quantity
```

```
          End Get
      End Property
   End Class

   Class ForeignOrder
      Inherits Order

      Public ConversionRate As Double

      Public Overrides ReadOnly Property Total() As Double
         Get
            Return MyBase.Total * ConversionRate
         End Get
      End Property
   End Class
```

When you are overriding a read-write property, both the Get and the Set accessors must be provided, even if you wish to override only one of them. Only methods and properties can be overridden, and they can be overridden *only* if they specify the Overrides keyword in their declaration. This is to prevent programmers from accidentally letting derived classes override methods that they did not intend to be overridden.

Only accessible members from a base type can be overridden. Thus, a Friend Overridable method cannot be overridden outside the assembly it is declared in. (It is not valid to declare a method Private Overridable, because no derived type could override such a method.) When you are overriding a method, the access of the overriding method must be the same as the method being overridden.

> **■ NOTE**
> When you are overriding a Protected Friend method from a derived class that is not in the same assembly as the class, the overriding method specifies just Protected instead of Protected Friend.

Sometimes it is desirable to override a method but prevent any further derived classes from overriding the method. Adding the NotOverridable keyword to a method that is overriding another method prevents any further derived classes from overriding the method.

MyBase and MyClass

In the example in the previous section, `Employee.Print` had to supply the entire implementation of `Person.Print` so that the name and address would still be printed—if it hadn't done that, only the salary would have been printed. In this situation, the keyword `MyBase` can be used to call the methods of the base class, allowing `Employee.Print` to call `Person.Print`. Calling methods off of `MyBase` calls the base class's implementation of a method, even if the derived class has overridden it. So the example could be rewritten as follows.

```
Class Person
  Public Name As String
  Public Address As String
  Public City As String
  Public State As String
  Public ZIP As String

  Overridable Sub Print()
    Console.WriteLine(Name)
    Console.WriteLine(Address)
    Console.WriteLine(City & ", " & State & " " & ZIP)
  End Sub
End Class

Class Employee
  Inherits Person

  Overrides Sub Print()
    MyBase.Print()
    Console.WriteLine("Salary = " & Salary)
  End Sub

  Public Salary As Integer
End Class
```

The result would be the same: First, `Person.Print` would be called to print the name and address, and then `Employee.Print` would print the salary.

Sometimes it is desirable to call the particular implementation of a method that your class provides, regardless of whether the instance might be of a type that overrides it. Qualifying the method call with the keyword

MyClass will always call the containing class's implementation of a method, ignoring any further implementation. The following example:

```
Class Person
  Public Name As String
  Public Address As String
  Public City As String
  Public State As String
  Public ZIP As String

  Sub CallPrint()
    Print()
  End Sub

  Sub CallMyClassPrint()
    MyClass.Print()
  End Sub

  Overridable Sub Print()
    Console.WriteLine(Name)
    Console.WriteLine(Address)
    Console.WriteLine(City & ", " & State & " " & ZIP)
  End Sub
End Class

Class Employee
  Inherits Person

  Overrides Sub Print()
    Console.WriteLine(Name)
    Console.WriteLine(Address)
    Console.WriteLine(City & ", " & State & " " & ZIP)
    Console.WriteLine("Salary = " & Salary)
  End Sub

  Public Salary As Integer
End Class

Module Test
  Sub Main()
    Dim e As Employee = New Employee()
    Dim p As Person

    e.Name = "John Doe"
    e.Address = "123 Main St."
    e.City = "Toledo"
    e.State = "OH"
    e.ZIP = "48312"
    e.Salary = 43912

    p = e
```

```
        Console.WriteLine("CallPrint:")
        p.CallPrint()

        Console.WriteLine()
        Console.WriteLine("CallMyClassPrint:")
        p.CallMyClassPrint()
    End Sub
End Module
```

will print the following information.

```
CallPrint:
John Doe
123 Main St.
Toledo, OH 48312
Salary = 43912

CallMyPrint:
John Doe
123 Main St.
Toledo, OH 48312
```

When the method `Person.CallPrint` calls the overridable `Print` method, what `Print` method ends up getting called depends on the actual type instance at runtime. Since the instance in this case is actually an `Employee`, `Person.CallPrint` ends up calling `Employee.Print`. However, because `CallMyClassPrint` qualifies the call to `Print` with `MyClass`, it always calls `Person.Print`, even if the instance is a more derived class.

Abstract Classes and Methods

In the examples we've been using so far in this chapter, `Person`, `Employee`, and `Customer` have all been classes that can be created using the `New` operator. However, there may be situations where a base class should never be created—perhaps there should only be instances of the `Employee` type and `Customer` type and never an instance of the `Person` type. It's possible just to add a comment saying `Person` should never be created, or `Person` might have a `Private` constructor to make it impossible to create. However, `Person` can also be designated as an *abstract* type. An abstract type is the same as a regular (or *concrete*) type in all respects except for one: An abstract type can never directly be created. In the following example, `Person` is now declared as an abstract type, using the `MustInherit` modifier.

```
MustInherit Class Person
   Public Name As String
   Public Address As String
   Public City As String
   Public State As String
   Public ZIP As String

   Sub Print()
     Console.WriteLine(Name)
     Console.WriteLine(Address)
     Console.WriteLine(City & ", " & State & " " & ZIP)
   End Sub
End Class

Class Customer
   Inherits Person

   Public CustomerID As Integer
End Class

Class Employee
   Inherits Person

   Public Salary As Integer
End Class
```

> ■ **NOTE**
> Just because a class is abstract and cannot be created, it does not mean that it cannot have constructors. An abstract class may have constructors to initialize methods or pass values along to base class constructors.

Abstract classes are special in that they can also define *abstract methods*. Abstract methods are overridable methods that are declared with the `MustOverride` keyword and provide no implementation. A class that inherits from a class with abstract methods must provide an implementation for the abstract methods or must be abstract itself. For example, the

Person class could define an abstract PrintName method that each derived class has to implement to display the person's name correctly.

```
MustInherit Class Person
  Public Name As String
  Public Address As String
  Public City As String
  Public State As String
  Public ZIP As String

  MustOverride Sub PrintName()

  Sub Print()
    PrintName()
    Console.WriteLine(Address)
    Console.WriteLine(City & ", " & State & " " & ZIP)
  End Sub
End Class

Class Customer
  Inherits Person

  Overrides Sub PrintName()
    Console.Write("Customer ")
    Console.WriteLine(Name)
  End Sub

  Public CustomerID As Integer
End Class

Class Employee
  Inherits Person

  Overrides Sub PrintName()
    Console.Write("Employee ")
    Console.WriteLine(Name)
  End Sub

  Public Salary As Integer
End Class
```

In this example, Person.Print can call the PrintName method, even though Person supplies no implementation for the method, because it is guaranteed that any derived class that can be instanced must provide an implementation.

Conclusion

Inheritance is a powerful way of expressing the relationships between types and reusing code across multiple types. The .NET Framework class libraries make extensive use of inheritance, and understanding inheritance is essential to understanding those libraries. Overridable methods and abstract methods provide a way for derived classes to specialize the behavior of their base classes. In the next chapter, we will discuss another way of reusing code across types: interfaces.

Here are some style points to keep in mind.

* The `Object` type combines the capabilities that used to be split between the `Object` type and the `Variant` type in previous versions of Visual Basic.
* Unless code is particularly performance sensitive and doing a lot of unboxing, `CType` is more general than `DirectCast` and is preferred.

■ 14■
Interfaces

In the previous chapter, we discussed inheritance as a way of abstracting common attributes of types into base types. Inheritance is a good way of expressing the essential nature of a type; for example, an `Employee` *is* a `Person` and a `Manager` *is* an `Employee`. But because types can only have a single base class, inheritance cannot be used to express general capabilities of types. For example, many types are "comparable," which is the property of having values that can be "less than" or "greater than" other values. (For example, both numbers and dates are comparable types.) Comparable types have many useful attributes, not the least of which is that they can be sorted into an order.

However, inheritance is usually not sufficient to express the "comparability" of a type. In an order-tracking system, a `Customer` object may be comparable on the basis of the customer's `CustomerID`, while an `Order` object may be comparable on the basis of the order's `OrderID`. However, it would probably not make sense to have both the `Customer` object and the `Order` object share the same base class, because they share no other attributes. Even worse, comparability is not the only capability that a type can express. Another capability that a type can have is "enumerability," which is the property of containing values that can be enumerated using the `For Each` statement. An `Order` object may also be enumerable, allowing the `For Each` statement to enumerate through the various products that make up the order. Because `Order` can only inherit from a single base class, it isn't possible to express both comparability and enumerability through inheritance.

Interfaces allow types to support general capabilities without having to be limited by inheritance. An interface defines a set of methods, properties, and events that make up a particular capability, such as comparability. For example, comparability is defined in the .NET Framework through the `System.IComparable` interface.

```
Interface IComparable
   Function CompareTo(ByVal obj As Object) As Integer
End Interface
```

In this case, the `IComparable` interface defines a method, `CompareTo`, that a "comparable" type must supply. Any type that implements this interface can be considered comparable, irrespective of its base types.

Defining Interfaces

An interface defines a *contract* that a type fulfills when it *implements* the interface. The type must supply an implementation for all the members of the interface—the interface provides no implementation of its own. An interface is defined using the `Interface` keyword. Interfaces may only contain methods, events, and properties. Methods and properties that appear in an interface declaration do not have a body, because they do not have an implementation in the interface. Also, members of interfaces never specify an access level, because they are always implicitly `Public`.

For example, the following declaration defines an `ISizeable` interface that defines a number of capabilities that a type that has a size should support.

```
Interface ISizeable
   ReadOnly Property Height() As Integer
   ReadOnly Property Width() As Integer

   Sub Resize(ByVal NewWidth As Integer, ByVal NewHeight As Integer)

   Event Resized(ByVal NewWidth As Integer, ByVal NewHeight As Integer)
End Interface
```

The `Height` and `Width` properties will return the size, while the `Resize` method will change the size. When the size are changed, the `Resized` event will be fired.

> ### Style
>
> By convention, all interface names start with the uppercase letter `I`.

Implementing Interfaces

A type *implements* an interface by specifying the name of the interface in an `Implements` statement. There is no limit on the number of interfaces that a type can implement; a type can implement multiple interfaces in a single `Implements` statement or can contain multiple `Implements` statements. For example, the following code defines two classes, `Square` and `Rectangle`, which each implement the `ISizeable` interface and the `IComparable` interface.

```
Class Square
  Implements ISizeable, IComparable

  . . .
End Class

Class Rectangle
  Implements ISizeable
  Implements IComparable

  . . .
End Class
```

When a type implements an interface, it must provide an implementation for each member of the interface. A type implements a member of an interface by adding an `Implements` clause on a type member that has the same signature (i.e., parameter list and return type) as the interface member. In the following example, the `Square` class provides an implementation for each member of the `ISizeable` interface.

```
Class Square
  Implements ISizeable

  Private _Height, _Width As Integer

  Public ReadOnly Property Height() As Integer _
      Implements ISizeable.Height
    Get
      Return _Height
    End Get
  End Property

  Public ReadOnly Property Width() As Integer _
      Implements ISizeable.Width
    Get
      Return _Width
    End Get
  End Property

  Public Sub Resize(ByVal NewWidth As Integer, _
      ByVal NewHeight As Integer) Implements ISizeable.Resize
    _Height = NewHeight
    _Width = NewWidth

    RaiseEvent Resized(NewWidth, NewHeight)
  End Sub

  Public Event Resized(ByVal NewWidth As Integer, _
    ByVal NewHeight As Integer) Implements ISizeable.Resized
End Class
```

It is worth noting that the name of a member and the name of the interface member that it implements do not have to match, although they usually do. For example, the previous example could have been written instead as follows.

```
Class Square
  Implements ISizeable

  Private _Height, _Width As Integer

  Public ReadOnly Property SquareHeight() As Integer _
      Implements ISizeable.Height
    Get
      Return _Height
    End Get
  End Property
```

```
  Public ReadOnly Property SquareWidth() As Integer _
      Implements ISizeable.Width
    Get
      Return _Width
    End Get
  End Property

  Public Sub SquareResize(ByVal NewWidth As Integer, _
      ByVal NewHeight As Integer) Implements ISizeable.Resize
    _Height = NewHeight
    _Width = NewWidth

    RaiseEvent SquareResized(NewWidth, NewHeight)
  End Sub

  Public Event SquareResized(ByVal NewWidth As Integer, _
    ByVal NewHeight As Integer) Implements ISizeable.Resized
End Class
```

The fact that the Square.SquareHeight method and the ISizeable.Height method have different names makes no difference when you are implementing the interface. It does affect how the type and interface are used, as will be discussed in a subsequent section.

Style

Because it can be confusing to consumers of the type to have two names for the same method, it is generally best to use the same names when you are implementing an interface.

Private Interface Implementation

One thing to note is that the members of an interface are always Public even if the members implementing them are not. In other words, interface methods on a type can be called even if the members implementing them cannot be called (assuming, of course, that the type itself is accessible). For example, the following class implements the ISizeable interface in such a way that the ISizeable methods can *only* be called through the interface.

```
Class Square
  Implements ISizeable

  Private _Height, _Width As Integer

  Private ReadOnly Property Height() As Integer _
      Implements ISizeable.Height
    Get
      Return _Height
    End Get
  End Property

  Private ReadOnly Property Width() As Integer _
      Implements ISizeable.Width
    Get
      Return _Width
    End Get
  End Property

  Private Sub Resize(ByVal NewWidth As Integer, _
      ByVal NewHeight As Integer) Implements ISizeable.Resize
    _Height = NewHeight
    _Width = NewWidth

    RaiseEvent Resized(NewWidth, NewHeight)
  End Sub

  Private Event Resized(ByVal NewWidth As Integer, _
    ByVal NewHeight As Integer) Implements ISizeable.Resized
End Class

Module Test
  Sub Main()
    Dim s As Square = New Square()
    Dim i As ISizeable = s

    ' Error: Resize is not accessible
    s.Resize(10, 10)

    ' OK: Resize is always accessible through interface
    i.Resize(10, 10)
  End Sub
End Module
```

In the previous example, the Square class uses a *private interface imple-mentation* to implement the ISizeable interface without exposing any of the interface methods directly. Private interface implementations are useful when a type wishes to implement an interface but not expose the methods as a part of the type. A common use of private interface implementation is to implement a general interface while providing a more specific version of the interface's methods. For example, a `Point` structure may implement the `IComparable` interface (which takes `Object`) while exposing a `CompareTo` method that takes `Point` values.

```
Structure Point
  Implements IComparable

  Private Function CompareTo(ByVal obj As Object) As Integer _
      Implements IComparable.CompareTo
    ...
  End Function

  Public Function CompareTo(ByVal p As Point) As Integer
    ...
  End Function

  ...
End Structure
```

In this example, the `CompareTo(Object)` function is less desirable than the `CompareTo(Point)` method because converting a `Point` structure to `Object` would require boxing. However, there is still benefit in implementing the `IComparable` interface, since many Framework methods use it. A private interface implementation allows implementing the interface while only exposing the strongly typed `CompareTo` to code using the `Point` class directly.

Event Implementation

When a type implements an interface event, the delegate type of the event in the interface must match the delegate type of the event in the type. When the delegate type is stated explicitly, this is relatively straightforward.

```
Interface IClickable
  Event Click As EventHandler
End Interface

Class Square
  Implements IClickable

  Event Click As EventHandler Implements IClickable.Click
End Class
```

However, when an event implicitly defines its own delegate, things get more complicated. An event that implements an interface event but doesn't explicitly declare its delegate type picks up its delegate type from the interface event.

```
Interface IClickable
  Event Click As EventHandler
End Interface

Class Square
  Implements IClickable

  Event Click(ByVal sender As Object, ByVal e As EventArgs) _
    Implements IClickable.Click
End Class
```

In this example, the `Square.Click` event implicitly picks up its delegate type from `IClickable.Click`. So the underlying delegate type of `Square.Click` will be `System.EventHandler` and not an auto-generated `ClickEventHandler` type. Note that the parameters to the event still must match the arguments of the event delegate.

If an event attempts to implement two events that use different delegate types, an error will occur because there is no way for an event to have two different delegate types.

```
Interface IClickable
  Event Click(ByVal sender As Object, ByVal e As EventArgs)
  Event Release(ByVal sender As Object, ByVal e As EventArgs)
End Interface

Class Square
  Implements IClickable

  ' Error, delegate types conflict
  Event Click(ByVal sender As Object, ByVal e As EventArgs) _
    Implements IClickable.Click, IClickable.Release
End Class
```

Even though `IClickable.Click` and `IClickable.Release` have the same parameters, they each declare their own implicit delegate type. When `Square.Click` attempts to implement both of the events, it cannot choose between the two delegate types, so an error results.

Consuming Interfaces

When a type implements an interface, instances of that type can be converted to the interface type. This allows all types that implement the interface to be treated in the same way. For example, the following code takes an instance of a type that implements the ISizeable interface and prints its size.

```
Module Test
  Sub PrintSize(ByVal Shape As ISizeable)
    Console.WriteLine(Shape.Width & "," & Shape.Height)
  End Sub

  Sub Main()
    Dim s As Square = New Square()
    Dim r As Rectangle = New Rectangle()

    PrintSize(s)
    PrintSize(r)
  End Sub
End Module
```

Both an instance of Square and an instance of Rectangle can be passed to the PrintSize method because both types implement the ISizeable interface.

As noted in the previous section, a type can implement an interface with different names than the ones the interface uses. If the Square class implements the Width and Height properties with properties named SquareWidth and SquareHeight (see the previous section for an example of this), the names used to access the property depend on whether the instance is being accessed as a class or as an interface. For example:

```
Module Test
  Sub PrintSize(ByVal Shape As ISizeable)
    Console.WriteLine(Shape.Width & "," & Shape.Height)
  End Sub

  Sub PrintSquareSize(ByVal Square As Square)
    Console.WriteLine(Square.SquareWidth & "," & Square.SquareHeight)
  End Sub

  Sub Main()
    Dim s As Square = New Square()
```

```
      PrintSize(s)
      PrintSquareSize(s)
    End Sub
  End Module
```

In this example, the `PrintSize` method does not have to change, because it deals with the interface `ISizeable`, whose property names are `Width` and `Height`. But because the `PrintSquareSize` method deals with an instance of `Square`, it has to use the property names as they are defined in `Square`—that is, `SquareWidth` and `SquareHeight`.

The conversion from a type to an interface it implements is widening because the conversion can never fail. The conversion from an interface to a type that implements it is narrowing because an interface can be implemented by many different types. For example, converting from `ISizeable` to `Square` may fail because the `ISizeable` instance may really be an instance of `Rectangle` (which cannot be converted to `Square`).

Interoperability

Because COM classes do not always declare every interface that they support, it is valid to convert a class to an interface that it does not explicitly implement, and vice versa. If the class is a COM class, this turns into a runtime `QueryInterface` call for the particular interface. If the class is not a COM class, the conversion will fail at runtime.

Interface Inheritance

Unlike classes, interfaces support multiple inheritance. That is, a single interface can inherit from multiple base interfaces.

```
Interface IDrawable
  Sub Draw()
End Interface

Interface IMoveable
  Sub Move(ByVal X As Integer, ByVal Y As Integer)
End Interface
```

```
Interface IShape
    Inherits IDrawable, IMoveable
End Interface
```

In this situation, the derived interface IShape contains members from its two base interfaces, IDrawable and IMoveable. So the IShape interface contains two members: IShape.Draw and IShape.Move.

Because an interface can inherit from multiple base interfaces, it is possible for the same interface to show up multiple times in the base interfaces of an interface (although an interface still cannot derive from itself). In that case, the interface is inherited from only once, not multiple times. For example:

```
Interface ISizeable
    Sub GetSize(ByRef X As Integer, ByRef Y As Integer)
End Interface

Interface IDrawable
    Inherits ISizeable

    Sub Draw()
End Interface

Interface IMoveable
    Inherits ISizeable

    Sub Move(ByVal X As Integer, ByVal Y As Integer)
End Interface

Interface IShape
    Inherits IDrawable, IMoveable
End Interface
```

The IShape interface inherits GetSize only once, even though it derives from ISize through two separate paths. Types that implement interfaces that inherit the same interface multiple times have to implement the interface only once, as well.

```
Class Square
    Implements IShape

    Sub GetSize(ByRef X As Integer, ByRef Y As Integer) _
        Implements IShape.GetSize
        ...
    End Sub
```

```
    Sub Draw() Implements IShape.Draw
      ...
    End Sub

    Sub Move(ByVal X As Integer, ByVal Y As Integer) _
      Implements IShape.Move
      ...
    End Sub
End Class
```

If an interface inherits members with the same name from two separate, unrelated interfaces, the conflicting members cannot be used in the derived interface without casting to one of the base interfaces. This is because there is no way for the compiler to know which method is supposed to be called. For example:

```
Interface IDrawable
  Sub GetSize(ByRef X As Integer, ByRef Y As Integer)
  Sub Draw()
End Interface

Interface IMoveable
  Sub GetSize(ByRef X As Integer, ByRef Y As Integer)
  Sub Move(ByVal X As Integer, ByVal Y As Integer)
End Interface

Interface IShape
  Inherits IDrawable, IMoveable
End Interface

Module Test
  Sub Main()
    Dim Shape As IShape = New Square()
    Dim X, Y As Integer

    ' Error: GetSize is multiply inherited.
    Shape.GetSize(X, Y)

    ' OK: Calls IDrawable.GetSize
    CType(Shape, IDrawable).GetSize(X, Y)
  End Sub
End Module
```

Conclusion

Whereas inheritance is a powerful way of using the relationships between *related* types to reuse code, interfaces are powerful a way of using commonalities between *unrelated* types to reuse code. Interfaces are useful to express generalized capabilities that any type can have, and they are used extensively in the .NET Framework for this purpose. Now that we have covered all the major types in the Framework, the next chapter starts a discussion of advanced language topics. First up is a discussion of attributes, which allow programmers to attach user-defined information to types in an assembly.

Here are some style points to consider.

- By convention, all interface names start with the uppercase letter I.
- Because it can be confusing to consumers of the type to have two names for the same method, it is generally best to use the same names when you are implementing an interface.
- Because COM classes do not always declare every interface that they support, it is valid to convert a class to an interface that it does not explicitly implement, and vice versa. If the class is a COM class, this turns into a runtime `QueryInterface` call for the particular interface. If the class is not a COM class, the conversion will fail at runtime.

▪ 15 ▪
Attributes

Declarations often have modifiers, such as `Public` or `Overridable` or `ReadOnly`, attached to them. These modifiers give the compiler and the .NET Framework extra information about the declaration, such as its accessibility, whether it can be overridden, and whether its value can be changed.

Modifiers have two problems, however. One is that modifiers have to be a part of the language—that is, the compiler has to understand them specially, and they cannot be used in programs to name things (unless they are escaped, of course). This is a problem because the .NET Framework has many places where modifiers are desirable to change the Framework's runtime behavior, but it would be a large burden on the language to define new modifiers for all of them.

For example, the Framework can automatically synchronize access to a field by multiple threads. It would be desirable to have a modifier that could be applied to fields that would indicate that access should synchronized, but that would require adding a new keyword and new code to the compiler to understand it. Multiply this case by a hundred other kinds of Framework modifiers, and the language would quickly become unmanageable.

The other problem is that modifiers cannot be used to store programmer-defined information about the declarations in a program. For example, when defining a Windows control, a programmer might want to attach some information to the class that indicates to a development environment how to show the control in the toolbox. Or a programmer might want to attach some information to the classes in a class library so that an automated test tool could test the classes. But because modifiers are defined as part of the language and must be understood by the compiler, a programmer cannot add new modifiers.

These problems can be solved through the use of *attributes*. Attributes are classes that can be attached to declarations, just like modifiers. And like modifiers, the information stored in attributes is stored as part of the assembly and can be retrieved at runtime by the Framework or a program. Attributes allow the Framework to define new modifiers without requiring them to be defined in the Visual Basic .NET language, and they allow programmers to attach arbitrary information to their declarations.

Applying Attributes

An instance of an attribute class is applied to a declaration by enclosing a constructor call in angle brackets (`<>`). Attributes always come before any regular modifiers. The following example applies the `System.Thread-StaticAttribute` attribute (which makes a `Shared` field's storage unique for each thread) to a field.

```
Class Test
  <ThreadStatic> Public Shared x As Integer
End Class
```

Style

Instead of using the full name of an attribute, such as `System.Thread-StaticAttribute`, for readability and simplicity you can leave off the "Attribute" suffix when applying the attribute.

Frequently, attribute constructors will have parameters that allow extra information to be specified as part of the attribute application. Arguments to an attribute follow the name of the attribute in parentheses, exactly as if they were constructor arguments. For example, the `System.Obsolete-Attribute` attribute (which is used to mark methods that are obsolete) takes a `String` as a parameter.

```
<System.Obsolete("This API should not be called.")> _
Sub Test()
  ...
End Sub
```

> **■ NOTE**
> Like language-defined modifiers, attributes have to be on the same source code line as the declaration that they modify. If you wish to put attributes on a separate line, you have to use a line continuation to connect the two lines into a single line.

Attributes also can have properties that can be used to store optional information. For example, the `System.AttributeUsageAttribute` attribute (which is used to define new attributes, as shown in the next section) has two properties, `AllowMultiple` and `Inherited`, which are optional values. Values are assigned to properties in the same way that named arguments are used in normal method invocation: The name of the property is followed by a colon equals (`:=`) and the value. Like named arguments, properties must follow regular arguments in the argument list. The following code shows two uses of `AttributeUsage`, one with values set to the properties, one without.

```
<System.AttributeUsage(AttributeTargets.All)> _
Class FirstAttribute
  Inherits Attribute
End Class

<AttributeUsage(AttributeTargets.All, _
                AllowMultiple := True, _
                Inherited := False)> _
Class SecondAttribute
  Inherits Attribute
End Class
```

Attributes can be placed anywhere that access modifiers, such as Public and Private, can be placed. In addition, attributes can be placed

- On members of enumerations.
- On parameters.
- On individual property accessors (i.e., before the Get or Set). In this case, the attribute applies to the underlying Get or Set method that the compiler generates for the property.
- On the return type of a function.
- On an assembly or .NET Framework module.

The last two points bear some discussion. Attributes may be placed on the return type of a function primarily so that COM marshalling information (using the System.Runtime.InteropServices.MarshalAs-Attribute) can be applied to function return types. The attribute is placed right before the function return type's name. For example, the following declaration applies an attribute to the return type of the function F.

```
Imports System.Runtime.InteropServices

Class Test
  Function F() As <MarshalAs(UnmanagedType.I4)> Integer
    ...
  End Function
End Class
```

It is also possible to define attributes that apply to the assembly or .NET Framework module being produced by the compiler. (.NET Framework modules are a special type of assembly that can be linked together to produce a single assembly. Their usage is beyond the scope of this book.) To apply an attribute to the assembly or Framework module as a whole, you can specify an attribute by itself after any Option or Imports statements. The attribute name must be preceded by "assembly:" for attributes that apply to the assembly, or "module:" for attributes that apply to Framework modules. At compile time, all the attributes applied to the assembly or Framework module are combined. For example, the following code shows the usage of the `System.Reflection.AssemblyDescriptionAttribute` attribute.

```
Imports System.Reflection

<Assembly: AssemblyDescription("A test program.")>

Module Test
  Sub Main()
    Console.WriteLine("Test.")
  End Sub
End Module
```

Some attributes can be applied multiple times to a declaration. For example, the `System.ObsoleteAttribute` attribute can be applied only once, but the `System.Diagnostics.ConditionalAttribute` attribute (which allows method calls to be compiled on a conditional basis) can be applied multiple times.

```
Module Test
<Obsolete("Don't call this API."), _
 Diagnostics.Conditional("DEBUG"), _
 Diagnostics.Conditional("TEST")> _
  Sub Main()
    Console.WriteLine("Test.")
  End Sub
End Module
```

Attributes applied to a class are, by default, inherited by any classes that derive from that class. Overriding a method does not remove the attributes applied to the method being overridden. If an overriding method specifies the same attribute as the method being overridden, the behavior depends on whether or not the attribute can be applied multiple times: If the attribute can be used multiple times, the overriding attribute complements the overridden attribute; if the attribute is single-use, the overriding attribute replaces the overridden attribute.

Defining Attributes

Attribute classes define attributes that can be applied to declarations. Attribute classes always inherit from the class `System.Attribute`, and by convention the name of the attribute class should end in the word "Attribute." (For example, if you wanted to define a `Help` attribute, the name of the class would be `HelpAttribute`.)

Style

It is strongly recommended that attribute class names always end in "Attribute." When looking for an attribute with a particular name, the compiler will first look for the name with "Attribute" added to the end and, if that fails, will look up the name as provided. This means that if an X attribute class and an `XAttribute` attribute class are defined, `<X>` will always refer to `XAttribute`, and there will be no way to refer to X.

An attribute class must also have a `System.AttributeUsage-Attribute` attribute applied to it. The `ValidOn` parameter of the `AttributeUsage` constructor specifies what kinds of declarations the attribute may be placed on and whether the attribute is multiuse and/or inherited. Table 15-1 lists the types of declarations that attributes may be placed on and the corresponding values that can be passed to the `ValidOn` parameter.

■ NOTE

The `AttributeTargets` enumeration values are flags and can be combined using the `Or` operator.

The parameters of an attribute are defined by the parameters of the instance constructors of the attribute. The following example defines an attribute that can take either a `String` value or a `String` value and an `Integer` value as arguments, and shows a use of the attribute.

```
<System.AttributeUsage(System.AttributeTargets.All)> _
Public Class HelpAttribute
   Inherits Attribute

   Public ReadOnly Message As String
   Public ReadOnly TopicNumber As Integer
```

TABLE 15-1: AttributeTargets Values

Values	Description
AttributeTargets.All	Attribute can be applied to anything in this list.
AttributeTargets.Assembly	Attribute can be applied to an assembly as a whole.
AttributeTargets.Class	Attribute can be applied to a class or module.
AttributeTargets.Constructor	Attribute can be applied to instance and shared constructors.
AttributeTargets.Delegate	Attribute can be applied to a delegate.
AttributeTargets.Enum	Attribute can be applied to an enumeration.
AttributeTargets.Event	Attribute can be applied to an event.
AttributeTargets.Field	Attribute can be applied to a field.
AttributeTargets.Interface	Attribute can be applied to an interface.
AttributeTargets.Method	Attribute can be applied to a method.
AttributeTargets.Module	Attribute can be applied to a .NET Framework module.
AttributeTargets.Parameter	Attribute can be applied to a parameter.
AttributeTargets.Property	Attribute can be applied to a property.
AttributeTargets.ReturnValue	Attribute can be applied the return value of a function.
AttributeTargets.Struct	Attribute can be applied to a structure.

```
Public Sub New(ByVal Message As String)
  Me.Message = Message
End Sub

Public Sub New(ByVal Message As String, ByVal TopicNumber As Integer)
  Me.Message = Message
```

```
        Me.TopicNumber = TopicNumber
    End Sub
End Class

<Help("This is a test class.", 5393)> _
Class Test
End Class
```

Attribute properties represent optional values for the attribute and are defined by instance fields and properties in the attribute class. To be used when an attribute is applied, the field or property cannot be ReadOnly. The following example rewrites the previous example using a property for the TopicNumber instead of constructor arguments.

```
<System.AttributeUsage(System.AttributeTargets.All)> _
Public Class HelpAttribute
  Inherits Attribute

  Public ReadOnly Message As String

  Private _TopicNumber As Integer
  Public Property TopicNumber() As Integer
    Get
      Return _TopicNumber
    End Get

    Set (Value As Integer)
      _TopicNumber = Value
    End Set
  End Property

  Public Sub New(ByVal Message As String)
    Me.Message = Message
  End Sub
End Class

<Help("This is a test class.", TopicNumber := 5393)> _
Class Test
End Class
```

Only certain types can be stored in attributes. Fields, properties, and constructor arguments in an attribute class can only be one of the following types:

- The fundamental types `Boolean`, `Byte`, `Short`, `Integer`, `Long`, `Single`, `Double`, `Char`, and `String`. (Note that this list does not include `Date` or `Decimal`.)
- The base .NET Framework reflection type `System.Type`.
- Any enumeration.

If a field, property, or constructor uses a type that isn't in this list (or if they use an enumeration that isn't accessible), the field, property, or constructor cannot be used when the attribute is applied to a declaration.

Advanced

The list of types that can be used in attributes is the same as those allowed by the Common Language Specification (CLS). Other languages, however, may allow using types such as `Object` or one-dimensional arrays in attributes even though those attributes would not be CLS compliant. Non-CLS-compliant attributes cannot be used in Visual Basic .NET.

Storing and Reading Attributes

The manner in which attributes are stored and retrieved is defined by the .NET Framework, so a detailed discussion is beyond the scope of this book. However, it is worth briefly discussing how attributes work, to give a better understanding about them. Take the following example.

```
<System.AttributeUsage(System.AttributeTargets.All)> _
Public Class HelpAttribute
  Inherits Attribute

  Public ReadOnly Message As String

  Private _TopicNumber As Integer
  Public Property TopicNumber() As Integer
    Get
      Return _TopicNumber
```

```
        End Get

    Set (Value As Integer)
      _TopicNumber = Value
    End Set
  End Property

  Public Sub New(ByVal Message As String)
    Me.Message = Message
  End Sub
End Class

<Help("This is a test class.", TopicNumber := 5393)> _
Class Test
End Class
```

When the Test class is compiled, the values specified as the arguments to the Help attribute are serialized into a binary form that is stored with the Test class definition in the assembly.

When a program asks for the attribute through reflection, the serialized attribute information is retrieved from the assembly. The method Get-CustomAttributes on the class System.Type or on the class System.Reflection.Assembly can be used to retrieve attributes. This method returns an array of Object values that represent the custom attributes defined on the particular type or assembly. When the .NET Runtime builds the array of values, it takes each serialized attribute and then creates an instance of the attribute class, passing in the specified arguments and assigning the specified values to the fields and properties.

The following example shows how the GetCustomAttributes method can be used to retrieve attributes at runtime.

```
Imports System

<AttributeUsage(AttributeTargets.All)> _
Public Class HelpAttribute
  Inherits Attribute

  Public ReadOnly Message As String

  Private _TopicNumber As Integer
  Public Property TopicNumber() As Integer
    Get
```

```
      Return _TopicNumber
    End Get

    Set (Value As Integer)
      _TopicNumber = Value
    End Set
  End Property

  Public Sub New(ByVal Message As String)
    Me.Message = Message
  End Sub
End Class

<Help("This is a test class.", TopicNumber := 5393)> _
Class Test
End Class

Module Main
  Sub Main()
    Dim T As Type = GetType(Test)
    Dim HelpAttribute As HelpAttribute

    HelpAttribute = CType(T.GetCustomAttributes(True)(0), _
      HelpAttribute)
    Console.WriteLine(HelpAttribute.Message & ": " & _
      HelpAttribute.TopicNumber)
  End Sub
End Module
```

This example fetches the first attribute that was applied to Test, casts it to a HelpAttribute, and then prints the value of the attribute.

Conclusion

Attributes allow the .NET Framework and the programmer to define new kinds of information that can be specified on declarations without requiring changes in the language. Given their widespread use in the Framework, understanding how to apply attributes is important. Defining new attributes is primarily of interest to programmers writing tools to analyze or process other assemblies. The next chapter covers another advanced topic: versioning.

Here are some style points to consider.

- Instead of using the full name of an attribute, such as `System.ThreadStaticAttribute`, for readability and simplicity you can leave off the "Attribute" suffix when applying the attribute.

- It is strongly recommended that attribute class names always end in "Attribute." When looking for an attribute with a particular name, the compiler will first look for the name with "Attribute" added to the end and, if that fails, will look up the name as provided. This means that if an `X` attribute class and an `XAttribute` attribute class are defined, `<X>` will always refer to `XAttribute` and there will be no way to refer to `X`.

■ 16 ■
Versioning

Developers as a group tend to think about only a single release at a time—nothing exists beyond the version of the code that they are working on. As nice as this fantasy is, it usually does not fit with reality. Rare is the application or class library that does not undergo multiple revisions during its life cycle. Failing to consider how an application will grow and change over time can cause severe programming challenges further down the road. Visual Basic .NET has several features that help developers manage versioning of applications as they evolve over time.

It is important to note up front that this chapter only discusses *language* features that relate to application versioning and that there is much more to versioning than just what is discussed here. This chapter deals with how different versions of *types* work with one another, but does not get into how different versions of *assemblies* work with one another. The .NET Framework manages assembly versioning, so for more information on that topic, I recommend reading the excellent *Essential .NET Volume 1: The Common Language Runtime,* by Don Box (Addison-Wesley, 2003).

Shadowing

In general, derived classes should not declare members with the same name as a base class member. When the same programmer defines both the base class and the derived classes, this rule is fairly easily followed. But when two programmers (or even two companies) define the base class and derived classes separately, avoiding name collisions is difficult or impossible.

For example, imagine a class library sold by SmithCorp that contains the following class.

```
Class Base
  . . .
End Class
```

A developer from DoeCorp purchases the class library and uses it to build an application. In that application, the developer derives a class from the Base class and defines a Print method.

```
Class Derived
   Inherits Base

   Sub Print()
     . . .
   End Sub
End Class
```

Everyone's happy. A year later, SmithCorp releases version 2.0 of its class library. This new version contains many bug fixes and new features, and DoeCorp wants to use the new version as the basis for version 2.0 of their application. So they buy the new version and rebuild their application. However, unbeknownst to DoeCorp, the developers at SmithCorp have added a new method, Print, to the class Base.

```
Class Base
  . . .

   Sub Print()
     . . .
   End Sub
End Class
```

This new method has the same name and signature as the method that DoeCorp defined in their derived class. What happens now?

One solution in this case would be to simply rename `Derived.Print` to something else. However, this may not be practical—it's possible that DoeCorp is writing a class library that other customers already are using, or the cost of replacing all calls to `Derived.Print` may be too great (especially if this problem occurs with each new version of `Base`). Instead, when a member in a derived class has the same name as a member in a base class, the derived member *hides* the base member. This is also called *shadowing* one member with another. Shadowing is automatically done by the compiler, but it will give a warning unless the code explicitly acknowledges that the shadowing is occurring.

```
Class Derived
   Inherits Base

   Shadows Sub Print()
      . . .
   End Sub
End Class
```

The `Shadows` keyword applied to the declaration of `Derived.Print` states that the method shadows any base members by the same name. The one situation in which the `Shadows` keyword can be omitted without getting a warning is when a derived class member shadows an inaccessible base class member.

`Shadows` is allowed on a declaration even if the declaration doesn't shadow anything in a base class. Adding `Shadows` to a declaration that doesn't shadow anything allows "preemptive" name hiding, to protect against likely future conflicts. It's also important to note that `Shadows` can be used on any kind of declaration and that `Shadows` can be used to hide any kind of declaration. In the following example, the `Print` field shadows the base `Print` method.

```
Class Derived
   Inherits Base

   Shadows Print As Boolean
End Class
```

If one overloaded method is declared as `Shadows`, they all have to be, since they all hide the same name. For example, if `Print` were overloaded in `Derived`, it would have to be declared as follows.

```
Class Derived
  Inherits Base

  Shadows Sub Print()
    ...
  End Sub

  Shadows Sub Print(ByVal o As Object)
    ...
  End Sub
End Class
```

Shadowing and Overriding

It is easy to get confused over the differences between shadowing and overriding, so it is worth discussing this one point in detail. When a method in a derived class overrides a base class method, it *replaces* the base class's implementation of the method. When the method is called, the base class method is still the one being called. In the following code, the `Main` method is still calling the `Base.Print` method—it is just that the actual implementation of the method called at runtime is the one supplied by `Derived.Print`.

```
Class Base
  Overridable Sub Print()
    ...
  End Sub
End Class

Class Derived
  Inherits Base

  Overrides Sub Print()
    ...
  End Sub
End Class

Module Test
  Sub Main()
    Dim d As Derived = New d()
    Dim b As Base = d
```

```
    ' This calls the implementation supplied by Derived.Print
    b.Print()

    ' This also calls the implementation supplied by Derived.Print
    d.Print()
  End Sub
End Module
```

Whether the instance is typed as `Base` or `Derived` makes no difference in this case, because what `Derived` did was replace `Base`'s implementation of the method `Print`.

In contrast, when a method in a derived class shadows a base class method, it only *hides* the base class method. Because of this, the stated type of an instance is significant. If an instance is typed as the derived class, the base class method is hidden. If an instance is typed as the *base* class, the base class method suddenly becomes visible again because the derived class no longer hides the method. In the following code, the `Main` method calls the `Base.Print` method in the first call and the `Derived.Print` method in the second.

```
Class Base
  Sub Print()
    ...
  End Sub
End Class

Class Derived
  Inherits Base

  Shadows Sub Print()
    ...
  End Sub
End Class

Module Test
  Sub Main()
    Dim d As Derived = New Derived()
    Dim b As Base = d

    ' This calls Base.Print
    b.Print()

    ' This calls Derived.Print
    d.Print()
  End Sub
End Module
```

In this case, whether the instance is typed as `Base` or `Derived` matters very much as to which `Print` method is visible at any one time.

This is an extremely subtle point but one that's important to understand. Shadowing is not a way to "override" a method that was not declared overridable.

Shadowing and Accessibility

Another important point to keep in mind is that when a derived member shadows a base member, it only hides the base member in contexts where the derived member is accessible. For example, in the following situation, the `Main` method calls `Base.Print` because `Derived.Print` is declared as `Private`. Since `Derived.Print` is not accessible to `Main`, it does not hide `Base.Print` from `Main`'s perspective.

```
Class Base
  Public Sub Print()
    ...
  End Sub
End Class

Class Derived
  Inherits Base

  Private Shadows Sub Print()
    ...
  End Sub
End Class

Module Test
  Sub Main()
    Dim d As Derived = New Derived()

    ' This calls Base.Print because Derived.Print is not accessible
    d.Print()
  End Sub
End Module
```

This rule may seem obscure, but it allows new members to be added to a base class without an inaccessible derived class member "blocking" the new member. Without this rule, there would be no way for the preceding `Main` class to access `Base.Print` through the type `Derived`, something that would be unfortunate given that `Derived.Print` is `Private` and can never be accessed outside of `Derived`.

Default Properties

Default properties have an interesting interaction with shadowing. Default properties can be accessed in two ways: as the default property of a type and as a regular property. As a result, a member can shadow the default property's property name but still allow the property to be accessed as the default property of a type.

```
Class Base
  Default ReadOnly Property Item(ByVal Index As Integer) As Integer
    Get
      ...
    End Get
  End Property
End Class

Class Derived
  Inherits Base

  ' This only shadows the Item name because it's not declared as
    Default
  Shadows ReadOnly Property Item(ByVal Index As Integer) As Integer
    Get
      ...
    End Get
  End Property
End Class

Module Test
  Sub Main()
    Dim x As Derived = New Derived()

    ' This calls Base.Item
    Console.WriteLine(x(10))

    ' This calls Derived.Item
    Console.WriteLine(x.Item(10))
  End Sub
End Module
```

Similarly, a default property in a derived class can shadow a base class default property but not shadow the base default property's name.

```
Class Base
  Default ReadOnly Property Item(ByVal Index As Integer) As Integer
    Get
      ...
```

```
         End Get
      End Property
   End Class

   Class Derived
      Inherits Base

      ' This only shadows the default property because it has a different
      ' name
      Shadows Default ReadOnly Property Value(ByVal Index As Integer) _
         As Integer
         Get
            ...
         End Get
      End Property
   End Class

   Module Test
      Sub Main()
         Dim x As Derived = New Derived()

         ' This calls Derived.Value
         Console.WriteLine(x(10))

         ' This calls Base.Item
         Console.WriteLine(x.Item(10))
      End Sub
   End Module
```

Overloading

When a member in a derived class shadows a method in the base class, it hides that method in the derived class. This handles the situation where a base class is versioned, but what about the situation in which the programmer does not wish to hide the base class method? For instance, given a base class that defines a `Print` method, the programmer may wish to add another `Print` overload. However, shadowing defeats this.

```
   Class Base
      Sub Print(ByVal s As String)
      End Sub
   End Class

   Class Derived
      Inherits Base
```

```
      ' This hides Base.Print(String)
      Shadows Sub Print(ByVal d As Decimal)
      End Sub
End Class

Module Test
   Sub Main()
      Dim d As Derived = New Derived()

      ' Error: Derived.Print(Decimal) hides Base.Print(Object)
      d.Print("abc")
   End Sub
End Module
```

Instead of declaring a derived method or property with the Shadows keyword, you can declare it with the Overloads keyword. This causes the derived method or property only to hide methods or properties in the base class *with the same name and parameter list as the method*. In the following example, the method Derived.Print no longer hides the method Base.Print.

```
Class Base
   Sub Print(ByVal s As String)
   End Sub
End Class

Class Derived
   Inherits Base

   Overloads Sub Print(ByVal d As Decimal)
   End Sub
End Class

Module Test
   Sub Main()
      Dim d As Derived = New Derived()

      ' OK: Calls Base.Print(String)
      d.Print("abc")
   End Sub
End Module
```

The keyword Overloads is used because it allows methods and properties to be overloaded across the inheritance hierarchy.

Style

The `Overloads` keyword is required only when you are doing overloading across the inheritance hierarchy. It is never required when you are doing overloading within a class.

Only methods and properties can use the `Overloads` keyword, because they are the only kinds of members that can be overloaded. If a member declared as `Overloads` conflicts with a base class member that is not the same kind of member, `Overloads` is the equivalent to `Shadows`. In the following example, `Derived.Value` hides `Base.Value` even though it is declared as `Overloads`, because one is a property and the other is a method.

```
Class Base
  ReadOnly Property Value() As Integer
    Get
      ...
    End Get
  End Property
End Class

Class Derived
  Inherits Base

  ' This hides Base.Value
  Overloads Function Value() As Integer
  End Function
End Class
```

Also remember that a method declared as `Overloads` will still hide a member with the same name and parameter list in the base class. This is because it would otherwise be impossible for the compiler to choose between two methods with exactly the same name and parameter list. In the following example, the method `Derived.Print` will be called because it has exactly the same parameter list as the method `Base.Print`.

```
Class Base
  Sub Print(ByVal s As String)
  End Sub
End Class
```

```
Class Derived
   Inherits Base

   Overloads Sub Print(ByVal s As String)
   End Sub
End Class

Module Test
   Sub Main()
      Dim d As Derived = New Derived()

      ' Calls Derived.Print(String)
      d.Print("abc")
   End Sub
End Module
```

As with `Shadows`, if one overloaded method is declared as `Overloads`, they all have to be. For example, if `Print` were overloaded in `Derived`, it would have to be declared as follows.

```
Class Derived
   Inherits Base

   Overloads Sub Print()
      ...
   End Sub

   Overloads Sub Print(ByVal s As String)
      ...
   End Sub
End Class
```

Obsolete

Over time, it is inevitable that types and type members in an assembly will become obsolete or no longer used. Just removing obsolete code from an assembly, however, is an abrupt all-or-nothing transition—any application that depends on the obsolete code will immediately cease to run, and any code that depends on the obsolete code will fail to compile. To help developers gradually obsolete types and type members, the .NET Framework defines an attribute, `System.ObsoleteAttribute`, that can be applied to declarations to indicate that a type or type member is obsolete. When a type or type member that is marked with the attribute is used in a program, the Visual Basic .NET compiler gives a warning or an error (depending on how

the attribute is applied) and prints the message specified in the attribute.
For example:

```
Class Customer
  Public Name As String

  <Obsolete("Call Print(True) instead.")> _
  Public Sub Print()
    Print(True)
  End Sub

  Public Sub Print(ByVal WriteLine As Boolean)
    If WriteLine Then
      Console.WriteLine(Name)
    Else
      Console.Write(Name)
    End If
  End Sub
End Class

Module Test
  Sub Main()
    Dim c As Customer = New Customer()

    ' Prints out the warning: "Call Print(True) instead."
    c.Print()
  End Sub
End Module
```

In this example, the `Customer.Print` method that takes no parameters
has been replaced with a new method that takes a `Boolean` parameter.
Because the obsolete method should eventually be removed, an `Obsolete`
attribute is applied to the obsolete method. This causes a message to be displayed when the method is used, pointing developers to the new method.

Conclusion

Versioning is a fact of life for most developers. Designing code that versions
well and handles changes to the libraries that it uses (including the .NET
Framework libraries) can be a challenging task. `Shadows` and `Overloads`
are intended to help developers deal with versioning.

A style point to consider is that the `Overloads` keyword is required only
when you are doing overloading across the inheritance hierarchy. It is never
required when you are doing overloading within a class.

A

Runtime Functions

The .NET Framework class libraries contain functions and subroutines designed specifically for Visual Basic .NET programmers. These methods provide functionality not found in other places in the Framework, or they provide functionality that is compatible with previous versions of Visual Basic. Although they are designed for Visual Basic .NET programmers, they are usable by any language supported on the .NET Framework and are considered part of the Framework. They will always be available anywhere the .NET Framework is installed.

All the Visual Basic .NET runtime functions are defined in the `Microsoft.VisualBasic` namespace. The methods themselves are contained within the `Microsoft.VisualBasic.DLL` assembly, which is always available in the Visual Studio IDE and on the command line.

AppWinStyle Enumeration

The `AppWinStyle` enumeration is used by the `Shell` function to indicate what window state should be used when the process is started. The enumeration's underlying type is `Short`.

```
Hide = 0
```

The new process's window should be hidden. Constant equivalent: `vbHide`.

```
NormalFocus = 1
```

The new process's window should be given the focus. Constant equivalent: vbNormalFocus.

```
MinimizedFocus = 2
```

The new process's window should be minimized and given the focus. Constant equivalent: vbMinimizedFocus.

```
MaximizedFocus = 3
```

The new process's window should be maximized and given the focus. Constant equivalent: vbMaximizedFocus.

```
NormalNoFocus = 4
```

The new process's window should not be given the focus. Constant equivalent: vbNormalNoFocus.

```
MinimizedNoFocus = 6
```

The new process's window should be minimized and not given the focus. Constant equivalent: vbMinimzedNoFocus.

CallType Enumeration

The CallType enumeration is used by the CallByName function to indicate the call type to make.

```
Method = 1
```

The call is a method call. Constant equivalent: vbMethod.

```
Get = 2
```

The call is a property get. Constant equivalent: vbGet.

```
Let = 4
```

The call is a property value assignment. Constant equivalent: `vbLet`.

Advanced

This value is valid only when you are calling a property on a COM object that has a property `Let` accessor.

```
Set = 8
```

The call is a property set. Constant equivalent: `vbSet`.

Collection Class

The `Collection` object stores lists of objects. Objects in a collection can be assigned an optional key value and can be retrieved either by position (like an array) or by key (like a dictionary). Unlike the collection objects such as `ArrayList` and `HashTable` in `System.Collections`, values can be removed from a `Collection` object while the collection is being enumerated. When a value is removed from a `Collection`, all enumerators are automatically updated.

■ NOTE

The methods defined directly on `Collection` are 1-based, which means that items in the collection are indexed starting with 1. This is different from `ArrayList` or `HashTable`, which are 0-based and are indexed starting with 0. Note that `Collection` also implements the interface `System.IList`, which is 0-based.

```
Public Sub New()
```

This constructor creates a new, empty collection object.

```
Public Sub Add(ByVal Item As Object, _
   Optional ByVal Key As String = Nothing, _
   Optional ByVal Before As Object = Nothing, _
   Optional ByVal After As Object = Nothing)
```

The Add method adds a new value to the collection, with an optional key specified by the Key parameter. The item can be inserted before or after an item with a particular key by supplying the Before or After parameters; Before and After cannot both be specified at the same time.

```
Public Sub Remove(ByVal Index As Integer)
Public Sub Remove(ByVal Key As String)
```

The Remove method removes a value from the collection either by index or by key. The Collection type allows removing methods while the collection is being iterated, unlike other collection types, such as ArrayList.

```
Public Property Count() As Integer
```

The read-only Count property returns the number of items stored in the collection.

```
Public ReadOnly Default Property Item(ByVal Index As Integer) As Object
Public ReadOnly Default Property Item(ByVal Key As String) As Object
```

The Item property allows fetching a particular item from the collection by index or by key.

ComClassAttribute Attribute

The ComClassAttribute attribute indicates that a class should be exposed as a COM coclass.

```
Public ReadOnly Property ClassID() As String
```

The ClassID property is the COM class ID of the class.

```
Public ReadOnly Property EventID() As String
```

The EventID property is the COM interface ID of the class's COM event interface.

```
Public ReadOnly Property InterfaceID() As String
```

The `InterfaceID` property is the COM interface ID of the class's default interface.

```
Public Property InterfaceShadows() As Boolean
```

The `InterfaceShadows` property indicates whether the COM interface name shadows another member of the class or base class.

```
Public Sub New()
Public Sub New(ByVal _ClassID As String)
Public Sub New(ByVal _ClassID As String, ByVal _InterfaceID As String)
Public Sub New(ByVal _ClassID As String, ByVal _InterfaceID As String, _
  ByVal _EventID As String)
```

The `ComClassAttribute` constructor applies an instance of the attribute to a class. If any of the three ID parameters are omitted, a compiler-generated GUID will be used in their place.

CompareMethod Enumeration

The `CompareMethod` enumeration is used by several functions to indicate whether string comparisons should be done using binary comparisons or text comparisons.

Advanced

If the `CompareMethod` enumeration is not supplied to a Visual Basic .NET runtime function, the compiler will substitute the current `Option Compare` value instead.

```
Binary = 0
```

Binary comparisons should be used. Constant equivalent: `vbBinary-Compare`.

```
Text = 1
```

Text comparisons should be used. Constant equivalent: `vbText-Compare`.

Constants Module

The `Constants` module contains a set of constants that provide alternate names to the values of the various enumerations discussed in this appendix. For example, the constant `vbExclamation` has the same value (48) as the enumerated value `MsgBoxStyle.Exclamation`. Each enumeration discussed in this appendix lists the constants in the `Constants` module that correspond to its enumerated values.

Compatibility

The constants in the `Constants` module are provided to assist in conversion of code from previous versions of Visual Basic. Programmers are encouraged to use the enumerations rather than the constants for greater clarity.

```
vbNullString = Nothing
```

A null reference to a string.

```
vbObjectError = &H80040000
```

The first user-defined error number. All user-defined error numbers must be greater than this.

ControlChars Class

The `ControlChars` class contains a set of character constants that are useful when you are composing strings.

```
Public Const Back As Char = ChrW(8)
```

A backspace character. Constant equivalent: `vbBack`.

```
Public Const Cr As Char = ChrW(13)
```

A carriage return character. Constant equivalent: `vbCr`.

```
Public Const CrLf As String = ChrW(13) & ChrW(10)
```

A carriage return followed by a line feed. Constant equivalent: vbCrLf.

```
Public Const FormFeed As Char = ChrW(12)
```

A form feed character. Constant equivalent: vbFormFeed.

```
Public Const Lf As Char = ChrW(10)
```

A line feed character. Constant equivalent: vbLf.

```
Public Const NewLine As String = ChrW(13) & ChrW(10)
```

A carriage return followed by a line feed. Constant equivalent: vbNewLine.

```
Public Const NullChar As Char = ChrW(0)
```

A null character. Constant equivalent: vbNullChar.

```
Public Const Quote As Char = ChrW(34)
```

A double quote character.

```
Public Const Tab As Char = ChrW(9)
```

A tab character. Constant equivalent: vbTab.

```
Public Const VerticalTab As Char = ChrW(11)
```

A vertical tab character. Constant equivalent: vbVerticalTab.

Conversion Module

The Conversion module contains methods useful for converting values from one type to another.

```
Public Function ErrorToString() As String
Public Function ErrorToString(ByVal ErrorNumber As Integer) As String
```

The `ErrorToString` function returns a text description of the last exception if no parameter is specified, or a text description of the exception corresponding to the error number.

```
Public Function Fix(ByVal Number As Short) As Short
Public Function Fix(ByVal Number As Integer) As Integer
Public Function Fix(ByVal Number As Long) As Long
Public Function Fix(ByVal Number As Decimal) As Decimal
Public Function Fix(ByVal Number As Single) As Single
Public Function Fix(ByVal Number As Double) As Double
Public Function Fix(ByVal Number As Object) As Object
```

The `Fix` function removes the fractional part of a number and returns the whole part of the number. For negative numbers, `Fix` returns the first negative integer greater than or equal to the number (i.e., –5.5 to –5).

```
Public Function Hex(ByVal Number As Byte) As String
Public Function Hex(ByVal Number As Short) As String
Public Function Hex(ByVal Number As Integer) As String
Public Function Hex(ByVal Number As Long) As String
Public Function Hex(ByVal Number As Object) As String
```

The `Hex` function converts an integral number into hexadecimal (base 16).

```
Public Function Int(ByVal Number As Short) As Short
Public Function Int(ByVal Number As Integer) As Integer
Public Function Int(ByVal Number As Long) As Long
Public Function Int(ByVal Number As Decimal) As Decimal
Public Function Int(ByVal Number As Single) As Single
Public Function Int(ByVal Number As Double) As Double
Public Function Int(ByVal Number As Object) As Object
```

The `Int` function removes the fractional part of a number and returns the whole part of the number. For negative numbers, `Int` will return the first negative number less than or equal to the number (i.e., –5.5 to –6).

```
Public Function Oct(ByVal Number As Byte) As String
Public Function Oct(ByVal Number As Short) As String
Public Function Oct(ByVal Number As Integer) As String
Public Function Oct(ByVal Number As Long) As String
Public Function Oct(ByVal Number As Object) As String
```

The `Oct` function converts an integral number into octal (base 8).

```
Public Function Str(ByVal Number As Object) As String
```

The Str function converts a number or a Boolean value into a string. If the number is positive, a leading space will be added to represent the sign of the number.

```
Public Function Val(ByVal Expression As String) As Double
Public Function Val(ByVal Expression As Char) As Integer
Public Function Val(ByVal Expression As Object) As Double
```

The Val function converts a string into a number. The function will read until the first nonwhitespace, nonnumeric value, ignoring all whitespace. It also recognizes hex and octal literals (i.e., &H3A or &O23).

DateAndTime Module

The DateAndTime module contains methods useful for manipulating date and time values.

```
Public ReadOnly Property Now() As Date
```

The Now property returns the current date and time.

```
Public Function DateAdd(ByVal Interval As DateInterval, _
   ByVal Number As Double, ByVal DateValue As Date) As Date
Public Function DateAdd(ByVal Interval As String, _
   ByVal Number As Double, ByVal DateValue As Object) As Date
```

The DateAdd function adds (or subtracts) the specified number of units from the supplied date.

```
Public Function DateDiff(ByVal Interval As DateInterval, _
   ByVal Date1 As Date, ByVal Date2 As Date, _
   Optional ByVal DayOfWeek As FirstDayOfWeek = FirstDayOfWeek.Sunday, _
   Optional ByVal WeekOfYear As FirstWeekOfYear = FirstWeekOfYear.Jan1) _
   As Long
Public Function DateDiff(ByVal Interval As String, _
   ByVal Date1 As Object, ByVal Date2 As Object, _
   Optional ByVal DayOfWeek As FirstDayOfWeek = FirstDayOfWeek.Sunday, _
   Optional ByVal WeekOfYear As FirstWeekOfYear = FirstWeekOfYear.Jan1) _
   As Long
```

The DateDiff function returns the number of specified units that the two dates differ by. The DayOfWeek and WeekOfYear parameters can be used to specify the behavior of the calendar used to determine the result.

```
Public Function DatePart(ByVal Interval As DateInterval, _
    ByVal DateValue As Date, _
    Optional ByVal FirstDayOfWeekValue As FirstDayOfWeek = _
        vbSunday, _
    Optional ByVal FirstWeekOfYearValue As FirstWeekOfYear =
        vbFirstJan1) As Integer
Public Function DatePart(ByVal Interval As String, _
    ByVal DateValue As Object, _
    Optional ByVal DayOfWeek As FirstDayOfWeek = _
        FirstDayOfWeek.Sunday, _
    Optional ByVal WeekOfYear As FirstWeekOfYear = _
        FirstWeekOfYear.Jan1) As Integer
```

The DatePart function returns the number of specified units that are in the date value. The FirstDayOfWeekValue and FirstWeekOfYearValue parameters can be used to specify the behavior of the calendar used to determine the result.

```
Public Function DateSerial(ByVal Year As Integer, _
    ByVal Month As Integer, ByVal Day As Integer) As Date
```

The DateSerial function returns a date made up of the Month, Day, and Year values given. If Year is less than 1, the value is subtracted from the current year. The Month value represents the specified month in the current year. Month values less than 1 represent months in previous years (0 is December in the previous year, –1 is November in the previous year, etc.); Month values greater than 12 represent months in the following years (13 is January in the next year). The Day value represents the specified day in the specified month. Day values less than 1 represent days in previous months (0 is the last day of the previous month); Day values greater than the number of days in the month represent days in the following months.

```
Public Property DateString() As String
```

The DateString property returns the current date as a string.

```
Public Function DateValue(ByVal StringDate As String) As Date
```

The `DateValue` function returns the date that corresponds to the given string.

```
Public Function Day(ByVal DateValue As Date) As Integer
```

The `Day` function returns the days value of the given date.

```
Public Function Hour(ByVal TimeValue As Date) As Integer
```

The `Hour` function returns the hours value of the given date.

```
Public Function Minute(ByVal TimeValue As Date) As Integer
```

The `Minute` function returns the minutes value of the given date.

```
Public Function Month(ByVal DateValue As Date) As Integer
```

The `Month` function returns the months value of the given date.

```
Public Function MonthName(ByVal Month As Integer, _
    Optional ByVal Abbreviate As Boolean = False) As String
```

The `MonthName` function returns the name of the given month in the current culture of the thread. The `Abbreviate` parameter determines whether the string returned is the full name or the abbreviated name of the month (i.e., "January" versus "Jan").

```
Public Function Second(ByVal TimeValue As Date) As Integer
```

The `Second` function returns the seconds value of the given date.

```
Public ReadOnly Property Timer() As Double
```

The `Timer` property returns a value that represents the number of clock ticks since midnight.

```
Public Function TimeSerial(ByVal Hour As Integer, _
    ByVal Minute As Integer, ByVal Second As Integer) As Date
```

The `TimeSerial` function returns a time during the day representing the `Hour`, `Minute`, and `Second` values given. If any of the values are less than 0 or greater than their maximum possible value, the values wrap around (i.e., a `Minute` value of 65 will add one hour and 15 minutes).

```
Public Property TimeString() As String
```

The `TimeString` property returns the current time as a string.

```
Public Function TimeValue(ByVal StringTime As String) As Date
```

The `TimeValue` function returns the time that corresponds to the given string.

```
Public Property Today() As Date
```

The `Today` property returns the current date. Assigning a date value to this property sets the date for the machine.

```
Public Property TimeOfDay() As Date
```

The `TimeOfDay` property returns the current time. Assigning a time value to this property sets the time for the machine.

```
Public Function Weekday(ByVal DateValue As Date, _
    Optional ByVal DayOfWeek As FirstDayOfWeek = FirstDayOfWeek.Sunday) _
    As Integer
```

The `Weekday` function returns the day of the week of the given date. The `DayOfWeek` parameter can be used to specify the behavior of the calendar used to determine the result.

```
Public Function Year(ByVal DateValue As Date) As Integer
```

The `Year` function returns the years value of the given date.

```
Public Function WeekdayName(ByVal Weekday As Integer, _
    Optional ByVal Abbreviate As Boolean = False, _
    Optional ByVal FirstDayOfWeekValue As FirstDayOfWeek = _
      FirstDayOfWeek.System) As String
```

The `WeekdayName` function returns the name of the given day of the week in the current culture of the thread. The `Abbreviate` parameter determines whether the string returned is the full name or the abbreviated name of the month (i.e., "Monday" versus "Mon"). The `FirstDayOfWeek-Value` parameter can be used to specify the behavior of the calendar used to determine the result.

DateFormat Enumeration

The `DateFormat` enumeration is used by the `FormatDate` function to indicate the date format to use for a date value.

```
GeneralDate = 0
```

Use the general date format as specified by the computer's regional settings at runtime. Constant equivalent: `vbGeneralDate`.

```
LongDate - 1
```

Use the long date format as specified by the computer's regional settings at runtime. Constant equivalent: `vbLongDate`.

```
ShortDate = 2
```

Use the short date format as specified by the computer's regional settings at runtime. Constant equivalent: `vbShortDate`.

```
LongTime = 3
```

Use the long time format as specified by the computer's regional settings at runtime. Constant equivalent: `vbLongTime`.

```
ShortTime = 4
```

Use the short time format as specified by the computer's regional settings at runtime. Constant equivalent: `vbShortTime`.

DateInterval Enumeration

The `DateInterval` enumeration is used by the `DateAdd`, `DateDiff`, and `DatePart` functions to indicate which part of a date/time value should be used. The `DateInterval` enumeration values have no constant equivalents, but they do have string equivalents that can be used in place of the enumeration in the overloaded functions.

```
Year = 0
```

The year of the date should be used. String equivalent: "yyyy".

```
Quarter = 1
```

The quarter of the year (1 through 4) should be used. String equivalent: "q".

```
Month = 2
```

The month of the year should be used. String equivalent: "m".

```
DayOfYear = 3
```

The day of the year (1 through 366) should be used. String equivalent: "y".

```
Day = 4
```

The day of the month should be used. String equivalent: "d".

```
WeekOfYear = 5
```

The week of the year (1 through 53) should be used. String equivalent: "ww".

```
Weekday = 6
```

The day of the week (1 through 7) should be used. String equivalent: "w".

```
Hour = 7
```

The hour of the day should be used. String equivalent: "h".

```
Minute = 8
```

The minute of the hour should be used. String equivalent: "n".

```
Second = 9
```

The second of the minute should be used. String equivalent: "s".

DueDate Enumeration

The `DueDate` enumeration is used by the functions in the `Financial` module to indicate whether a payment is due at the beginning or at the end of a period. The `DueDate` enumeration values have no constant equivalents.

```
BegOfPeriod = 1
```

The payment is due at the beginning of a period.

```
EndOfPeriod = 0
```

The payment is due at the end of a period.

ErrObject Class

An instance of the `ErrObject` class is returned by the `Err` function of the `Information` module. The `ErrObject` class represents the last exception caught by an `On Error` statement or by a `Try` statement.

```
Public Sub Clear()
```

The `Clear` subroutine clears all information about the last exception.

```
Public Property Description() As String
```

The `Description` property provides a text description of the last exception. If no description was supplied for the last exception, the result (if any) of the `ErrorToString` function will be returned.

```
Public ReadOnly Property Erl() As Integer
```

The `Erl` property returns the number of the last numeric label before an exception occurred.

Compatibility

The `Erl` function is provided only for backward compatibility and should not be used. The method `System.Exception.StackTrace` provides more comprehensive information about where an exception occurred.

```
Public Function GetException() As System.Exception
```

The `GetException` function returns the underlying `System.Exception` instance of the last exception.

```
Public Property HelpContext() As Integer
```

The `HelpContext` property provides the help context ID of the last exception.

```
Public Property HelpFile() As String
```

The `HelpFile` property provides the help file of the last exception.

```
Public ReadOnly Property LastDllError() As Integer
```

The `LastDllError` property returns the Win32 error code, if any, set by the last call to a `Declare` statement.

```
Public Property Number() As Integer
```

The `Number` property provides the error number of the last exception.

Compatibility

Error numbers are provided only for exceptions that have equivalent numbers in previous versions of Visual Basic. New exceptions will return the general error number 5. In general, error numbers should not be used in Visual Basic .NET.

```
Public Sub Raise(ByVal Number As Integer, _
  Optional ByVal Source As Object = Nothing, _
  Optional ByVal Description As Object = Nothing, _
  Optional ByVal HelpFile As Object = Nothing, _
  Optional ByVal HelpContext As Object = Nothing)
```

The `Raise` subroutine throws a new exception.

Compatibility

The `Raise` function is provided solely for backward compatibility. The `Throw` statement is the preferred way to throw exceptions.

```
Public Property Source() As String
```

The `Source` property provides the name of the object or application that caused the last exception.

FileAttribute Enumeration

The `FileAttribute` enumeration defines attributes of files used by the `Dir`, `GetAttr`, and `SetAttr` functions in the `FileSystem` module.

```
Normal = 0
```

The file has normal attributes. Constant equivalent: `vbNormal`.

```
ReadOnly = 1
```

The file is read-only. Constant equivalent: `vbReadOnly`.

```
Hidden = 2
```

The file is hidden. Constant equivalent: `vbHidden`.

```
System = 4
```

The file is a system file. Constant equivalent: `vbSystem`.

```
Volume = 8
```

The file is a volume label. Constant equivalent: `vbVolume`.

```
Directory = 16
```

The file is a directory. Constant equivalent: `vbDirectory`.

```
Archive = 32
```

The file has its archive bit set. Constant equivalent: `vbArchive`.

FileSystem Module

The `FileSystem` module contains methods useful for interacting with the file system.

Compatibility

The `FileSystem` module contains methods that replace the file I/O statements (`Open`, `Close`, `Print`, `Write`, `Seek`, etc.) that are no longer supported in Visual Basic .NET. Table A-1 gives the equivalent method for each statement. These methods are provided for backward compatibility use, and their general use is discouraged in favor of the methods in the `System.IO` namespace.

Many of the `FileSystem` methods take a file number as a parameter. File numbers can be any number between 1 and 255.

Warning

File numbers are shared across all threads of execution at runtime. Caution should be exercised when you are using file numbers in a multithreaded program.

```
Public Sub ChDir(ByVal Path As String)
```

TABLE A-1: FileSystem Equivalents

Visual Basic 6.0 Statement	FileSystem Method
Close	FileClose
Get	FileGet, FileGetObject
Input	Input, InputString
Line Input	LineInput
Lock	Lock
Open	FileOpen
Print	Print, PrintLine
Put	FilePut, FilePutObject
Seek	Seek
Spc	SPC
Tab	Tab
Unlock	Unlock
Width	FileWidth
Write	Write, WriteLine

The ChDir subroutine changes the current directory on the current drive.

```
Public Sub ChDrive(ByVal Drive As Char)
Public Sub ChDrive(ByVal Drive As String)
```

The ChDrive subroutine changes the current drive.

```
Public Function CurDir() As String
Public Function CurDir(ByVal Drive As Char) As String
```

The CurDir function returns the current directory for the specified drive, or the current drive if none is specified.

```
Public Function Dir(ByVal Pathname As String, _
  Optional ByVal Attributes As FileAttribute = FileAttribute.Normal) _
  As String
Public Function Dir() As String
```

The `Dir` function allows iterating through all the files in a directory or volume, or all the files in the current directory. Calling the `Dir` function with a string starts the search. The `Pathname` parameter specifies the directory or volume to iterate; if no directory or volume name is given, the current directory is iterated. The directory or volume name can be followed by a file name to match. The file name can contain the wildcard characters `?` (to match one character) and `*` (to match multiple characters). The `Attributes` parameter can further restrict the scope of the iteration. Once `Dir` has been called with a string, subsequent calls to the parameterless `Dir` will return the next file name in the specified location that matches the given file name.

```
Public Function EOF(ByVal FileNumber As Integer) As Boolean
```

The `EOF` function returns whether the end of the specified file has been reached.

```
Public Function FileAttr(ByVal FileNumber As Integer) As OpenMode
```

The `FileAttr` function returns the `OpenMode` used to open the specified file number.

```
Public Sub FileClose(ByVal ParamArray FileNumbers() As Integer)
```

The `FileClose` subroutine closes the specified file numbers.

```
Public Sub FileCopy(ByVal Source As String, ByVal Destination As String)
```

The `FileCopy` subroutine copies the `Source` file to the `Destination` directory.

```
Public Function FileDateTime(ByVal PathName As String) As Date
```

The `FileDateTime` function returns the date and time the specified file was created or last accessed.

```
Public Sub FileGet(ByVal FileNumber As Integer, _
  ByRef Value As ValueType, Optional ByVal RecordNumber As Long = -1)
Public Sub FileGet(ByVal FileNumber As Integer, _
  ByRef Value As Array, Optional ByVal RecordNumber As Long = -1, _
  Optional ByVal ArrayIsDynamic As Boolean = False, _
  Optional ByVal StringIsFixedLength As Boolean = False)
Public Sub FileGet(ByVal FileNumber As Integer, _
  ByRef Value As Boolean, Optional ByVal RecordNumber As Long = -1)
Public Sub FileGet(ByVal FileNumber As Integer, _
  ByRef Value As Byte, Optional ByVal RecordNumber As Long = -1)
Public Sub FileGet(ByVal FileNumber As Integer, _
  ByRef Value As Short, Optional ByVal RecordNumber As Long = -1)
Public Sub FileGet(ByVal FileNumber As Integer, _
  ByRef Value As Integer, Optional ByVal RecordNumber As Long = -1)
Public Sub FileGet(ByVal FileNumber As Integer, _
  ByRef Value As Long, Optional ByVal RecordNumber As Long = -1)
Public Sub FileGet(ByVal FileNumber As Integer, _
  ByRef Value As Char, Optional ByVal RecordNumber As Long = -1)
Public Sub FileGet(ByVal FileNumber As Integer, _
  ByRef Value As Single, Optional ByVal RecordNumber As Long = -1)
Public Sub FileGet(ByVal FileNumber As Integer, _
  ByRef Value As Double, Optional ByVal RecordNumber As Long = -1)
Public Sub FileGet(ByVal FileNumber As Integer, _
  ByRef Value As Decimal, Optional ByVal RecordNumber As Long = -1)
Public Sub FileGet(ByVal FileNumber As Integer, _
  ByRef Value As String, Optional ByVal RecordNumber As Long = -1, _
  Optional ByVal StringIsFixedLength As Boolean = False)
Public Sub FileGet(ByVal FileNumber As Integer, _
  ByRef Value As Date, Optional ByVal RecordNumber As Long = -1)
```

The `FileGet` function reads a value of the specified type from the given file number. The `RecordNumber` parameter specifies the record to use for files that were opened for `Random` access. The `ArrayIsDynamic` parameter specifies whether the array being read was stored as a dynamic array using `FilePut`. The `StringIsFixedLength` specifies whether the string (or array of strings) being read was stored as fixed-length strings using `FilePut`.

```
Public Sub FileGetObject(ByVal FileNumber As Integer, _
  ByRef Value As Object, Optional ByVal RecordNumber As Long = -1)
```

The `FileGetObject` function reads a value whose type is unknown from the given file number. The `RecordNumber` parameter specifies the record to use for files that were opened for `Random` access.

```
Public Function FileLen(ByVal PathName As String) As Long
```

The `FileLen` function returns the length of the specified file in bytes.

```
Public Sub FileOpen(ByVal FileNumber As Integer, _
  ByVal FileName As String, ByVal Mode As OpenMode, _
  Optional ByVal Access As OpenAccess = OpenAccess.Default, _
  Optional ByVal Share As OpenShare = OpenShare.Default, _
  Optional ByVal RecordLength As Integer = -1)
```

The `FileOpen` function opens a file for input or output. The `Mode`, `Access`, and `Share` parameters specify the type of operations that will be performed on the file. If the open mode is `OpenMode.Binary`, the `RecordLength` parameter specifies the size of buffer used to read from the file. If the open mode is `OpenMode.Random`, the `RecordLength` parameter specifies the size of a single record in the file.

```
Public Sub FilePut(ByVal FileNumber As Integer, _
  ByVal Value As ValueType, Optional ByVal RecordNumber As Long = -1)
Public Sub FilePut(ByVal FileNumber As Integer, _
  ByVal Value As Array, Optional ByVal RecordNumber As Long = -1, _
  Optional ByVal ArrayIsDynamic As Boolean = False, _
  Optional ByVal StringIsFixedLength As Boolean = False)
Public Sub FilePut(ByVal FileNumber As Integer, _
  ByVal Value As Boolean, Optional ByVal RecordNumber As Long = -1)
Public Sub FilePut(ByVal FileNumber As Integer, _
  ByVal Value As Byte, Optional ByVal RecordNumber As Long = -1)
Public Sub FilePut(ByVal FileNumber As Integer, _
  ByVal Value As Short, Optional ByVal RecordNumber As Long = -1)
Public Sub FilePut(ByVal FileNumber As Integer, _
  ByVal Value As Integer, Optional ByVal RecordNumber As Long = -1)
Public Sub FilePut(ByVal FileNumber As Integer, _
  ByVal Value As Long, Optional ByVal RecordNumber As Long = -1)
Public Sub FilePut(ByVal FileNumber As Integer, _
  ByVal Value As Char, Optional ByVal RecordNumber As Long = -1)
Public Sub FilePut(ByVal FileNumber As Integer, _
  ByVal Value As Single, Optional ByVal RecordNumber As Long = -1)
Public Sub FilePut(ByVal FileNumber As Integer, _
  ByVal Value As Double, Optional ByVal RecordNumber As Long = -1)
Public Sub FilePut(ByVal FileNumber As Integer, _
  ByVal Value As Decimal, Optional ByVal RecordNumber As Long = -1)
Public Sub FilePut(ByVal FileNumber As Integer, _
  ByVal Value As String, Optional ByVal RecordNumber As Long = -1, _
  Optional ByVal StringIsFixedLength As Boolean = False)
Public Sub FilePut(ByVal FileNumber As Integer, _
  ByVal Value As Date, Optional ByVal RecordNumber As Long = -1)
```

The `FilePut` function writes a value of the specified type to the given file number. The `RecordNumber` parameter specifies the record to use for files that were opened for Random access. The ArrayIsDynamic parameter specifies whether the array being written should be stored with a dynamic array header. The StringIsFixedLength specifies whether the string (or array of strings) being written should be stored with a fixed-length string header.

```
Public Sub FilePutObject(ByVal FileNumber As Integer, _
    ByVal Value As Object, Optional ByVal RecordNumber As Long = -1)
```

The FilePutObject function writes a value, whose type is unknown, to the given file number. The RecordNumber parameter specifies the record to use for files that were opened for Random access.

```
Public Sub FileWidth(ByVal FileNumber As Integer, _
    ByVal RecordWidth As Integer)
```

The FileWidth subroutine assigns an output line length to a given file number. The line length determines how many characters will be output before a new line is started. A line length of zero indicates that a line has no limit.

```
Public Function FreeFile() As Integer
```

The FreeFile function returns the next file number that is not currently in use.

```
Public Function GetAttr(ByVal PathName As String) As FileAttribute
```

The GetAttr function returns the attributes of the given file or directory.

```
Public Sub Input(ByVal FileNumber As Integer, ByRef Value As Object)
Public Sub Input(ByVal FileNumber As Integer, ByRef Value As Boolean)
Public Sub Input(ByVal FileNumber As Integer, ByRef Value As Byte)
Public Sub Input(ByVal FileNumber As Integer, ByRef Value As Short)
Public Sub Input(ByVal FileNumber As Integer, ByRef Value As Integer)
Public Sub Input(ByVal FileNumber As Integer, ByRef Value As Long)
Public Sub Input(ByVal FileNumber As Integer, ByRef Value As Char)
Public Sub Input(ByVal FileNumber As Integer, ByRef Value As Single)
Public Sub Input(ByVal FileNumber As Integer, ByRef Value As Double)
Public Sub Input(ByVal FileNumber As Integer, ByRef Value As Decimal)
Public Sub Input(ByVal FileNumber As Integer, ByRef Value As String)
Public Sub Input(ByVal FileNumber As Integer, ByRef Value As Date)
```

The Input function reads a value from a given file number.

```
Public Function InputString(ByVal FileNumber As Integer, _
    ByVal CharCount As Integer) As String
```

The Input function reads up to CharCount number of characters from the given file number.

```
Public Sub Kill(ByVal PathName As String)
```

The Kill subroutine deletes the specified file.

```
Public Function LineInput(ByVal FileNumber As Integer) As String
```

The LineInput function reads a string from a given file number.

```
Public Function Loc(ByVal FileNumber As Integer) As Long
```

The Loc function returns the current position in the specified file number.

```
Public Sub Lock(ByVal FileNumber As Integer)
Public Sub Lock(ByVal FileNumber As Integer, ByVal Record As Long)
Public Sub Lock(ByVal FileNumber As Integer, _
    ByVal FromRecord As Long, ByVal ToRecord As Long)
```

The Lock function prevents other processes from accessing all or part of the specified file number.

```
Public Function LOF(ByVal FileNumber As Integer) As Long
```

The LOF function returns the length, in bytes, of the specified file number.

```
Public Sub MkDir(ByVal Path As String)
```

The MkDir subroutine creates a new directory.

```
Public Sub Print(ByVal FileNumber As Integer, _
    ByVal ParamArray Output() As Object)
```

The `Print` subroutine outputs the information to the specified file number in a display-formatted manner.

```
Public Sub PrintLine(ByVal FileNumber As Integer, _
   ByVal ParamArray Output() As Object)
```

The `PrintLine` subroutine outputs the information to the specified file number in a display-formatted manner, followed by a line feed.

```
Public Sub Rename(ByVal OldPath As String, ByVal NewPath As String)
```

The `Rename` subroutine renames a file or directory.

```
Public Sub Reset()
```

The `Reset` subroutine closes all open file numbers.

```
Public Sub RmDir(ByVal Path As String)
```

The `RmDir` subroutine deletes a directory.

```
Public Sub Seek(ByVal FileNumber As Integer, ByVal Position As Long)
Public Function Seek(ByVal FileNumber As Integer) As Long
```

The `Seek` function returns the current position of the specified file number. The `Seek` subroutine sets the current position for the specified file number.

```
Public Sub SetAttr(ByVal PathName As String, _
   ByVal Attributes As FileAttribute)
```

The `SetAttr` subroutine sets the file attributes for the specified file or directory.

```
Public Function SPC(ByVal Count As Short) As SpcInfo
```

The `SPC` function is used with the `Print` and `PrintLine` subroutines to output a specified number of spaces in the output.

```
Public Function TAB() As TabInfo
Public Function TAB(ByVal Column As Short) As TabInfo
```

The TAB function is used with the Print and PrintLine subroutines to output one or more tab spaces in the output.

```
Public Sub Unlock(ByVal FileNumber As Integer)
Public Sub Unlock(ByVal FileNumber As Integer, ByVal Record As Long)
Public Sub Unlock(ByVal FileNumber As Integer, _
   ByVal FromRecord As Long, ByVal ToRecord As Long)
```

The Unlock subroutine allows other processes to access some or all of the specified file number. An Unlock call must exactly match a previous Lock call.

```
Public Sub Write(ByVal FileNumber As Integer, _
   ByVal ParamArray Output() As Object)
```

The Write subroutine outputs the information to the specified file number.

```
Public Sub WriteLine(ByVal FileNumber As Integer, _
   ByVal ParamArray Output() As Object)
```

The WriteLine subroutine outputs the information to the specified file number followed by a line feed.

Financial Module

The Financial module contains functions that perform useful financial calculations.

Historical

It may seem odd that the Visual Basic .NET runtime library contains financial functions, since the .NET Framework in general does not provide specialized financial functionality. Although the history is somewhat unclear, the financial functions are most likely a legacy of Visual Basic's use as Microsoft Excel's scripting language.

```
Public Function DDB(ByVal Cost As Double, ByVal Salvage As Double, _
    ByVal Life As Double, ByVal Period As Double, _
    Optional ByVal Factor As Double = 2.0) As Double
```

The DDB function calculates the depreciation of an asset for a specific time period using the double-declining balance method.

```
Public Function FV(ByVal Rate As Double, ByVal NPer As Double, _
    ByVal Pmt As Double, Optional ByVal PV As Double = 0, _
    Optional ByVal Due As DueDate = DueDate.EndOfPeriod) As Double
```

The FV function calculates the future value of an annuity based on periodic, fixed payments and a fixed interest rate.

```
Public Function IPmt(ByVal Rate As Double, ByVal Per As Double, _
    ByVal NPer As Double, ByVal PV As Double, _
    Optional ByVal FV As Double = 0, _
    Optional ByVal Due As DueDate = DueDate.EndOfPeriod) As Double
```

The IPmt function calculates the interest payment for a given period of an annuity based on periodic, fixed payments and a fixed interest rate.

```
Public Function IRR(ByRef ValueArray() As Double, _
    Optional ByVal Guess As Double - 0.1) As Double
```

The IRR function calculates the internal rate of return for a series of periodic cash flows (payments and receipts).

```
Public Function MIRR(ByRef ValueArray() As Double, _
    ByVal FinanceRate As Double, ByVal ReinvestRate As Double) As Double
```

The MIRR function calculates the modified internal rate of return for a series of periodic cash flows (payments and receipts).

```
Public Function NPer(ByVal Rate As Double, ByVal Pmt As Double, _
    ByVal PV As Double, Optional ByVal FV As Double = 0, _
    Optional ByVal Due As DueDate = DueDate.EndOfPeriod) As Double
```

The NPer function calculates the number of periods for an annuity based on periodic, fixed payments and a fixed interest rate.

```
Public Function NPV(ByVal Rate As Double, _
    ByRef ValueArray() As Double) As Double
```

The NPV function calculates the net present value of an investment based on a series of periodic cash flows (payments and receipts) and a discount rate.

```
Public Function Pmt(ByVal Rate As Double, ByVal NPer As Double, _
    ByVal PV As Double, Optional ByVal FV As Double = 0, _
    Optional ByVal Due As DueDate = DueDate.EndOfPeriod) As Double
```

The Pmt function calculates the payment for an annuity based on periodic, fixed payments and a fixed interest rate.

```
Public Function PPmt(ByVal Rate As Double, ByVal Per As Double, _
    ByVal NPer As Double, ByVal PV As Double, _
    Optional ByVal FV As Double = 0, _
    Optional ByVal Due As DueDate = DueDate.EndOfPeriod) As Double
```

The PPmt function calculates the principal payment for a given period of an annuity based on periodic, fixed payments and a fixed interest rate.

```
Public Function PV(ByVal Rate As Double, ByVal NPer As Double, _
    ByVal Pmt As Double, Optional ByVal FV As Double = 0, _
    Optional ByVal Due As DueDate = DueDate.EndOfPeriod) As Double
```

The PV function calculates the present value of an annuity based on periodic, fixed payments to be paid in the future and a fixed interest rate.

```
Public Function Rate(ByVal NPer As Double, ByVal Pmt As Double, _
    ByVal PV As Double, Optional ByVal FV As Double = 0, _
    Optional ByVal Due As DueDate = DueDate.EndOfPeriod, _
    Optional ByVal Guess As Double = 0.1) As Double
```

The Rate function calculates the interest rate per period for an annuity.

```
Public Function SLN(ByVal Cost As Double, ByVal Salvage As Double, _
    ByVal Life As Double) As Double
```

The SLN function calculates the straight-line depreciation of an asset for a single period.

```
Public Function SYD(ByVal Cost As Double, ByVal Salvage As Double, _
    ByVal Life As Double, ByVal Period As Double) As Double
```

The SYD function calculates the sum-of-years digits depreciation of an asset for a specified period.

FirstDayOfWeek Enumeration

The `FirstDayOfWeek` enumeration is used by functions in the `DateAnd-Time` module to indicate what day should be considered the first day of the week.

```
System = 0
```

The first day of the week is specified by the system settings at runtime. Equivalent constant: `vbUseSystemDayOfWeek`.

```
Sunday = 1
```

The first day of the week is Sunday. Equivalent constant: `vbSunday`.

```
Monday = 2
```

The first day of the week is Monday. Equivalent constant: `vbMonday`.

```
Tuesday = 3
```

The first day of the week is Tuesday. Equivalent constant: `vbTuesday`.

```
Wednesday = 4
```

The first day of the week is Wednesday. Equivalent constant: `vbWednesday`.

```
Thursday = 5
```

The first day of the week is Thursday. Equivalent constant: `vbThursday`.

```
Friday = 6
```

The first day of the week is Friday. Equivalent constant: `vbFriday`.

```
Saturday = 7
```

The first day of the week is Saturday. Equivalent constant: `vbSaturday`.

FirstWeekOfYear Enumeration

The `FirstWeekOfYear` enumeration is used by functions in the `DateAnd-Time` module to indicate what week should be considered the first week of the year.

```
System = 0
```

The first week of the year is specified by the system settings at runtime. Equivalent constant: `vbUseSystem`.

```
Jan1 = 1
```

The first week of the year is the first week that contains January 1. Equivalent constant: `vbFirstJan1`.

```
FirstFourDays = 2
```

The first week of the year is the first week that has at least four days. Equivalent constant: `vbFirstFourDays`.

```
FirstFullWeek = 3
```

The first week of the year is the first full week of the year. Equivalent constant: `vbFirstFullWeek`.

Globals Module

The `Globals` module contains functions that provide global information about the runtime environment.

```
Public ReadOnly Property ScriptEngine() As String
```

The `ScriptEngine` property returns the name of the current language. This will always return the string "VB".

```
Public ReadOnly Property ScriptEngineMajorVersion() As Integer
```

The `ScriptEngineMajorVersion` property returns the major version of the current language. For example, if the language version is 7.0, the major version is 7.

```
Public ReadOnly Property ScriptEngineMinorVersion() As Integer
```

The `ScriptEngineMinorVersion` property returns the minor version of the current language. For example, if the language version is 7.0, the minor version is 0.

```
Public ReadOnly Property ScriptEngineBuildVersion() As Integer
```

The `ScriptEngineBuildVersion` property returns the build version of the current language.

Information Module

The `Information` module contains functions that provide information about values and exceptions.

```
Public Function Erl() As Integer
```

The `Erl` function returns the number of the last numeric label before an exception occurred.

Compatibility

The `Erl` function is provided only for backward compatibility and should not be used. The method `System.Exception.StackTrace` provides more comprehensive information about where an exception occurred.

```
Public Function Err() As ErrObject
```

The `Err` function returns an object that contains information about the last exception that occurred.

```
Public Function IsArray(ByVal VarName As Object) As Boolean
```

The `IsArray` function returns whether the value passed in is an array reference.

```
Public Function IsDate(ByVal Expression As Object) As Boolean
```

The `IsDate` function returns whether the value passed in is a `Date` value.

```
Public Function IsDBNull(ByVal Expression As Object) As Boolean
```

The `IsDBNull` function returns whether the value passed in is `System.DBNull.Value`.

```
Public Function IsNothing(ByVal Expression As Object) As Boolean
```

The `IsNothing` function returns whether the value passed in is `Nothing`.

```
Public Function IsError(ByVal Expression As Object) As Boolean
```

The `IsError` function returns whether the value passed in is an exception (i.e., inherits from `System.Exception`).

```
Public Function IsReference(ByVal Expression As Object) As Boolean
```

The `IsReference` function returns whether the value passed in is a reference.

```
Public Function IsNumeric(ByVal Expression As Object) As Boolean
```

The `IsNumeric` function returns whether the value passed in is a numeric value. If the value passed in is a string, this function determines whether the string can be converted to a numeric value.

```
Public Function LBound(ByVal Array As System.Array, _
    Optional ByVal Rank As Integer = 1) As Integer
```

The `LBound` function returns the lower bound of the specified rank of the given array.

```
Public Function QBColor(ByVal Color As Integer) As Integer
```

The QBColor function returns the RGB color code corresponding to the specified QuickBasic color code.

Historical

It is a reasonable question why this function still exists in Visual Basic .NET. Unfortunately, there is no good answer to that question!

```
Public Function RGB(ByVal Red As Integer, ByVal Green As Integer, _
    ByVal Blue As Integer) As Integer
```

The RGB function returns the RGB color code corresponding to the specified red, green, and blue values. Although the three parameters are typed as Integer, each value must be between 0 and 255.

```
Public Function SystemTypeName(ByVal VbName As String) As String
```

The SystemTypeName function returns the .NET Framework type name for a Visual Basic .NET fundamental type. For example, SystemTypeName("Integer") returns the string System.Int32.

```
Public Function TypeName(ByVal VarName As Object) As String
```

The TypeName function returns the fully qualified name of the type of the value passed in.

```
Public Function UBound(ByVal Array As System.Array, _
    Optional ByVal Rank As Integer = 1) As Integer
```

The UBound function returns the upper bound of the specified rank of the given array.

Performance

If the array is one-dimensional, it is often faster to use the Length property of the array to calculate the upper bound. For example, the expression a.Length - 1 may be faster than the expression UBound(a).

```
Public Function VarType(ByVal VarName As Object) As VariantType
```

The `VarType` function returns the equivalent COM `Variant` type of the given value.

```
Public Function VbTypeName(ByVal UrtName As String) As String
```

The `VbTypeName` function returns the Visual Basic .NET fundamental type name, if any, for a .NET Framework type. For example, `VbType-Name("System.Int32")` returns the string `Integer`.

Interaction Module

The `Interaction` module contains subroutines and functions that assist in interacting with the runtime environment.

```
Public Sub AppActivate(ByVal ProcessId As Integer)
Public Sub AppActivate(ByVal Title As String)
```

The `AppActivate` subroutine switches the active application on the desktop to the specified application. The argument can be either the `Integer` process ID of the process to switch to or the title of the window.

```
Public Sub Beep()
```

The `Beep` subroutine makes a lovely sound through the computer's speakers.

```
Public Function CallByName(ByVal ObjectRef As Object, _
    ByVal ProcName As String, ByVal UseCallType As CallType, _
    ByVal ParamArray Args() As Object) As Object
```

The `CallByName` function simulates a late-bound method call or a late-bound index. The `ObjectRef` parameter is the instance on which the call will be made. The `ProcName` parameter specifies the name of the method to call (this parameter should be `Nothing` to call the default property). The `UseCallType` parameter specifies the type of call to be made, and the `Args` parameter array specifies the arguments to pass to the call. The function returns the value returned by the call.

```
Public Function Choose(ByVal Index As Double, _
    ByVal ParamArray Choice() As Object) As Object
```

The Choose function selects and returns a value from among the parameter array. The Index parameter indicates which of the parameters to return.

```
Public Function Command() As String
```

The Command function returns the argument portion of the command line used to start the current program.

```
Public Function CreateObject(ByVal ProgId As String, _
    Optional ByVal ServerName As String = "") As Object
```

The CreateObject function creates and returns a reference to a COM object. The ProgId parameter specifies the type of COM object to create, and the ServerName parameter specifies the name of the network server where the object should be created (an empty string specifies that the local machine should be used).

> **▪ NOTE**
>
> To create a .NET Framework object at runtime, you can use the function System.Activator.CreateInstance.

```
Public Sub DeleteSetting(ByVal AppName As String, _
    Optional ByVal Section As String = Nothing, _
    Optional ByVal Key As String = Nothing)
```

The DeleteSetting subroutine deletes a section or a key from the application's section in the Windows registry.

```
Public Function Environ(ByVal Expression As Integer) As String
Public Function Environ(ByVal Expression As String) As String
```

The Environ function returns the value of the specified environment variable. If Expression is an Integer, the variable is fetched by position. If Expression is a String, the variable is fetched by name.

```
Public Function GetAllSettings(ByVal AppName As String, _
    ByVal Section As String) As String(,)
```

The GetAllSettings function returns all the values from an application's section in the Windows registry. The return value is a two-dimensional array of keys and settings.

```
Public Function GetObject(Optional ByVal PathName As String = Nothing, _
    Optional ByVal [Class] As String = Nothing) As Object
```

The GetObject function returns a reference to an object provided by a COM component. The PathName parameter specifies the path from which to load the object. If PathName is not specified, the Class parameter must be specified. The Class parameter specifies the class of the object to load.

```
Public Function GetSetting(ByVal AppName As String, _
    ByVal Section As String, ByVal Key As String, _
    Optional ByVal [Default] As String = "") As String
```

The GetSetting function returns the value of a specified key from the application's section in the Windows registry.

```
Public Function IIf(ByVal Expression As Boolean, _
    ByVal TruePart As Object, ByVal FalsePart As Object) As Object
```

The IIf function returns a value based on a Boolean expression. (IIf stands for "Immediate If.") If Expression is True, IIf returns the TruePart parameter. If Expression is False, IIf returns the FalsePart parameter.

> **■ NOTE**
>
> IIf does not short-circuit. Both the TruePart and FalsePart expressions will be evaluated, regardless of the value of Expression.

```
Public Function InputBox(ByVal Prompt As String, _
    Optional ByVal Title As String = "", _
    Optional ByVal DefaultResponse As String = "", _
    Optional ByVal XPos As Integer = -1, _
    Optional ByVal YPos As Integer = -1) As String
```

The InputBox function displays a prompt, waits for the user to input text or click a button, and then returns a string containing the contents of the text box.

```
Public Function MsgBox(ByVal Prompt As Object, _
    Optional ByVal Buttons As MsgBoxStyle = MsgBoxStyle.OKOnly, _
    Optional ByVal Title As Object = Nothing) As MsgBoxResult
```

The MsgBox displays a message, waits for the user to click a button, and then returns which button the user clicked.

```
Public Function Partition(ByVal Number As Long, ByVal Start As Long, _
    ByVal [Stop] As Long, ByVal Interval As Long) As String
```

The Partition function returns a string that represents the calculated range that contains a number.

```
Public Sub SaveSetting(ByVal AppName As String, _
    ByVal Section As String, ByVal Key As String, ByVal Setting As String)
```

The SaveSetting function sets a key value in the application's section in the Windows registry.

```
Public Function Shell(ByVal Pathname As String, _
    Optional ByVal Style As AppWinStyle = AppWinStyle.MinimizedFocus, _
    Optional ByVal Wait As Boolean = False, _
    Optional ByVal Timeout As Integer - -1) As Integer
```

The Shell function starts a new process and returns the new process's ID, if it is still running.

```
Public Function Switch(ByVal ParamArray VarExpr() As Object) As Object
```

The Switch function returns the first parameter in the parameter array that evaluates to True. The parameter array must contain a set of paired values: The first value specifies the True/False value, and the second value is the value to return if the first value is True.

MsgBoxResult Enumeration

The MsgBoxResult enumeration is used by the MsgBox function in the Interaction module to indicate which button in a message box was pressed.

```
OK = 1
```

The OK button was pressed. Constant equivalent: vbOK.

```
Cancel = 2
```

The Cancel button was pressed. Constant equivalent: vbCancel.

```
Abort = 3
```

The Abort button was pressed. Constant equivalent: vbAbort.

```
Retry = 4
```

The Retry button was pressed. Constant equivalent: vbRetry.

```
Ignore = 5
```

The Ignore button was pressed. Constant equivalent: vbIgnore.

```
Yes = 6
```

The Yes button was pressed. Constant equivalent: vbYes.

```
No = 7
```

The No button was pressed. Constant equivalent: vbNo.

MsgBoxStyle Enumeration

The MsgBoxStyle enumeration is used by the MsgBox function in the Interaction module to indicate the look and behavior of the message box. The values in the MsgBoxStyle enumeration are flags, and one flag from each group can be combined.

Button Flags

```
OKOnly = 0
```

The OK button should be shown. Constant equivalent: vbOKOnly.

```
OKCancel = 1
```

The OK and Cancel buttons should be shown. Constant equivalent: `vbOKCancel`.

```
AbortRetryIgnore = 2
```

The Abort, Retry, and Ignore buttons should be shown. Constant equivalent: `vbAbortRetryIgnore`.

```
YesNoCancel = 3
```

The Yes, No, and Cancel buttons should be shown. Constant equivalent: `vbYesNoCancel`.

```
YesNo = 4
```

The Yes and No buttons should be shown. Constant equivalent: `vbYesNo`.

```
RetryCancel = 5
```

The Retry and Cancel buttons should be shown. Constant equivalent: `vbRetryCancel`.

Icon Flags

```
Critical = 16
```

The Critical icon should be shown. Constant equivalent: `vbCritical`.

```
Question = 32
```

The Question icon should be shown. Constant equivalent: `vbQuestion`.

```
Exclamation = 48
```

The Exclamation icon should be shown. Constant equivalent: `vbExclamation`.

```
Information = 64
```

The Information icon should be shown. Constant equivalent: `vbInformation`.

Default Button Flags

```
DefaultButton1 = 0
```

The first button should be the default button. Constant equivalent: vbDefaultButton1.

```
DefaultButton2 = 256
```

The second button should be the default button. Constant equivalent: vbDefaultButton2.

```
DefaultButton3 = 512
```

The third button should be the default button. Constant equivalent: vbDefaultButton3.

Message Box Behavior Flags

```
ApplicationModal = 0
```

The message box should be application modal. Constant equivalent: vbApplicationModal.

```
SystemModal = 4096
```

The message box should be system modal. Constant equivalent: vbSystemModal.

Miscellaneous Flags

```
MsgBoxHelp = 16384
```

The message box should have a Help button. Constant equivalent: vbMsgBoxHelp.

```
MsgBoxRight = 524288
```

The message box text should be right justified. Constant equivalent: vbMsgBoxRight.

```
MsgBoxRtlReading = 1048576
```

The message box text is right-to-left on Hebrew and Arabic systems. Constant equivalent: vbMsgBoxRtlReading.

```
MsgBoxSetForeground = 65536
```

The message box should be the foreground window. Constant equivalent: vbSetForeground.

OpenAccess Enumeration

The OpenAccess enumeration is used by the FileOpen method in the FileSystem module to indicate what access should be used when opening a file. The OpenAccess enumeration values have no constant equivalents.

```
Default = -1
```

Reads and writes should be permitted.

```
Read = 1
```

Only reads should be permitted.

```
ReadWrite = 3
```

Reads and writes should be permitted.

```
Write = 2
```

Only writes should be permitted.

OpenMode Enumeration

The OpenMode enumeration is used by the FileOpen and FileAttr methods in the FileSystem module to indicate the way in which the file will be used. The OpenMode enumeration values have no constant equivalents.

```
Input = 1
```

The file will be used for input.

```
Output = 2
```

The file will be used for output.

```
Random = 4
```

The file will be used for random access.

```
Append = 8
```

The file will be used to append output to the file.

```
Binary = 32
```

The file will be used for binary reads and writes.

OpenShare Enumeration

The OpenShare enumeration is used by the FileOpen method in the FileSystem module to indicate the permitted sharing for the file. The OpenShare enumeration values have no constant equivalents.

```
Default = -1
```

The file is shared for reading and writing.

```
Shared = 3
```

The file is shared for reading and writing.

```
LockRead = 2
```

The file is locked for reading. Other processes cannot read from the file.

```
LockReadWrite = 0
```

The file is locked for reading and writing. Other processes cannot read from or write to the file.

```
LockWrite = 1
```

The file is locked for writing. Other processes cannot write to the file.

Strings Module

The `Strings` module contains functions useful for manipulating string values.

```
Public Function Asc(ByVal [String] As Char) As Integer
Public Function Asc(ByVal [String] As String) As Integer
```

The `Asc` function returns the ASCII value of the character or the first character in the string.

> **■ NOTE**
> The ASCII value returned depends on the current ASCII codepage being used by the current thread.

```
Public Function AscW(ByVal [String] As String) As Integer
Public Function AscW(ByVal [String] As Char) As Integer
```

The `AscW` function returns the Unicode value of the character or the first character in the string.

```
Public Function Chr(ByVal CharCode As Integer) As Char
```

The `Chr` function returns a character representing the given ASCII character value.

> **■ NOTE**
> The ASCII value returned depends on the current ASCII codepage being used by the current thread.

```
Public Function ChrW(ByVal CharCode As Integer) As Char
```

The `ChrW` function returns a character representing the given Unicode character value.

```
Public Function Filter(ByVal Source() As Object, _
```

```
      ByVal Match As String, Optional ByVal Include As Boolean = True, _
      Optional ByVal Compare As CompareMethod = CompareMethod.Binary) _
      As String()
   Public Function Filter(ByVal Source() As String, _
      ByVal Match As String, Optional ByVal Include As Boolean = True, _
      Optional ByVal Compare As CompareMethod = CompareMethod.Binary) _
      As String()
```

The `Filter` function returns a one-dimensional array of strings representing the members of the `Source` array filtered on the `Match` parameter. If `Include` is `True`, the array contains all elements of `Source` that contain `Match` as a substring. If `Include` is `False`, the array contains all elements of `Source` that do not contain `Match` as a substring.

```
   Public Function Format(ByVal Expression As Object, _
      Optional ByVal Style As String = "") As String
```

The `Format` function formats a value based on the specified format string. See Format Strings at the end of this section for more information on format strings.

```
   Public Function FormatCurrency(ByVal Expression As Object, _
      Optional ByVal NumDigitsAfterDecimal As Integer = -1, _
      Optional ByVal IncludeLeadingDigit As TriState = _
        TriState.UseDefault, _
      Optional ByVal UseParensForNegativeNumbers As TriState = _
        TriState.UseDefault, _
      Optional ByVal GroupDigits As TriState = TriState.UseDefault) _
      As String
```

The `FormatCurrency` function formats a value into a currency string. The currency format used is the current system currency format at runtime.

```
   Public Function FormatDate(ByVal Expression As Date, _
      Optional ByVal NamedFormat As DateFormat = DateFormat.GeneralDate) _
      As String
```

The `FormatDate` function formats a value based on the specified date format.

```
   Public Function FormatNumber(ByVal Expression As Object, _
      Optional ByVal NumDigitsAfterDecimal As Integer = -1, _
      Optional ByVal IncludeLeadingDigit As TriState = _
        TriState.UseDefault, _
```

```
    Optional ByVal UseParensForNegativeNumbers As TriState = _
      TriState.UseDefault, _
    Optional ByVal GroupDigits As TriState = TriState.UseDefault) _
    As String
```

The `FormatNumber` function formats a value into a number string. The number format used is the current system number format at runtime.

```
Public Function FormatPercent(ByVal Expression As Object, _
    Optional ByVal NumDigitsAfterDecimal As Integer = -1, _
    Optional ByVal IncludeLeadingDigit As TriState = _
      TriState.UseDefault, _
    Optional ByVal UseParensForNegativeNumbers As TriState = _
      TriState.UseDefault, _
    Optional ByVal GroupDigits As TriState = TriState.UseDefault) _
    As String
```

The `FormatPercent` function formats a value into a percentage string. The number format used is the current system number format at runtime.

```
Public Function GetChar(ByVal str As String, ByVal Index As Integer) _
    As Char
```

The `GetChar` function returns the character position specified by `Index`.

```
Public Function InStr(ByVal String1 As String, _
    ByVal String2 As String, _
    Optional ByVal Compare As CompareMethod = CompareMethod.Binary) _
    As Integer
Public Function InStr(ByVal Start As Integer, _
    ByVal String1 As String, ByVal String2 As String, _
    Optional ByVal Compare As CompareMethod = CompareMethod.Binary) _
    As Integer
```

The `InStr` function returns an `Integer` specifying the start position of the first occurrence of one string within another.

```
Public Function InStrRev(ByVal StringCheck As String, _
    ByVal StringMatch As String, Optional ByVal Start As Integer = -1, _
    Optional ByVal Compare As CompareMethod = CompareMethod.Binary) _
    As Integer
```

The `InStrRev` function returns an `Integer` specifying the start position of the last occurrence of one string within another.

```
Public Function Join(ByVal SourceArray() As Object, _
   Optional ByVal Delimiter As String = " ") As String
Public Function Join(ByVal SourceArray() As String, _
   Optional ByVal Delimiter As String = " ") As String
```

The `Join` function returns a string that represents the concatenation of all the values passed in. If `Delimiter` is supplied, the string is used to separate each value in the string.

```
Public Function LCase(ByVal Value As String) As String
Public Function LCase(ByVal Value As Char) As Char
```

The `LCase` function converts a string into all lowercase.

```
Public Function Left(ByVal str As String, ByVal Length As Integer) _
   As String
```

The `Left` function returns the specified number of characters in the string, starting from the beginning of the string.

```
Public Function Len(ByVal Expression As String) As Integer
Public Function Len(ByVal Expression As Byte) As Integer
Public Function Len(ByVal Expression As Char) As Integer
Public Function Len(ByVal Expression As Int16) As Integer
Public Function Len(ByVal Expression As Int32) As Integer
Public Function Len(ByVal Expression As Int64) As Integer
Public Function Len(ByVal Expression As Single) As Integer
Public Function Len(ByVal Expression As Double) As Integer
Public Function Len(ByVal Expression As Boolean) As Integer
Public Function Len(ByVal Expression As Decimal) As Integer
Public Function Len(ByVal Expression As Date) As Integer
Public Function Len(ByVal Expression As Object) As Integer
```

The `Len` function returns the number of characters required to store the value in a file using the functions in the `FileSystem` module.

```
Public Function LSet(ByVal Source As String, ByVal Length As Integer) _
   As String
```

The `LSet` function returns a string of the specified length. If the `Source` parameter is less than `Length` characters long, the returned string is padded at the end with spaces.

```
Public Function LTrim(ByVal str As String) As String
```

The `LTrim` function returns the `str` parameter with all leading spaces removed.

```
Public Function Mid(ByVal str As String, ByVal Start As Integer) _
   As String
Public Function Mid(ByVal str As String, ByVal Start As Integer, _
   ByVal Length As Integer) As String
```

The `Mid` function returns the specified number of characters from the middle of a string. If no `Length` parameter is specified, the rest of the string is returned.

It is also possible to use the `Mid` function to assign a string into another string. The following example prints the string `abxxef`.

```
Dim s As String = "abcdef"

Mid(s, 3, 2) = "xx"
Console.WriteLine(s)
```

When `Mid` assignment is done, the string value on the right-hand side of the assignment replaces the characters in the right-hand side string indicated by the `Start` and `Length` parameters of the function. Only the number of characters in the right-hand side string is replaced, and no more than the number of characters selected by the `Mid` function are replaced.

Style

In previous versions of Visual Basic, `Mid` assignment could be faster than using `Left`, `Mid`, and `Right` to compose a new string. However, in Visual Basic .NET, there is no performance advantage to `Mid` assignment. The `System.Text.StringBuilder` class can be used instead when changes need to be made to a string and performance is important.

```
Public Function Replace(ByVal Expression As String, _
   ByVal Find As String, ByVal Replacement As String, _
   Optional ByVal Start As Integer = 1, _
   Optional ByVal Count As Integer = -1, _
```

```
        Optional ByVal Compare As CompareMethod = CompareMethod.Binary) _
        As String
```

The `Replace` function returns a string in which a specified substring has been replaced with another substring a specified number of times.

```
    Public Function Right(ByVal str As String, ByVal Length As Integer) _
        As String
```

The `Right` function returns the specified number of characters in the string, starting from the end of the string.

```
    Public Function RSet(ByVal Source As String, ByVal Length As Integer) _
        As String
```

The `RSet` function returns a string of the specified length. If the `Source` parameter is less than `Length` characters long, the returned string is padded at the beginning with spaces.

```
    Public Function RTrim(ByVal str As String) As String
```

The `RTrim` function returns the `str` parameter with all trailing spaces removed.

```
    Public Function Space(ByVal Number As Integer) As String
```

The `Space` function returns a string consisting of the specified number of spaces.

```
    Public Function Split(ByVal Expression As String, _
        Optional ByVal Delimiter As String = " ", _
        Optional ByVal Limit As Integer = -1, _
        Optional ByVal Compare As CompareMethod = CompareMethod.Binary) _
        As String()
```

The `Split` function returns an array of substrings that represent the partitioning of the original string. The original string is partitioned based on the `Delimiter` parameter. The `Limit` parameter determines how many substrings will be returned.

```
    Public Function StrComp(ByVal String1 As String, _
        ByVal String2 As String, _
```

```
    Optional ByVal Compare As CompareMethod = CompareMethod.Binary) _
    As Integer
```

The `StrComp` function compares two strings using the alphanumeric sort values of the corresponding character of each string. If `String1` sorts before `String2`, the function returns –1. If `String1` sorts after `String2`, the function returns 1. If the two strings sort the same, the function returns 0.

```
Public Function StrConv(ByVal str As String, _
    ByVal Conversion As VbStrConv, _
    Optional ByVal LocaleID As Integer = 0) As String
```

The `StrConv` function converts the specified string into a new string using the specified conversion and locale.

```
Public Function StrDup(ByVal Number As Integer, _
    ByVal Character As Object) As Object
Public Function StrDup(ByVal Number As Integer, _
    ByVal Character As Char) As String
Public Function StrDup(ByVal Number As Integer, _
    ByVal Character As String) As String
```

The `StrDup` function returns a string that consists of the given character repeated a specified number of times.

```
Public Function StrReverse(ByVal Expression As String) As String
```

The `StrReverse` function returns a string that is the reverse of the specified string.

```
Public Function Trim(ByVal str As String) As String
```

The `Trim` function returns the `str` parameter with all leading and trailing spaces removed.

```
Public Function UCase(ByVal Value As String) As String
Public Function UCase(ByVal Value As Char) As Char
```

The `UCase` function converts a string into all uppercase.

Format Strings

A format string controls how the Format function formats a value into a string. By default, an empty format string will convert the value to a string using the current regional settings of the computer at runtime. Format also has a set of predefined formats that can be used to format values in a standard way. And, finally, user-defined formats can be composed using special characters.

Predefined Formats

The predefined formats are *named* formats. To use a predefined format, you supply the name of the format as the Style parameter of the Format function. Tables A-2 through A-4 list the predefined formats.

TABLE A-2: Numeric Predefined Formats

Format Name	Description
"General Number", "G", or "g"	Displays a number with no thousands separator.
"Currency", "C", or "c"	Displays a number as a currency value, using the current regional settings.
"Fixed", "F", or "f"	Displays a number with at least one digit to the left of a decimal point and at least two digits to the right of a decimal point.
"Standard", "N", or "n"	Displays a number in the same format as the Fixed format, except that a thousands separator will be used if needed.
"Percent"	Displays a number as a percentage with the percentage sign.
"P" or "p"	Displays a number in the same format as the Percent format, except that a thousands separator will be used if needed.
"Scientific"	Displays a number in scientific format with two significant digits.
"E" or "e"	Displays a number in scientific format with six significant digits.
"D" or "d"	Displays a number as a whole decimal (base 10) number.
"X" or "x"	Displays a number as a whole hexadecimal (base 16) number.

TABLE A-3: Date/Time Predefined Formats

Format Name	Description
"General Date" or "G"	Displays a date and time using the current general date regional setting.
"Long Date" or "D"	Displays a date using the current long date regional setting.
"Medium Date"	Displays a date using a medium date format.
"Short Date" or "d"	Displays a date using the current short date regional setting.
"Long Time" or "T"	Displays a time using the current long time regional setting.
"Medium Time"	Displays a time in a 12-hour format with hours, minutes, seconds, and an AM/PM designator.
"Short Time" or "t"	Displays a time using the 24-hour format.
"f"	Displays a date and time using the long date and short time regional settings.
"F"	Displays a date and time using the long date and long time regional settings.
"g"	Displays a date and time using the short date and long time regional settings.
"M" or "m"	Displays the month and day of a date value.
"R" or "r"	Displays a date and time as Greenwich Mean Time (GMT).
"s"	Displays a date and time as a sortable index.
"u"	Displays a date and time as a GMT sortable index.
"U"	Displays a date and time as GMT using the long date and long time regional settings.
"Y" or "y"	Displays the year and month of a date value.

TABLE A-4: Other Predefined Formats

Format Name	Description
"Yes/No"	Displays "No" if the value is 0, "Yes" otherwise.
"True/False"	Displays "False" if the value is 0, "True" otherwise.
"On/Off"	Displays "Off" if the value is 0, "On" otherwise.

User-Defined Formats

A user-defined format string uses special characters to indicate how the value should be formatted. Tables A-5 and A-6 list the characters that can be used to create format strings.

These are some examples of user-defined numeric format strings.

```
Format(10, "")                      ' Result:10
Format(41, "000")                   ' Result: 041
Format(3.5, "0.00")                 ' Result: 3.50
Format(35, "#,##0")                 ' Result: 35
Format(1000, "#,##0")               ' Result: 1,000
Format(1394.34, "$#,##0.00")        ' Result: $1394.34
Format(.124, "0.00%")               ' Result: 12.40%
Format(.124, "0.00E-00")            ' Result: 1.24E-01
```

TABLE A-5: Numeric User-Defined Format Characters

Character	Description
None	Displays a number.
0	Displays a digit, or a zero if there is no matching digit.
#	Displays a digit, or nothing if there is no matching digit.
.	Displays a decimal point using the current regional setting. This character determines where characters to the right and to the left of the decimal point begin and end.
%	Displays a percentage sign and formats the number as a percentage.
,	Displays a thousands separator, if needed, using the current regional setting.

TABLE A-6: Date/Time User-Defined Format Characters

Character	Description
:	Displays a time separator using the current regional setting.
d or %d	Displays the day as a number without a leading zero.
dd	Displays the day as a number with a leading zero.
ddd	Displays the day as an abbreviated day of the week (for example, "Sun") using the current regional setting.
dddd	Displays the day as a day of the week (for example, "Sunday") using the current regional setting.
M or %M	Displays the month as a number without a leading zero.
MM	Displays the month as a number with a leading zero.
MMM	Displays the month as an abbreviated month name (for example, "Jan") using the current regional setting.
MMMM	Displays the month as a month name (for example, "January") using the current regional setting.
gg	Displays the period/era string of the date (for example, "A.D.").
h or %h	Displays the hour as a number without leading zeros.
hh	Displays the hour as a number with leading zeros using the 12-hour clock.
H or %H	Displays the hour as a number without leading zeros using the 24-hour clock.
HH	Displays the hour as a number with leading zeros using the 24-hour clock.
m or %m	Displays the minute as a number without leading zeros.
mm	Displays the minute as a number with leading zeros.
s or %s	Displays the seconds as a number without leading zeros.

continues

TABLE A-6: Date/Time User-Defined Format Characters (*continued*)

Character	Description
ss	Displays the seconds as a number with leading zeros.
f, ff, fff, etc., or %f	Displays the fractions of seconds. Each "f" represents a decimal place (so "f" is tenths of a second, "ff" is hundredths of a second, and so on). Up to seven f's can be used.
t or %t	Displays "a" for hours before noon, "p" for hours after noon but before midnight.
tt	Displays "AM" for hours before noon, "PM" for hours after noon but before midnight.
y or %y	Displays the year number (0–9) without leading zeros.
yy	Displays the year in two-digit numeric format with a leading zero.
yyy	Displays the year in four-digit numeric format without leading zeros.
yyyy	Displays the year in four-digit numeric format with leading zeros.
z or %z	Displays the time zone offset without a leading zero.
zz	Displays the time zone offset with a leading zero.
zzz	Displays the full time zone offset.

These are some examples of user-defined date format strings.

```
Format(#8/23/70 3:43:12AM#, "M/d/yy")     ' Result: 8/23/70
Format(#8/23/70 3:43:12AM#, "d-MMM")      ' Result: 23-Aug
Format(#8/23/70 3:43:12AM#, "d-MMMM-yy")  ' Result: 23-August-1970
Format(#8/23/70 3:43:12AM#, "d MMMM")     ' Result: 23 August
Format(#8/23/70 3:43:12AM#, "MMMM yy")    ' Result: August 70
Format(#8/23/70 3:43:12AM#, "hh:mm tt")   ' Result: 03:43 AM
Format(#8/23/70 3:43:12AM#, "h:mm:ss")    ' Result: 3:43:12
```

Within a format string, the backslash character (\) causes the next character to be put into the output instead of being interpreted as a format character. The backslash itself is not displayed. (To display a backslash, you have to use two backslashes.) For example:

```
' Result is: Phone # is 206-555-1212
Format(2065551212, "Phone \# is: ###-###-####")
' Result is: C:\Test10.txt
Format(10, "C\:\\Test10\.txt")
```

Strings in quotation marks are also copied directly into the output. The quotes themselves are not displayed. (To display a double quote character, you must precede it by a backslash.) For example:

```
' Result is: Phone # is 206-555-1212
Format(2065551212, "Phone ""#"" is: ###-###-####")
' Result is: The value is "10".
Format(10, "The value is \""##\""\.")
```

Numeric formats can format differently based on the value of the number being formatted. If the format string has two formats separated by a semicolon, the first format applies to values equal to or greater than zero, while the second format applies to values less than zero. If the format string has three formats separated by semicolons, the first format applies to positive values, the second format applies to negative values, and the third format applies to zero values. If a format string with three formats omits the second format, the first format is used for both positive and negative numbers. For example:

```
Format(1234, "$#,##0;($#,##0)")              ' Result: $1,234
Format(-1234, "$#,##0;($#,##0)")             ' Result: ($1,234)
Format(1234, "$#,##0;($#,##0);\Z\e\r\o")     ' Result: $1,234
Format(0, "$#,##0;($#,##0);\Z\e\r\o")        ' Result: Zero
Format(1234, "$#,##0;;\Z\e\r\o")             ' Result: $1,234
Format(0, "$#,##0;;\Z\e\r\o")                ' Result: Zero
```

TriState Enumeration

The `TriState` enumeration is used by parameters that are `Boolean` but can have a default setting.

```
False = 0
```

The value is `False`. Constant equivalent: `vbFalse`.

```
True = -1
```

The value is `True`. Constant equivalent: `vbTrue`.

```
UseDefault = -2
```

The value is the default value. Constant equivalent: `vbUseDefault`.

VariantType Enumeration

The `VariantType` enumeration is used by the `VarType` function in the `Information` module to indicate the equivalent COM `Variant` type of a value.

```
Empty = 0
```

Equivalent to the `Variant` type Empty. Constant equivalent: `vbEmpty`.

```
Null = 1
```

Equivalent to the `Variant` type Null. Constant equivalent: `vbNull`.

```
Short = 2
```

Equivalent to the `Variant` type Short. Constant equivalent: `vbShort`.

```
Integer = 3
```

Equivalent to the `Variant` type Integer. Constant equivalent: `vbInteger`.

```
Single = 4
```

Equivalent to the `Variant` type Single. Constant equivalent: `vbSingle`.

```
Double = 5
```

Equivalent to the `Variant` type Double. Constant equivalent: `vbDouble`.

```
Currency = 6
```

Equivalent to the `Variant` type Currency. Constant equivalent: `vbCurrency`.

```
Date = 7
```

Equivalent to the `Variant` type Date. Constant equivalent: `vbDate`.

```
String = 8
```

Equivalent to the `Variant` type String. Constant equivalent: `vbString`.

```
Object = 9
```

Equivalent to the `Variant` type Object. Constant equivalent: `vbObject`.

```
Error = 10
```

Equivalent to the `Variant` type Error. Constant equivalent: `vbError`.

```
Boolean = 11
```

Equivalent to the `Variant` type Boolean. Constant equivalent: `vbBoolean`.

```
Variant = 12
```

Equivalent to the `Variant` type Variant. Constant equivalent: `vbVariant`.

```
DataObject = 13
```

Equivalent to the `Variant` type DataObject. Constant equivalent: `vbDataObject`.

```
Decimal = 14
```

Equivalent to the `Variant` type Decimal. Constant equivalent: `vbDecimal`.

```
Byte = 17
```

Equivalent to the `Variant` type Byte. Constant equivalent: `vbByte`.

```
Char = 18
```

Equivalent to the `Variant` type Char. Constant equivalent: `vbChar`.

```
Long = 20
```

Equivalent to the `Variant` type Long. Constant equivalent: `vbLong`.

```
UserDefinedType = 36
```

Equivalent to the `Variant` type UserDefinedType. Constant equivalent: `vbUserDefinedType`.

```
Array = 8192
```

Equivalent to a SafeArray of the specified type. Constant equivalent: `vbArray`.

VbStrConv Enumeration

The `VbStrConv` enumeration indicates the type of string conversion the `StrConv` function in the `Strings` module should do. The members of the `VbStrConv` enumeration are flags and can be combined.

```
None = 0
```

No conversion is to be performed.

```
UpperCase = 1
```

The string should be converted to uppercase. Constant equivalent: `vbUpperCase`.

```
LowerCase = 2
```

The string should be converted to lowercase. Constant equivalent: `vbLowerCase`.

```
ProperCase = 3
```

The first letter of every word in the string should be converted to upper-case. Constant equivalent: `vbProperCase`.

```
Wide = 4
```

Single-byte characters should be converted to double-byte characters. Constant equivalent: `vbWide`.

```
Narrow = 8
```

Double-byte characters should be converted to single byte characters. Constant equivalent: `vbNarrow`.

```
Katakana = 16
```

Hiragana characters in the string should be converted to Katakana characters. Applies to Japanese locale only. Constant equivalent: `vbKatakana`.

```
Hiragana = 32
```

Katakana characters in the string should be converted to Hiragana characters. Applies to Japanese locale only. Constant equivalent: `vbHiragana`.

```
SimplifiedChinese = 256
```

The string should be converted to Simplified Chinese characters. Constant equivalent: `vbSimplifiedChinese`.

```
TraditionalChinese = 512
```

The string should be converted to Traditional Chinese characters. Constant equivalent: `vbTraditionalChinese`.

```
LinguisticCasing = 1024
```

The string should be converted from file system rules for casing to linguistic rules. Constant equivalent: `vbLinguisticCasing`.

VBMath Module

The VBMath module contains useful mathematical functions and subroutines.

Compatibility

Most of the members of the Math module in previous versions of Visual Basic have moved to the System.Math class.

```
Public Sub Randomize()
Public Sub Randomize(ByVal Number As Double)
```

The Randomize subroutine seeds the Rnd function's random number generator. If a seed is not specified, the current time is used as the seed.

```
Public Function Rnd() As Single
Public Function Rnd(ByVal Number As Single) As Single
```

The Rnd function returns a random floating-point number greater than or equal to 0, but less than 1. If the Number argument is supplied, the behavior of the function depends on the value of Number. If Number is less than 0, Rnd returns a random number using Number as the seed. If Number is 0, Rnd returns the most recent random number returned by Rnd. If Number is greater than 0, Rnd returns a new random number. To produce a random number between a lower bound (e.g., 0) and an upper bound (e.g., 10), you can use the expression CInt(Int((upperbound - lowerbound + 1) * Rnd() + lowerbound)).

■ NOTE

The .NET Framework class System.Random can also be used to generate random numbers. The Rnd function and the Random class use different random number generation algorithms, so each one will generate a different sequence of random numbers, given the same starting seed.

VBFixedArrayAttribute Attribute

The VBFixedArrayAttribute attribute is used to ensure that files written using the FileSystem methods are compatible with previous versions of Visual Basic. A fixed-size array in previous versions of Visual Basic was an array declared with a size in a user-defined type.

```
Type Team
  Members(10) As String
End Type
```

This example shows a user-defined type with a fixed-size array of strings in it. When a user-defined type with a fixed-size array was written to disk, it included a special header containing the size of the array. For the array to be read properly in Visual Basic .NET, the corresponding class or structure has to specify the VBFixedArrayAttribute.

```
Class Team
  <VBFixedArrayAttribute(10)> Public Members() As String
End Class

Module Test
  Sub Main()
    Dim x As Team

    FileOpen(FileNum, "team.txt", OpenMode.Binary, _
      OpenAccess.Write, OpenShare.Default)
    FileGet(1, x)
    FileClose(1)
  End Sub
End Module

Public ReadOnly Property Bounds() As Integer()
```

The Bounds property returns a one-dimensional array of the upper bounds of each dimension.

```
Public ReadOnly Property Length() As Integer
```

The Length property returns the number of dimensions of the fixed-size array.

```
Public Sub New(ByVal UpperBound1 As Integer)
Public Sub New(ByVal UpperBound1 As Integer, _
  ByVal UpperBound2 As Integer)
```

The VBFixedArrayAttribute constructor specifies the upper bound or upper bounds of the array.

VBFixedStringAttribute Attribute

The VBFixedStringAttribute attribute is used to ensure that files written using the FileSystem methods are compatible with previous versions of Visual Basic. A fixed-size string in previous versions of Visual Basic was a string declared with a fixed size in a user-defined type.

```
Type Team
  Name As String * 10
End Type
```

This example shows a user-defined type with a fixed-size string of length 10 in it. When a user-defined type with a fixed-size string was written to disk, it included a special header containing the size of the string. For the string to be read properly in Visual Basic .NET, the corresponding class or structure has to specify the VBFixedStringAttribute.

```
Class Team
  <VBFixedStringAttribute(10)> Public Name As String
End Class

Module Test
  Sub Main()
    Dim x As Team

    FileOpen(FileNum, "team.txt", OpenMode.Binary, _
      OpenAccess.Write, OpenShare.Default)
    FileGet(1, x)
    FileClose(1)
  End Sub
End Module
```

```
Public ReadOnly Length() As Integer
```

The Length property returns the number of characters in the fixed-size string.

```
Public Sub New(ByVal Length As Integer)
```

The VBFixedStringAttribute constructor specifies the length of the fixed-size string.

▪ B ▪
Making the Transition from COM to the CLR

The move from the Common Object Model (COM) to the Common Language Runtime (CLR) as the underlying technology of the Visual Basic language was a significant one, requiring many changes to the language, large and small. This appendix discusses some of the major issues related to this transition that we encountered when designing Visual Basic .NET. A full and complete discussion of all the issues and changes between Visual Basic 6.0 and Visual Basic .NET is well beyond the scope of this appendix—it could easily fill a book in its own right. However, the issues discussed are intended to give an idea of the kinds of problems and solutions that we dealt with as we moved from Visual Basic 6.0 to Visual Basic .NET 2002.

Type System Additions

The CLR type system is considerably richer than the COM type system, which required a number of concepts to be added to the Visual Basic language. The most important was inheritance, but overloading, namespaces, and name hiding were also significant changes.

Classes

In previous versions of Visual Basic, a class was equivalent to a COM *coclass*. A coclass is a collection of supported interfaces without a distinct identity—when creating a coclass, the creator always requests one of the interfaces that the coclass implements and never requests the coclass itself. Given one interface supported by a coclass, it is possible to request other supported interfaces through the IUnknown interface that all coclasses support. In general, though, it is not possible to know what coclass an object is, given just an interface pointer.

Previous versions of Visual Basic simplified this situation slightly through the concept of *default interfaces*. When a class was defined in Visual Basic 6.0, a hidden interface was created that contained all the public members defined in the class. The class then implemented that default interface. Because everything had to be exposed in COM through interfaces, fields had to be exposed as properties. For example, given the following class definition in Visual Basic 6.0:

```
Public Value As Integer

Public Sub PrintValue()
  . . .
End Sub

Public Function CalculateValue() As Integer
  . . .
End Function
```

the following would have been generated:

- An interface named _Class1 that contained four members: a property Get method for Value, a property Let method for Value, a subroutine PrintValue, and a function CalculateValue
- A coclass named Class1 that implemented _Class1

In contrast to a COM coclass, a CLR class is a first-class type with its own identity and storage managed by the runtime. Classes can implement interfaces, but a reference—even to an interface—always refers to a particular instance of a *class*. It is never possible to refer to just an interface on its own. There are many benefits to this scheme (not the least of which is that data members do not have to be expressed as properties), but it does make interoperability between versions of Visual Basic a little more difficult.

Because the unit of identity changed between COM and the CLR, Visual Basic's behavior changed subtly in how references to interfaces and classes work. For example, given a class, Class1, that implements an interface, Interface1, the following code will produce two different answers on COM and on the CLR.

```
Sub Main()
  Dim c As Class1
  Set c = New Class1       ' VB6 syntax used

  Dim i As Interface1
  Set i = c                ' VB6 syntax used

  Debug.Print TypeName(i) ' VB6 syntax used
End Sub
```

Under COM, the name printed will be Interface1 because that is the unit of identity in COM (i.e., there is no true concept of Class1). On the CLR, however, the name printed will be Class1 because the thing that holds identity is the class, not the interface. No matter what interface a class is cast to, the CLR still knows what class the instance is.

The question then became how the COM concepts should be mapped to the CLR concepts when a COM object is being accessed from the CLR. The simplest answer would be to map a COM coclass to a CLR class and a COM interface to a CLR interface. However, in this case the tricks that Visual Basic 6.0 played in COM become troublesome on the CLR. Because the unit of identity in COM is the interface, that is what is used when a COM method is called in COM. So, given a coclass, Class1, a method taking a Class1 would actually be expressed as taking the default interface, _Class1. This was fine in Visual Basic 6.0 because the compiler hid the distinction. But since both classes and interfaces are first-class types in Visual Basic .NET, this means that using COM objects would require a lot of casting if strict type checking (new in Visual Basic .NET) is used. For example, given the following class, named Class1, defined in Visual Basic 6.0:

```
Private Value As Integer

Public Function CreateNewInstance() As Class1
  Set CreateNewInstance = New Class1()
End Function
```

the class would have to be used in Visual Basic .NET as such.

```
Option Strict On

Module Test
  Sub Main()
    Dim x As Class1 = New Class1()
    ' CType is required without extra work
    Dim y As Class1 = CType(x.CreateNewInstance(), Class1)
  End Sub
End Module
```

The return value of `CreateNewInstance` has to be explicitly cast to the class `Class1` because strict type checking requires that a cast from an interface to a class that supports the interface be explicit (since the instance might be of some other class type).

To avoid forcing the distinction between interfaces and classes on users as soon as they attempt to upgrade code (since it is likely that Visual Basic .NET code will want to use COM objects), we slightly modified the language rules to make this situation more straightforward. Instead of the simple mapping, the CLR itself changes the name of the default interface to the name of the coclass and appends the word "Class" onto the end of the name of the coclass. So the coclass `Class1` with the default interface `_Class1` would be mapped to the class `Class1Class` and the interface `Class1`.

The result of this is that a user creating an instance of a COM class will appear to actually be instantiating an instance of the default interface. Under the covers, the compiler then maps this to an instantiation of the coclass. But now the variable is correctly typed and will not require any casts to be assigned to by an API or passed to another API.

Inheritance

Adding inheritance to the Visual Basic .NET language was relatively straightforward. The main set of decisions that had to be made were how explicit to make the various inheritance concepts and what terms to use to refer to them. Since Visual Basic is a language that has a long history that does not include inheritance, we felt it was best to make the most conservative choices in regard to defaults. We also felt that it would be better to choose more descriptive (and more verbose) keywords rather than using C++-style keywords.

When implementing inheritance, we had to choose what kind of name hiding would be done across the inheritance chain. A robust name-hiding scheme was seen as critical to avoiding many of the versioning issues that Visual Basic had with COM. In particular, it was important to be able to "drop in" a new version of a base class library that contained new methods and have code compiled against it continue to work. The canonical example of this situation would be ASP.NET—it is essential to be able to upgrade ASP.NET without requiring all the Web pages on a Web site to be recoded.

For simplicity, the default name-hiding semantic we initially chose was *hide by name*. In other words, a member defined with a particular name would hide all members by that name in any base classes. The `Shadows` keyword was added to the language, but purely for developer awareness— all members were implicitly marked shadow by name, and omitting `Shadows` only caused a warning rather than an error.

This choice, however, presented a problem with overloading, which we were also adding to the language. Given a hide-by-name semantic, it is not possible for a method to be overloaded across a base and derived class, because the derived class members hide the base class members by the same name. At this point, it would have been possible to decide that overloading across inheritance was not allowed, but this didn't seem like a good solution. A more desirable result would be to allow developers to explicitly state that they wished to overload a method in a base class rather than hide it. To this end, we added the `Overloads` keyword. The `Overloads` keyword specifies that a member is *hide by name and signature* rather than hide by name. A method that hides by name and signature will only hide a method with the same name and exact signature, thus allowing overloading across the inheritance hierarchy.

```
Class Base
  Public Sub A(ByVal x As Integer)
    ...
  End Sub

  Public Sub B(ByVal x As Integer)
    ...
  End Sub
End Class
```

```
Class Derived
  Inherits Base

  Public Shadows Sub A(ByVal y As Double)
    ...
  End Sub

  Public Overloads Sub B(ByVal y As Double)
    ...
  End Sub

  Public Sub C()
    A(10)      ' Calls Derived.A
    B(10)      ' Calls Base.B
  End Sub
End Class
```

In this example, the method `Derived.A` shadows the member `Base.A` because it specifies the keyword `Shadows`. It does this even though the two signatures don't match. The method `Derived.B`, on the other hand, overloads the member `Base.B` because it specifies the keyword `Overloads`. Keep in mind, though, that if `Derived.A` and `Base.B` had the same signature, `Derived.B` would still hide `Base.B`. It's not possible to have two methods with the same signature be visible at the same time!

Design

In retrospect, our choice of the keyword `Overloads` in this situation was unfortunate. Although it accurately describes its function, people get easily confused into thinking that the keyword is required when they are doing overloading *within* a class, which isn't the case. This has confused even the most advanced Visual Basic .NET programmers.

Given that a method could have one of two separate name-hiding semantics associated with it, the question arose as to which should be the default. We had initially chosen `Shadows` as the default, but would it make more sense to choose `Overloads` as the default? Ultimately, we decided that it did *not* make more sense, because of the implications for overload resolution. Because overload resolution chooses among all the methods in the inheritance hierarchy with the same name (see the Overloading section for more details on overload resolution), a method marked as `Overloads` by default was vulnerable to changes in the base class.

For example, take the following situation: A base class vendor, Acme, produces a class, `Base`.

```
Class Base
  ...
End Class
```

Another company, MegaCorp, buys Acme's product and creates a derived class, `Derived`.

```
Class Derived
  Inherits Base

  Public Overloads Sub Print(ByVal y As Double)
    ...
  End Sub

  Public Overloads Sub Print(ByVal y As Integer)
    ...
  End Sub

  Public Sub DoWork()
    ...
    Print(4S)
    ...
  End Sub
End Class
```

In this example, the method `DoWork` calls `Print` with the `Short` value 4. Because there is no exact overload, the method `Print(Integer)` is chosen as the best overload.

Now, after some period of time, Acme releases an upgrade to class `Base`, adding a method called `Print` to the class.

```
Class Base
  Public Overloads Sub Print(ByVal s As Short)
    ...
  End Sub
End Class
```

MegaCorp purchases the new base class, installs it, and rebuilds `Derived`. The problem is that because `Derived.Print` was marked as `Overloads`, the method `Base.Print` will now be incorporated into the overload resolution for the name `Print`. In this case, `Base.Print(Short)` is the best overload, so now `Derived.DoWork` will silently start calling `Base.Print`, even though that method may do something radically different than `Derived.Print` does!

The only way to completely solve this issue would be to choose a method of overload resolution similar to the one that C# uses, as discussed in the Overloading section. Barring that, choosing `Shadows` as the default name-hiding semantic for methods seemed the safest choice. There is still some danger in using `Overloads`, but the risk can be assumed explicitly by the developer when adding the keyword.

Overloading

Because overloading is a fundamental part of the CLR, it was necessary to add it to the Visual Basic .NET language. Visual Basic already had a similar mechanism for dealing with optional parameters, but in most cases, overloading is a more robust way of accomplishing the same goals. This is especially true since the values of optional parameters are compiled into the caller rather than staying under the control of the method being called.

As discussed in the Inheritance section, the primary question that had to be answered regarding overloading was how overloading would interact with inheritance. We took what we thought was the simplest answer to the question, figuring that it would be the most straightforward and understandable: When doing overload resolution on a method, the language considers *all* the methods by a particular name in the inheritance hierarchy at once. This means that the most specific overload is always guaranteed to be chosen.

The downside of this is that, as previously discussed, it creates fragility in a derived class in the face of base class changes. An alternative method was considered that was closer to C#'s method of overload resolution: Consider all the methods overloaded on a name one class at a time, starting with the most derived class and moving to the most base class. This would have solved the fragility issue, but we felt that for Visual Basic programmers the results would be nonintuitive, because a less specific overload in a derived class might get chosen over a more specific overload in a base class. For example, C# and VB will choose different overloads in the following situation.

```
Class Base
  Public Overloads Sub Print(ByVal s As Short)
    . . .
  End Sub
End Class

Class Derived
  Inherits Base

  Public Overloads Sub Print(ByVal y As Double)
    . . .
  End Sub

  Public Overloads Sub Print(ByVal y As Integer)
    . . .
  End Sub

  Public Sub DoWork()
    Print(4S)
  End Sub
End Class
```

Because C# considers overloads one level at a time, it will choose `Derived.Print(Integer)` as the best overload. Because VB considers all the overloads at once, it will choose `Base.Print(Short)` because it most closely matches the argument.

One other interesting thing to note about overload resolution in Visual Basic .NET is the way that arguments typed as `Object` are treated. Overload resolution against arguments typed purely as `Object` will, given a straightforward set of resolution rules, result in an ambiguity. This is because `Object` is the root type of the type system, so a conversion from `Object` to any other type will be a narrowing conversion. Thus, the compiler will be unable to determine a most specific argument.

To enable calls to overloaded methods when a variable is typed as `Object` (especially when the `As` clause has been omitted), an additional rule was added. If overload resolution fails solely because of arguments typed as `Object`, the resolution of the call is deferred until runtime. In other words, the call is implicitly turned into a late-bound call (assuming strict semantics are not being used, because strict semantics disallow late binding). The late-bound method invocation code has the ability to perform overload resolution at runtime, allowing the resolution to be done on the actual type of the parameter at runtime.

Namespaces

Visual Basic already had an extremely rudimentary concept of a namespace—in previous versions, the name of the project functioned as a namespace for everything declared within it. This allowed for multiple projects to have something named `Class1` yet still reference one another. On the CLR, the concept just had to be extended to arbitrarily complex namespace schemes. We felt that most users would not want to see `Namespace` statements in their source code, so we still retained the original concept of a project-wide namespace. Essentially, every project defines a namespace that all declarations in the project are implicitly wrapped in. This allows users to define their own namespace hierarchies if they wish, but by default each project gets its own namespace. (The default namespace can be overridden, if needed.)

Type System Modifications

In addition to extensions to the Visual Basic type system, a number of modifications to the existing type system were required by the move to the CLR. For the most part, this was because many of the CLR types that corresponded to COM types (such as arrays and `Variant`) used different underlying storage.

Arrays

Arrays on the CLR are much more sophisticated than COM arrays (COM arrays are also called "SafeArrays"). There are two principal differences that caused changes from Visual Basic 6.0.

The first difference is that all arrays in the CLR encode their rank within their type. So a two-dimensional array of `Integer` is considered to be a different type from a one-dimensional array of `Integer` in the CLR. COM SafeArrays, however, encode their rank as an attribute of an array instance and not the array type. So a two-dimensional array of `Integer` is actually the same type as a one-dimensional array of `Integer` in COM; the instances just happen to have different ranks. Because of this difference between COM and the CLR, code from previous versions of Visual Basic that declares and uses arrays cannot be ported unchanged. In most cases, the differences between COM and the CLR don't cause serious problems—

most variables are ever assigned an array of only one particular rank, and the common case is that the rank of the array can be inferred easily from the code around it. For example, the following Visual Basic 6.0 code:

```
Sub Main()
  Dim x() As Integer

  ReDim x(10, 10)
  x(1, 1) = 10
End Sub
```

can pretty easily be rewritten as follows.

```
Module Test
  Sub Main()
    Dim x(,) As Integer   ' 2-dimensional array

    ReDim x(10, 10)
    x(1, 1) = 10
  End Sub
End Module
```

This difference between array types can cause problems, however, when you are trying to interoperate with COM. When you are transferring an array from the CLR to COM, it is impossible to know what rank array a COM method expects, because there is no way to inspect the API's code. Currently, the CLR treats all COM array parameters as one-dimensional arrays of the specified type. This takes care of the most common situations, but is not perfect. At this point, there is no simple way to specify the rank of an array parameter of an imported COM method.

The other difference between SafeArrays and CLR arrays is more problematic. A SafeArray type can contain a set of bounds for each dimension of the array, but those bounds are not considered to be part of the actual type, just as the rank of the array is not considered to be part of the type. In the CLR, however, the lower bounds of each dimension of the array are allowed to be (but not required to be) part of the type itself. So while there is, for example, a one-dimensional `Integer` array type that can have any lower bound, there are also one-dimensional `Integer` array types that have a fixed lower bound of zero, of one, of two, and so on. While any array of the particular rank and type can be assigned to the first kind of array type (i.e., the one without any fixed lower bound), only an array that has matching lower bounds can be assigned to the other kinds of array types (i.e., a one-dimensional `Integer` array with a lower bound of 5 cannot be assigned to a variable of type one-dimensional `Integer` array with a lower bound of 6).

Overall, this whole question would be academic if it was not for one fact—the Common Language Specification (CLS) decrees that all CLS-compliant languages must be able to use array types that have fixed lower bounds of zero. This is because languages such as C# and C++ do not allow the lower bounds of their arrays to be anything but zero. They could, conceivably, still use the array types that do not fix the lower bounds to represent an array that has a fixed lower bound of zero, but to do so would mean that several code optimizations based on knowing the lower bound of each dimension of an array would be lost. This was unacceptable to the designers of those languages.

A simple solution to this problem would be to say that Visual Basic .NET should use the array types that do not fix the lower bounds and just throw exceptions if you tried to pass one with nonzero lower bounds to a CLS-compliant method. The problem is that array types can make up part of the signatures of methods. So when you are overriding a method defined in C# that takes an array, the signature of the VB method has to match completely, including the fact that the array type has a fixed lower bound of zero. The result of this is that if Visual Basic .NET wishes to have nonzero lower bound arrays in the language, it must distinguish between array types that can have nonzero lower bounds and array types that have their lower bounds fixed at zero.

After much deliberation, it was decided that having two separate types of arrays in the language would be too confusing for most users. In many cases, it would be unclear which type should be used when declaring a method. Even worse, when errors occurred, it would be difficult to concisely explain exactly what was wrong. However, the removal of nonzero lower bound arrays is a significant issue for many users who routinely declared arrays with a lower bound other than zero.

Variant and Object

Previous versions of Visual Basic could be used in a loosely typed way through use of the `Variant` data type. A `Variant` is a structure that is a union of all the different COM types: `Integer`, `Double`, `BSTR`, `IDispatch`, and so on. This allows a `Variant` to contain any value expressible in Visual Basic. As a result, if you declared all variables as type `Variant` (implicitly or explicitly), Visual Basic became an almost "typeless" language.

This same scheme could not be used in the CLR, because the runtime does not allow reference types to be unioned with other types in a structure. This is because the CLR manages references to values on the heap and tracks them for garbage collection. To allow an `Integer` to be unioned with a reference to the heap would mean that the CLR would not be able to reliably know whether a particular instance of the type contained a reference or an `Integer`. This would cause safety and security issues, as well as making garbage collection impossible. It would have been possible for the CLR to instead expose a `Variant` type that it natively understood—in other words, the CLR would ensure that the "type" field of the `Variant` structure was always consistent with the "value" field. However, this was not ideal, because of the existence of the CLR `Object` type.

The CLR type system was designed as a single-root type system. What this means it that every type in the type system ultimately derives from `Object`. For reference types, this is no different from COM—in COM, every coclass implemented the `IUnknown` interface, which was equivalent to the `Object` type in Visual Basic 6.0. For value types (i.e., structures and primitive types), though, this is a big change. It is accomplished by something of a trick, as discussed in Chapter 9. Each value type can exist in one of two forms: its boxed form and its unboxed form. An unboxed value type is just a regular value type—it exists on the stack, in an array or within another type, and has no identity in and of itself. Unboxed value types are not managed by the CLR, because they are always part of something else. A boxed value type is the tricky part. When a value type is boxed, a copy of the value is made on the heap, and a reference to the heap location is returned. From this point on, the boxed value type can be treated just as if it were a reference type. Essentially, a value type is boxed when it is cast to `Object`, and unboxed when it is cast from `Object`.

The problem may be clearer at this point. Because every type in the CLR type system can be cast to `Object`, `Object` is in many ways functionally equivalent to `Variant`. But even though `Object` and `Variant` are *mostly* equivalent, they are not *exactly* equivalent. Assigning a value to a `Variant` variable only copies the value into the `Variant` itself, no matter how many values are assigned to the variable. Assigning a value to an `Object` variable allocates space on the heap and then copies the value into that space. Each time you assign a new value to the `Object` variable, an allocation occurs on the heap. Thus, there is more overhead to using `Object` than `Variant`.

Ultimately, we had a choice to make. We could keep `Variant` and live with the confusion over whether to use `Object` or `Variant` when a "universal" type was needed, or just use `Object` exclusively and suffer some performance penalty. After much analysis, we determined that in most cases the performance of `Object` would not appreciably affect applications. Additionally, we were concerned that even within Microsoft itself, the teams designing various parts of the .NET Framework would not be able to decide between using `Variant` and `Object` consistently in their APIs. It became clear that using `Object` exclusively was the best option.

A side effect of this decision relates to how `ByRef` parameters of type `Object` behave. The COM `Variant` type can not only store a value itself, it can also store a pointer to a value. This means that when a method in Visual Basic 6.0 calls a method declared with a `ByRef Variant` parameter, the argument passes a pointer to itself, allowing the called method to modify the original argument storage. Because of the complexity that would have been involved in allowing it, the CLR does not allow arbitrary pointers to storage locations to be passed around, unless the code is declared to be "unsafe." Visual Basic .NET does not support writing unsafe code, so there was no simple way to simulate the `ByRef Variant` behavior on the CLR.

There is a way to simulate the `ByRef Variant` behavior on the CLR in a safe way by using the `RefAny` type, but this type had some significant limitations and greatly complicated the implementation of the language. A simpler mechanism that we ultimately settled on was to instead pass values to `ByRef Object` parameters (the CLR equivalent to `ByRef Variant` parameters) using copy-in/copy-out semantics rather than true byref semantics, as covered in Chapter 10. What this briefly means is that instead of passing a pointer to the storage of the argument, a temporary `Object` variable is allocated, the argument is copied into, and a pointer to the temporary is passed to the method. Then, when the method returns, the value in the `Object` variable is cast back to the argument type and assigned back to the argument source. This means that changes to the parameter will not be reflected in the original argument location until the method returns. In practice, this distinction should not be often noticed. For example, the following code:

```
Module Test
  Public g As Integer = 10

  Function ChangeValue(ByRef o As Object)
    o = 20
    Console.WriteLine(g & " " & o)
  End Function

  Sub Main
    ChangeValue(g)
  End Sub
End Module
```

will print "10 20" because it is equivalent to the following.

```
Module Test
  Public g As Integer = 10

  Function ChangeValue(ByRef o As Object)
    o = 20
    Console.WriteLine(g & " " & o)
  End Function

  Sub Main()
    Dim Temp As Object

    Temp = g
    ChangeValue(Temp)
    g = Temp
  End Sub
End Module
```

Structures

User-defined types in Visual Basic 6.0 were renamed as structures and had their functionality significantly expanded in Visual Basic .NET. The name was changed both because structures can do more in the CLR and because the keyword Type conflicted with the type name System.Type. Because System.Type is the foundation of reflection (the .NET Framework system of runtime type inspection), keeping the keyword Type would have meant that writing code that uses reflection would require frequent use of escaping (i.e., [Type] instead of Type).

In Visual Basic .NET, structures are user-defined value types. Since there is no distinction in terms of *functionality* between value types and reference types (only a distinction in terms of storage and lifetime), structures can now have methods, events, properties, and so on, and their data members can now have accessibility modifiers placed on them. In Visual Basic .NET, the choice between a class and a structure boils down to only storage considerations and assignment behavior.

Date, Currency, and Decimal

A few other data type changes are worth noting. First, COM has both a Currency and a Decimal type. Because the Decimal type has a greater range and precision than Currency (i.e., it can store all the values that Currency can), we decided to replace the Currency type entirely with Decimal.

The other change was more subtle. In COM, a Date variable is stored using a double precision floating-point number. The number to the left of the decimal point represents the number of days since December 30, 1899. The number to the right of the decimal point represents the number of seconds since midnight. (This is a slightly simplified description of the actual representation, but should give the general idea.) Because the Date data type is represented as a floating-point number, the data type has the same limitations in terms of range and exactness that the underlying data type does.

The CLR DateTime class, in contrast, is stored using a signed 64-bit integer number representing the number of milliseconds since midnight, January 1, 1. This is a more precise representation and can represent a greater range of dates. This has two impacts on the Visual Basic language, however. First, it means that Double values can no longer implicitly be converted to and from Date values. Second, transferring dates from COM to the CLR and vice versa involves a translation. By and large, this is mostly a question of whether a DateTime value will fit into the range of the COM date, but there is one special situation that can cause problems.

In previous versions of Visual Basic, there was no way to express just a time value (i.e., a time of day not tied to a particular day). To work around this, Visual Basic would treat the time of day on the first day representable (December 30, 1899) as just a time value. In other words, printing the date constant #12/30/1899 1:43PM# would just print 1:43 PM. December 30, 1899, is also the zero day for the COM Date type—in other words, a Date variable that has no value assigned to it will by default represent midnight, December 30, 1899.

To preserve this behavior, Visual Basic .NET treats the zero day of the DateTime type (January 1, 1) as the "time only" date. In the case of code migrated from previous versions of Visual Basic, this preserves the semantics of the code. However, it does mean that transferring dates back and forth with COM is slightly complicated. Basically, any time during the zero date of DateTime is translated to the same time on the zero date of the COM Date, even though the two dates are different. Although this can cause some slightly anomalous results, by and large it produces the "expected" behavior.

Platform Changes

Above and beyond the changes to the type system in Visual Basic .NET, a number of changes were required by the underlying structure of the CLR itself.

Deterministic Finalization and Garbage Collection

The CLR was built from the ground up to be a garbage-collected system. That is to say that the CLR tracks all references to objects allocated on the heap. Periodically, the runtime checks to see if there are objects on the heap that no longer have any references to them. If there are any such objects, they are garbage collected—that is, freed. This scheme for freeing heap allocations is different from the scheme employed by COM. COM employed a reference-counting mechanism to track references to objects. When a reference to an object was copied, the copier would call the AddRef method on the object to let it know that there was another reference to it. When a piece of code was finished with a reference to an object, it called the Release method on the object to let it know that it was finished with the reference. When the number of references to an object reached zero, the object would free itself.

The advantage of the COM scheme is that all objects are *deterministically finalized*. That is, an object is freed at the very moment that the last reference to it is released. In the CLR, in comparison, an object will not be freed until sometime after the last reference was released—that is, probably the next time the garbage collector runs. Deterministic finalization is advantageous because an object itself may be holding onto references to other objects, some of which may be scarce (like a database connection). In that case, as soon as you free an object, you want the resources it holds to be freed as well. Even if the garbage collector runs every few milliseconds, that may not be fast enough to prevent resources from being used up.

The advantage of the CLR scheme is that it is very hard to get the COM scheme right. Many thousands of hours have been spent collectively in the software industry tracking down `AddRef/Release` problems. It is very easy when you are programming against a COM object to forget to do an `AddRef` when you copy a reference, resulting in a crash if the object is finalized too early. It is also even easier to forget to `Release` a reference once you are finished with it, resulting in memory leaks and objects hanging around forever and never releasing their resources.

Another advantage of the CLR scheme is that it easily solves the problem of *circular references*. A circular reference is when object A has a direct or indirect reference to object B and B has a direct or indirect reference to A; thus each object holds a reference to the other. Once a circular reference has been created, in COM the developer has to explicitly use some other mechanism to break the cycle and make the object finalize. However, because the CLR knows about all references between objects, the garbage collector can determine when a set of objects that contain circular references are no longer referenced outside the cycle and finalize all the objects at once.

By and large, the problems with the COM scheme listed above were hidden from Visual Basic developers by the compiler, except for circular references. The compiler would correctly insert `AddRef` or `Release` calls into the compiled Visual Basic code to manage the references. So the fact that the CLR uses garbage collection does not buy Visual Basic as much as it buys programmers who write in other languages such as C++, although there are still benefits such as circular reference finalization.

Unfortunately, there is no easy way to have deterministic finalization and garbage collection coexist easily within the same type system. A full discussion of this issue is beyond the scope of this appendix, but the core problem can be boiled down to a single question: is the type `Object` deterministically finalized or garbage collected? If the answer is that it is garbage collected, then casting an instance of a deterministically finalized to `Object` would have to cause the instance to lose its deterministic finalization property (because once it was typed as `Object`, `AddRef`/`Release` would not be called). Given that there are many situations (such as storing references in collections) where instances need to be cast to `Object`, this is not a workable solution. If `Object` is deterministically finalized, on the other hand, then effectively all types must be deterministically finalized, which means that garbage collection goes out the window. One could work around the question of `Object` by splitting the type system into two completely separate camps, garbage collected types and deterministically finalized types, but then there would have to be two different root `Object` types which would cause every type that takes `Object` (such as arrays and collections) to have two versions: one for deterministically finalized types and one for garbage collected types.

The end result of all this is that there is no solid replacement for deterministic finalization in Visual Basic .NET. An interface, `IDisposable`, has been added to the .NET Framework that a class should implement if it holds onto precious resources that should be disposed of as soon as possible, but the onus is on the developer to correctly call the `Dispose` method when they are finished with the instance.

Let and Set Assignment

In the past, Visual Basic has distinguished between value assignment (`Let`) and reference assignment (`Set`). While this can be a useful distinction, one of the reasons it was necessary in Visual Basic was because of parameterless default properties. In previous versions of Visual Basic, classes can expose a default property that has no parameters. In that case, the default property is considered the "value" property of the object (indeed, in most cases the parameterless default property is named `Value`). Because of this, there has to be two forms of assignment that distinguish whether you are assigning the "value" of an object or the actual reference to an object. For example:

```
Sub Main()
  Dim s As String
  Dim t1 As TextBox
  Dim t2 As TextBox

  Let s = t1    ' Assigns the value of the text box
  t2 = t1       ' Assigns the value of text box t1 to text box t2
  Set f2 = f1   ' Assigns the reference to t1 to t2
End Sub
```

Because COM distinguished between `Let` and `Set` style of assignments, properties had to be able to be defined with both kinds of accessors.

```
Property Set foo(Value As Variant)
End Property

Property Let foo(Value As Variant)
End Property
```

The problem is that the CLR does not distinguish between `Let` and `Set` types of assignment, so properties can only define one kind of assignment accessor. This is because most programming languages do not make a distinction between types of assignment, and in this case the majority won out. It would have been possible for Visual Basic to define both types of accessors but only expose one to other languages, but this was very problematic—if you had an `Object` property, which can take values and references, which one should be exposed? No matter which one was chosen, it would be wrong in many cases. And the reverse problem would occur with properties defined in other languages.

After much deliberation and considering of alternatives, we decided the simplest way was to drop the distinction between `Let` and `Set` forms of assignment. This meant that properties could only define one kind of assignment accessor. It also meant that parameterless default properties had to be removed from the language. Although parameterless default properties were useful, they could also be obscure and confusing, so this was not considered a huge loss. While the loss of the two distinct types of assignment tended to be not that significant for the Visual Basic .NET developer, it does create a headache when interoperating with COM. Just as Visual Basic .NET would have had to do, the CLR can only expose a `Let` or a `Set` accessor of a property in COM that has both. The decision was made to always expose the `Set` accessor of the property from the CLR, so this means that code that wants to call the `Let` accessor of the property has to do so by calling the accessor directly. For a property, `Foo`, that exposes both a `Let` and a `Set`, the interoperability layer will expose a method called `let_Foo` that allows calling the `Let` accessor directly.

Late Binding

Late binding is the mechanism by which resolution of a method call can be deferred until runtime. Essentially, when you are making a call on a variable typed as `Object`, the compiler instead emits a call to a helper, with all the relevant information about the method call. At runtime, the helper will resolve which method (if any) to call and then make the call itself.

The first challenge in implementing late binding was adapting to the change from COM to the CLR. In COM, late binding was handled by a component called OLE Automation through an interface called `IDispatch`. `IDispatch` relied on the information specified in a file called a *type library* that described a class. Type libraries were either compiled into or accompanied a COM component. In contrast, late binding in the CLR is done through a component called *reflection*. Whereas `IDispatch` and type libraries were not easily accessible in previous versions of Visual Basic and were considered more of an internal implementation detail, reflection is a full-fledged part of the .NET Framework. Reflection allows inspection of the type information that is part of every assembly (i.e., the equivalent of a type library compiled into the executable). It also has some mechanisms for doing late binding, but they are extremely simple, only allowing you to inspect the methods that an object has and then invoke one of them.

Because we needed to express the full set of Visual Basic binding semantics, we had to write special helpers that sit on top of reflection to do that binding. When a late-bound helper is invoked, it first goes through much the same process as the compiler does at compile time to determine what method to call. The runtime binder considers inheritance and name hiding, and does overload resolution. It understands Visual Basic's conversion rules and knows what calls are valid and which are not. It is a relatively complex piece of code.

Another challenge had to do with reference parameters. IDispatch was built using Variants, which, as noted before, have the ability to store pointers in them. This meant that when a late-bound call was made, Visual Basic could pass ByRef Variants to IDispatch for each argument. Then, if the actual parameter of the method being called was declared ByRef, the pointer could be passed in, and the method would work as expected. Because the CLR does not have a real equivalent to ByRef Variants, we had to employ the same copy-in/copy-out mechanism that we use for ByRef Object parameters, with an additional twist.

When you are making a call to a method early-bound, it is possible for the compiler to know which parameters are ByRef Object and which are not. So it can figure out which arguments, if any, need to be passed using copy-in/copy-out semantics. But when you are making a late-bound call, it's impossible to know until runtime which parameters are ByRef Object. So there is no way to know whether or not to generate code to do the copy-out. The ugly, but unavoidable, solution is to pass in an array of Boolean values corresponding to the argument list to the late-binding helper. Once the late-binding helper has determined which method it is going to call, it sets each element to True that corresponds to a ByRef parameter. Then, the compiler generates code to check the element for each argument that could do a copy-back (i.e., ignoring literals, read-only fields, and so on) and then do a copy-back if the element has been set to True.

It's also worth noting here that the change in the locus of identity from interfaces in COM to classes in the CLR affects late binding too. In COM, you would late bind to the particular interface that you happened to have in your hand when you made the call. However, since the CLR only sees instances of classes, it is never possible to have an instance of an interface in hand. This means that it is not possible to late bind to interfaces in the CLR, only classes. If a class, Foo, implements an interface, IBar, using a private member, there is no way to late bind to that interface member. This is an inescapable result of the design of the CLR type system.

On Error and Structured Exception Handling

The On Error style of error handling has always been built on top of exception handling mechanisms provided by the operating system. With Visual Basic .NET, we decided to expose the underlying exception handling mechanism, call *structured exception handling*, directly to programmers through the `Try` statement. Structured exception handling has two advantages over `On Error`–style error handling. First, its structured nature encourages more discriminating and precise use of exception handling, which can in some cases result in more optimized assembly output. Second, structured exception handling gives a much finer-grained control over which exceptions are handled and when. This is not to say that `On Error`–style error handling does not have advantages over structured exception handling. For example, there is no equivalent to `Resume` or `Resume Next` in structured exception handling.

Implementing `On Error`–style exception handling on top of structured exception handling was a relatively straightforward task (except for `Resume` and `Resume Next`, which will be discussed in a moment). Any method that contains an `On Error` statement is wrapped in a `Try` statement around all the code in the method. Then, a `Catch` handler is added that catches all exceptions. Each `On Error` statement sets a value in a local variable that indicates which `On Error` statement is currently active. When an exception occurs, the `Catch` handler switches on that local variable to determine where to go. For example:

```
Module Test
  Sub Main()
    Dim i As Integer

    On Error Goto Foo
    i = 20
Foo:
    On Error Goto Bar
    i = 30
Bar:
    On Error Goto 0
    i = 40
  End Sub
End Module
```

is equivalent to the following.

```
Module Test
  Sub Main()
    Dim CurrentHandler As Integer
```

```
      Try
        Dim i As Integer

        CurrentHandler = 1  ' On Error Goto Foo
        i = 20
   Foo:
        CurrentHandler = 2  ' On Error Goto Bar
        i = 30
   Bar:
        CurrentHandler = 0  ' On Error Goto 0
        i = 40
      Catch e As Exception When CurrentHandler > 0
        Select Case CurrentHandler
          Case 1
            Goto Foo
          Case 2
            Goto Bar
        End Select

        Throw  ' In case something goes wrong.
      End Try
    End Sub
  End Module
```

As noted earlier, `Resume` and `Resume Next` are slightly more complex cases. When compiling a method that contains a `Resume` or `Resume Next`, the compiler adds a local that tracks which statement is being processed. Code is inserted after each statement to increment the local. When an exception occurs and a `Resume` or `Resume Next` statement is executed (either through an `On Error` statement or on its own), the local is loaded (and incremented if `Resume Next`), and then a `Select` statement is executed to jump to the statement indicated by the local. For example:

```
  Module Test
    Sub Main()
      Dim i As Integer

      On Error Resume Next

      i = 20
      i = 30
      i = 40
    End Sub
  End Module
```

is equivalent to the following.

```
Module Test
 ·Sub Main()
    Dim CurrentHandler As Integer
    Dim CurrentLine As Integer

    Try
       Dim i As Integer

Line1:
       CurrentLine = 1
       CurrentHandler = -1   ' On Error Resume Next

Line2:
       CurrentLine = 2
       i = 20

Line3:
       CurrentLine = 3
       i = 30

Line4:
       CurrentLine = 4
       i = 40
    Catch e As Exception When CurrentHandler > 0
       Select Case CurrentHandler
         Case 1
           CurrentLine += 1

           Select Case CurrentLine
             Case 1
               Goto Line1
             Case 2
               Goto Line2
             Case 3
               Goto Line3
             Case 4
               Goto Line4
           End Select
       End Select

       Throw   ' In case something goes wrong.
    End Try
  End Sub
End Module
```

It's important to note that this can only be done by the compiler and not by the CLR—even if the CLR had a resume mechanism, it could only work based on IL instructions, whereas the `Resume` statement works based on statements. There's no way for the CLR to know where the "next" statement or "current" statement begins and ends.

Events and Delegates

Events in COM and the CLR are implemented very differently even though they have virtually the same functionality. In COM, a class that sources events exposes one or more *event interfaces*. An event interface defines callback methods to handle each event that the class exposes. A class that wished to handle the events would implement the event interface using the event handlers that it wished to use. The class handling the events would then give this event interface to the class that sourced the events (called a connection point). The sourcing class then invokes the appropriate methods when the event is raised.

In the CLR, events are built around delegates, which are managed function pointers. A delegate contains the address of a method and a particular instance of the containing class if the method is an instance method. A delegate can then invoke the method that it points to, given a list of arguments. Delegates are *multicast*, which is to say that a single delegate can point to more than one method. When the delegate is invoked, all the methods that the delegate points to are called in order.

It is worth noting that the semantics of the `AddressOf` expression were extended slightly in Visual Basic .NET to make working with delegates easier. The `AddressOf` operator can be applied to any method and produces, essentially, an unnamed delegate type representing that method's signature. Now, the CLR type system does not actually support unnamed delegate types, so this is merely a compiler trick—the result of an `AddressOf` expression must ultimately be converted to a named delegate type. The compiler then inserts an instantiation for the correct delegate type at the point of conversion. If the target delegate type is not specified (by converting the `AddressOf` expression to `Object`) or is ambiguous (as is possible in overload resolution), an error will result.

An event, then, is made up of three things in the CLR: a delegate type that defines the signature of the event, a method to add a new handler for the event, and a method that removes an existing handler for the event. When a class wishes to handle an event raised by a class, it first creates a new delegate of the type of the event on the method that will handle the event. It then passes this delegate to the add handler method of the event. The add handler method combines the delegate being passed in with all the other delegates that it has been called with to handle the event. When the event is raised, it simply invokes the delegate with the appropriate parameters, which calls each handler in turn. If a class wishes to stop handling the event, it simply creates another delegate on the handler that it wants to stop having called and calls the remove handler method with the delegate. The remove handler method then removes the particular delegate from the delegate list that it is maintaining for the event.

Visual Basic .NET significantly simplifies the process of defining and handling events. Although we give you access to most of the low-level definition of events, most of the time you don't need to bother with the inner guts. For example, you can declare an event with just a signature, and the compiler will define the event delegate for you under the covers. Also, if you declare a field with the WithEvents modifier, you can then declare methods in the class with the Handles clause, and the compiler will automatically call the add and remove event methods for you. For example:

```
Class Raiser
  Public Event E()

  Public Sub Raise()
    RaiseEvent E()
  End Sub
End Class

Class Handler
  Public WithEvents R As Raiser

  Public Sub New()
    R = New Raiser()
  End Sub

  Public Sub DoRaise()
    R.Raise()
  End Sub

  Public Sub HandleE() Handles R.E
  End Sub
End Class
```

is equivalent to the following.

```
Class Raiser
  Public Delegate Sub EEventHandler()
  Public Event E As EEventHandler

  Public Sub Raise()
    RaiseEvent E()
  End Sub
End Class

Class Handler
  Private RLocal As Raiser

  Public Property R As Raiser
    Get
      Return RLocal
    End Get
    Set (ByVal Value As Raiser)
      If Not RLocal Is Nothing Then
        R.remove_E(new EEventHandler(AddressOf HandleE))
      End If
      RLocal = Value
      If Not RLocal Is Nothing Then
        R.add_E(new EEventHandler(AddressOf HandleE))
      End If
    End Set
  End Property

  Public Sub DoRaise()
    R.Raise()
  End Sub

  Public Sub HandleE()
  End Sub
End Class
```

It is worth noting that there are some details, such as the add and remove methods of the event, that Visual Basic .NET does not allow you to define for yourself, although this may change in future versions.

Language Cleanup

As should be clear by now, moving to the CLR entailed some radical changes to the Visual Basic language. On top of the language changes, there were a number of library changes (such as the move from Visual Basic forms to .NET Windows Forms) that also significantly changed the way that code is written in Visual Basic .NET. Because of the magnitude of the changes necessitated by the CLR, it was clear that code from Visual Basic 6.0 would not be 100% forward compatible. Some migration and rewriting would be necessary to get code to compile, and even more would be necessary to fully move it to the CLR way of doing things.

Given this situation, the Visual Basic team decided to take the opportunity to make a few changes in the language that were not required by moving to the CLR. Each change was in response to specific feedback that the team had gathered over the years, and each was considered to be an improvement to the language when balanced against the cost of additional conversion requirements. For the most part, the changes involved removing support for anachronistic parts of the language. Examples of this would be the `Def` statements (such as `DefInt`) and `Gosub`. Both through feedback and experience, the pieces of the language that were dropped were ones that were rarely used by developers (in some cases, largely forgotten by users) and did not provide significant programmer benefit. A few of the other changes corrected quirks, like changing `Wend` to the more regular (and grammatical) `End While`. Most of these corrections are automatically handled by the migration tool and by the IDE editor (i.e., when you hit Enter after starting a `While` statement, `End While` is pasted in automatically).

Probably the most significant change was the redefinition of the `Integer` and `Long` types to 32 bits and 64 bits, respectively, and the addition of the 16-bit `Short` type. The primary problem with a 16-bit `Integer` type is that the CLR imposes performance penalties on 16-bit integers. There is no IL representation for a 16-bit integer on the stack—only 32-bit and 64-bit integers. This means that working with 16-bit integers puts code at a significant disadvantage, because every operation involves a conversion to catch overflow. For example, if a, b, c, and d are all 16-bit integer variables, the expression a = (b + c) * d results in two separate 16-bit conversion instructions (after the addition and the multiplication) to catch overflow. This overhead is nontrivial. When we were doing performance testing on early versions of the Visual Basic .NET compiler, Visual Basic performed at a disadvantage in relation to other languages. Much of that disadvantage was directly attributable to the fact that the test was written using `Integer`. Once a search and replace on `Integer` with `Long` was done, the performance problems vanished. The fact that `Integer` is the semantically default integral type made this issue a significant one.

The other main consideration was the fact that the CLR world is inherently multilingual. In previous versions, Visual Basic and C++ inhabited almost totally separate worlds. To move data between them or make cross-language calls was difficult at best. By and large, the Visual Basic developer had the easier time of it than the C++ developer—as long as they kept in mind that `int` was the same as `Long`, for the most part `Declare` statements would work. But because Visual Basic and C++ lived in such separate worlds, Visual Basic constantly lagged behind the curve—the Win32 world was so separate and relatively incompatible that to take advantage of new system features often required using black magic coding until the next version of Visual Basic was released.

Part of the promise of the Common Language Runtime, though, is that all languages now have a simple, straightforward way of dealing with each other because they're all working in the same world. As we move forward, new API sets will be rolled out as managed code, and when they do—with no intervention by any guru or wizard—those APIs will be immediately and fully usable by Visual Basic. By reducing the cross-language friction even further than has already been done by the CLR, we further encourage the connection between Visual Basic and the platform and the other languages on the CLR.

Index

Microsoft .NET Development Series

.NET Framework
Standard Library
Annotated Reference
Volume 1:

Microsoft .NET Framework
Class Libraries Team
Brad Abrams, Editor

0321154894

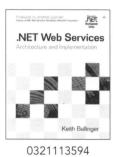

.NET Web Services
Architecture and Implementation

Keith Ballinger

0321113594

Essential .NET
Volume 1
The Common Language Runtime

Don Box
with Chris Sells

0201734117

Graphics
Programming
with GDI+

Mahesh Chand

0321160770

The C#
Programming
Language

Anders Hejlsberg
Scott Wiltamuth
Peter Golde

0321154916

A First Look at
ADO.NET and
System Xml v 2.0

Alex Homer
Dave Sussman
Mark Fussell

0321228391

A First Look at
ASP.NET v.2.0

Alex Homer
Dave Sussman
Rob Howard

0321228960

Common Language
Infrastructure
Annotated Standard

James S. Miller
Susann Ragsdale

0321154932

Essential ASP.NET
with Examples in C#

Fritz Onion

0201760401

Essential ASP.NET
with Examples in Visual Basic .NET

Fritz Onion

0201760398

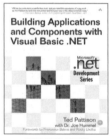

Building Applications
and Components with
Visual Basic .NET

Ted Pattison
with Dr. Joe Hummel

0201734958

Windows Forms
Programming in C#

Chris Sells

0321116208

Windows Forms
Programming in
Visual Basic .NET

Chris Sells
Justin Gehtland

0321125193

The Visual Basic
.NET Programming
Language

Paul Vick

0321169514

Programming
in the .NET
Environment

Damien Watkins
Mark Hammond
Brad Abrams

0201770180

Pragmatic ADO.NET
Data Access for the Internet World

Shawn Wildermuth

0201745682

For more information go to www.awprofessional.com/msdotnetseries/